P9-DJA-730
THOMAS A. EDISON
INCORPORATED

8694 NJ

8462

EDISON RECORDS

ECHO ALL OVER THE WORLD

Made at the Edison Laboratory

FALL RIVER PRESS

New York

An Imprint of Sterling Publishing Co., Inc.
1166 Avenue of the Americas
New York, NY 10036

FALL RIVER PRESS and the distinctive Fall River Press logo are registered trademarks of Barnes & Noble, Inc.

ISBN 978-1-4351-6123-8

Distributed in Canada by Sterling Publishing Co., Inc.
c/o Canadian Manda Group, 664 Annette Street
Toronto, Ontario, Canada M6S 2C8
Distributed in the United Kingdom by GMC Distribution Services
Castle Place, 166 High Street, Lewes, East Sussex, England BN7 1XU
Distributed in Australia by Capricorn Link (Australia) Pty. Ltd.
P.O. Box 704, Windsor, NSW 2756, Australia

For information about custom editions, special sales, and premium and corporate purchases, please contact
Sterling Special Sales at 800-805-5489 or specialsales@sterlingpublishing.com.

Manufactured in China

2 4 6 8 10 9 7 5 3 1

www.sterlingpublishing.com

Cover and interior design by Scott Russo

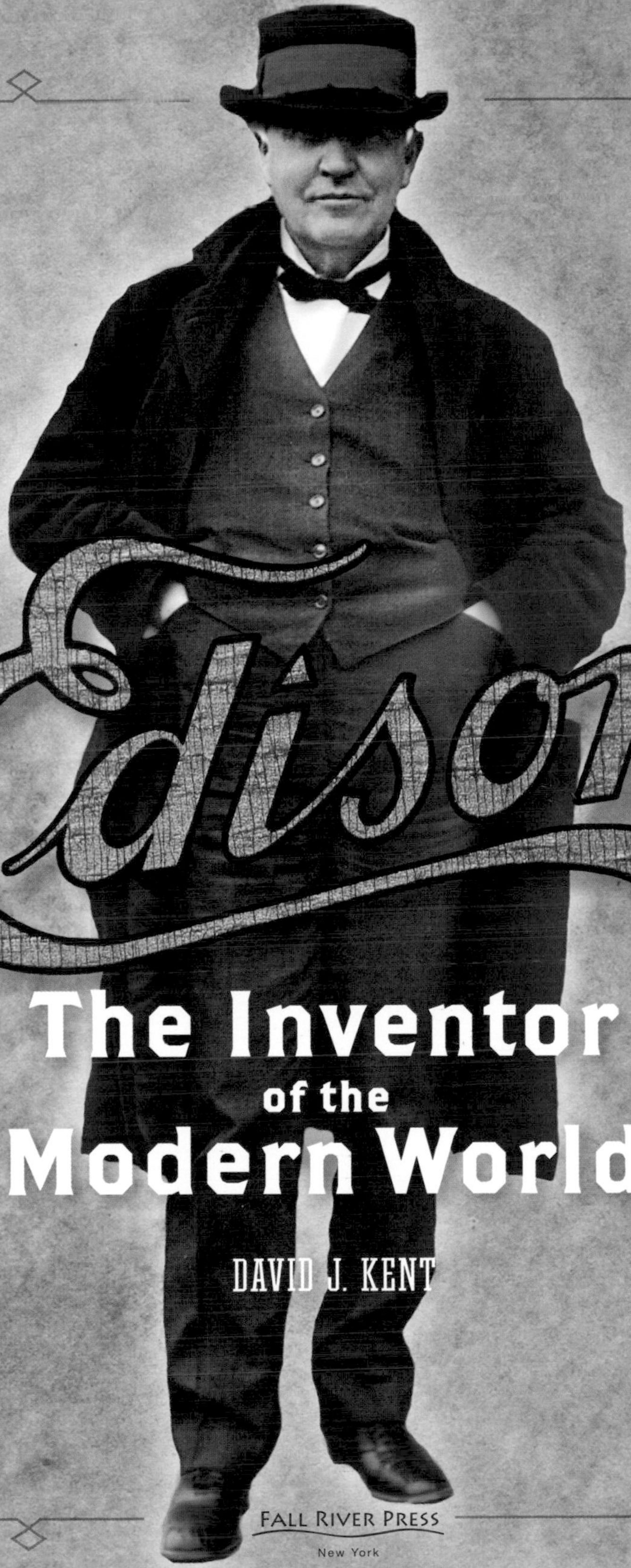

Edison

The Inventor of the Modern World

DAVID J. KENT

FALL RIVER PRESS
New York

Thomas A. Edison
HE HAD TO INVENT!
N IN MILAN, OHIO, IN 1847, TOM
RLY HELPED SUPPORT HIMSELF.
NUTS,
CORN,
NDY!
HE PUBLISHED A NEWSPAPER
HIMSELF IN A CORNER OF THE

CONTENTS

PROLOGUE

One misty morning in 1862, as the Civil War raged throughout the nation, the teenage Tom Edison saved a life, and in doing so set the stage for a career of invention that would change the lives of millions. Lingering at the train station in Mount Clemens, Michigan, Edison was gazing over the freight cars being moved around the rail yard. Suddenly, he noticed Jimmie MacKenzie, the stationmaster's young son, playing on the tracks and oblivious to a rail car speedily approaching. Recognizing the danger, Edison "made a dash for the child, whom he picked up and lifted to safety without a second to spare, as the wheel of the car struck his heel."[1] Falling hard along the gravel embankment, both Edison and Jimmie cut their faces and hands, but were otherwise unharmed. It was the scare of their young lives. In return for his heroic act, the stationmaster offered to teach Edison the art and science of telegraphy, and Edison accepted.[2] This decision would change his life—and ours.

Edison's train days may have also contributed to his deafness. He recounted once being roughly lifted onto a train by his ears, at which point he heard a "pop!" After that, his hearing steadily degenerated. Another report suggests a baggage master on the train "boxed his ears." Or perhaps it was a history of illness as a child or a congenital disease? Although the cause is unknown, Thomas Edison became progressively hard of hearing during his lifetime, which impacted both his inventive ability (he claimed the affliction helped him concentrate better) and his attitude (he would conveniently fail to hear critiques). His hearing impairment played a recurring, and sometimes ironic, role during his long career.

In an early biography, Frank Lewis Dyer and Thomas Commerford Martin describe the young Edison's life as "a youthful period marked by a capacity for doing things, and by an insatiable

Previous: **Portrait of Edison by Abraham Archibald Anderson, 1890**

Above: **Early 20th century "trade card" advertising Edison's phonograph**

thirst for knowledge." They write about a man who, after forty years of invention, was still "plunged deeply into work for which he has always had an incredible capacity" because of "his unsurpassed inventive ability, his keen reasoning powers, his tenacious memory, his fertility of resource."[3]

It makes for an impressively heroic tale, but the full story is much more complex, and not always so adoring of Thomas Edison the man. Nevertheless, Edison the endlessly inquisitive inventor played an unsurpassed role in improving telegraphy; inventing the telephone, the phonograph, and the motion picture camera; and developing a more reliable electric lighting system and lightbulb. Edison also less famously explored iron ore mining and milling, concrete building materials, and storage batteries for electric cars, and even launched the search for a domestic source of rubber for automobile and bicycle tires. Along the way he somehow found time for two wives and six children, although more often than not he worked through the night on his latest distraction.

Edison takes a complete tour of this great man's inventions, private life, personal struggles, and enduring legacy. Through fascinating anecdotes, illuminating stories, and many photographs, cartoons, and caricatures, this book brings to life one man's amazing career and incalculable contributions to humanity.

THOMAS A. EDISON IN HIS LABORATORY.

CHAPTER 1

BIRTH OF AN INVENTOR

Although he was the last of seven children, Thomas Alva Edison was born into a largely empty household. February 11, 1847, was a cold, snowy night in the tiny village of Milan, Ohio, not far from the shores of Lake Erie.[1] Edison's mother, Nancy, who seemed always to be wrapped in black mourning garb,[2] was eager to have more children to replace those who had not survived. One son, Carlile, died in 1842, when he was only six years old. A second son, three-year-old Samuel Ogden, perished a year later while Nancy was pregnant with daughter Eliza. She also lived only three years, passing away in late 1847, when Thomas was still an infant.[3]

The arrival of "Little Al," as he was known in his youth, was a welcome sight. Frail and burdened with an unusually large (though "well-shaped") head,[4] Edison struggled to survive a sickly childhood. The doctors feared he had something they called "brain fever."[5] Mostly he struggled alone; his eldest sister, Marion, often his only real companion, was already an adult when he was born. In 1849, when she was twenty and he just two years old, she married and moved away. Edison

Top: **Edison as a child**
Above: **Edison's father, Samuel, and mother, Nancy**

never forgave her new husband for taking Marion from him.[6] His older brother William Pitt (named for the English statesman)[7] and sister Harriet Ann moved out of the house not long after. Little Al was essentially raised as an only child.

His older siblings were born in Vienna, Ontario, a mirror of Milan on the northern shore of Lake Erie. Edison's great-grandfather John, who lived to be a feisty 102 years old, was a Tory fighting on the British side in the American Revolution before barely escaping into Canada ahead of the noose.[8] Edison's father, Samuel, continued the family tradition of rebellion, this time against the Canadian government. Many years later, Edison remarked that his father had "always been a rebel, a regular red-hot copperhead Democrat, and [had] General Jackson as his hero."[9] Samuel Edison's actions once again made emigration a necessary, and rather sudden, option for survival.[10] He had joined with the losing side of the short-lived Mackenzie Rebellion of 1837 and escaped Canada on the run, stopping off briefly in Michigan before settling in Milan.[11] John's family soon joined him. With new children on the way, Samuel began

Above: **Birthplace of Thomas Alva Edison in Milan, Ohio**

the next phase of his life.[12] Little Al—named Alva in honor of Captain Alva Bradley, a family friend and ship owner on the Great Lakes who had helped the family escape Canada—was the only one of the Milan-born children to survive.[13]

Milan seemed like an up-and-coming town. Samuel set up a shingle mill and a feed grain business.[14] He was also an active carpenter and land speculator successful enough that he built a nice house for his family and was considered quite well off.[15] Like many parts of Ohio, Indiana, and Illinois in the early 1800s, Milan was busy with "internal improvements," building canals and railroads to open up trade with the more commercially active East Coast.

Unfortunately, the expected railroad line was rerouted to bypass Milan, and the village began to fail as grain shippers ignored the town for the new thriving—and connected—port of Sandusky. With prospects falling in Milan, Samuel decided to uproot his family again and move back to his previous brief stop—Port Huron, Michigan.[16] There he sold lumber, speculated in real estate, and even built an observation tower and sold tickets to tourists eager for a grand view of Lake Huron.[17]

At seven years old, Edison had his first steamship ride. Almost immediately after arrival, he developed scarlet fever. While he survived the initial illness, he experienced almost constant colds, upper respiratory infections, and (perhaps worst of all, given his future invention of the phonograph) a further deterioration of his hearing.[18]

It was not easy for Edison to get an education. In the fall of 1854, he was enrolled in the school of Reverend G. B. Engle, a strict disciplinarian who taught by rote.[19] The easily distracted Edison didn't do

Top: **Edison at fourteen**
Above: **Young Edison with his sister**

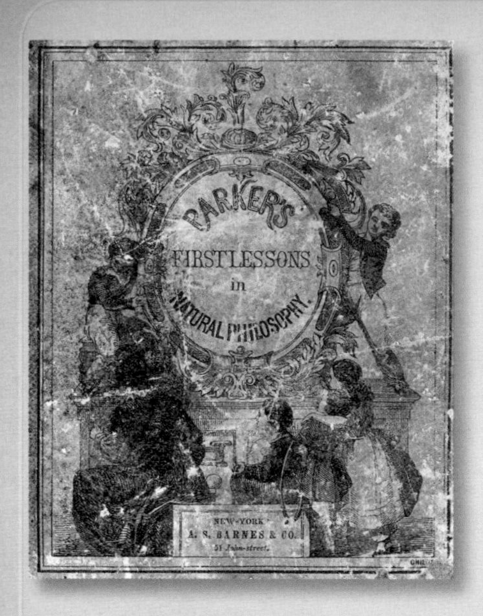

well under such conditions, and ran away. The reverend's wife called Edison "addled" and "dreamy," neither of which was intended as a compliment.[20] Furious, Edison's strong-willed mother pulled him from the school and home-schooled him with a rigorous regimen comprising studying a variety of subjects, reading literature, and memorizing. Above all else, Edison was a voracious reader. With his mother's guidance, he read Gibbon's *The History of the Decline and Fall of the Roman Empire*, Hume's *History of England*, Sears' *History of the World*, Burton's *Anatomy of Melancholy*, and the *Dictionary of Sciences*.[21]

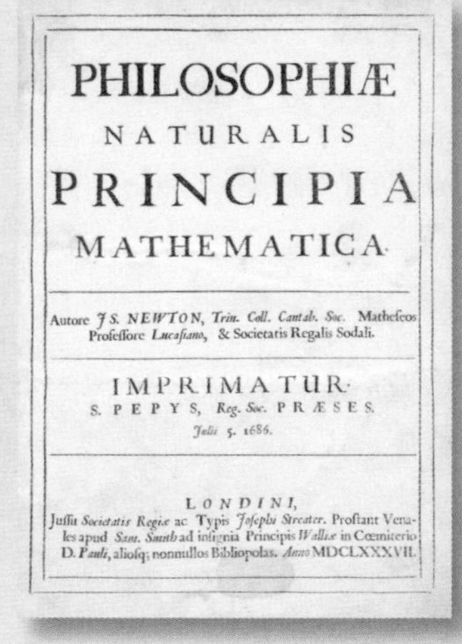
PHILOSOPHIÆ
NATURALIS
PRINCIPIA
MATHEMATICA.

Autore *J S.* NEWTON, *Trin. Coll. Cantab. Soc.* Matheseos Professore *Lucasiano*, & Societatis Regalis Sodali.

IMPRIMATUR.
S. PEPYS, *Reg. Soc.* PRÆSES.
Julii 5. 1686.

LONDINI,
Jussu *Societatis Regiæ* ac Typis *Josephi Streater*. Prostant Venales apud *Sam. Smith* ad insignia Principis *Walliæ* in Cœmiterio D. *Pauli*, aliosq; nonnullos Bibliopolas. *Anno* MDCLXXXVII.

Later, during a brief attendance at the Union School in Port Huron, Richard Green Parker's *A School Compendium of Natural and Experimental Philosophy* fed Edison's growing interest in science.[22] Another favorite book was Carl Fresenius' *System of Instruction in Chemical Analyses*.[23] He tried to read Newton's *Principia*, but later admitted he was stymied by the math, which was beyond his capability. With that exception, his excellent memory allowed him to retain virtually everything he read.[24]

> If ever there was a man who tore the heart out of books it is Edison, and what has been read by him is never forgotten if useful or worthy of submission to the test of experiment.[25]

Early on Edison displayed a trait that would bode well for his chosen avocation: He questioned everything. Ironically, this led his father to wonder if he was a bit dimwitted. Little Al had to know everything, and he nearly drove his father to exhaustion with his incessant inquiries. One early biographer described young Edison as having "the inquisitiveness of a red squirrel."[26] He hung around shipbuilders and asked them question after question about building ships, steam power, sailing, and whatever else he could think of. To say he was a curious child would be an understatement.[27]

Edison was adventurous and inventive. His ability to memorize long passages was illustrated by the ease with which he could acquire and recite "all the songs of the lumber gangs and canal men before he was five years old."[28] In the days before paving, when streets and walkways turned to mud with the slightest rain, Edison built "little plank roads out of the debris of yards and mills." The young inventor's curiosity sometimes got him into trouble. While investigating combustion, he accidentally burned down the family barn, which earned him a public whipping in the town square as a warning to others. He lost the tip of a finger to an axe while holding a skate strap for a friend. An irritated ram attacked him while he was digging out a bumblebee nest. He almost drowned in the canal on more than one occasion. He then almost "drowned" in a pile of wheat in a grain elevator.[29] On one occasion he was present when a childhood friend, George Lockwood, actually did drown.

Young Edison developed a profound interest in chemistry, building up a collection of some 200 bottles of chemicals in the family basement, duly labeled "Poison" to keep away prying eyes. Visits to local drug store proprietors, and his incessant inquisitiveness, made him knowledgeable about most chemicals. He began doing experiments from chemistry and physics books that he got from the local library, and had "tested to his satisfaction many of the statements encountered in his scientific reading."[30] His experiments made him familiar with the workings of early electrical batteries and the production of current, knowledge that would come in handy in his life as an electrical wizard.[31]

Extra!! Extra!!

While Milan was slow to grasp the growing importance of railroads, Port Huron was eager to engage the new technology, along with telegraphs, which grew in tandem. Railroads were springing up throughout the region, and Edison loved to spend time in the railway yards chatting up the conductors and engineers. At age eleven, he was selling vegetables out of the back of a horse-drawn wagon.[32] By the time he was twelve years old he had landed a job as a traveling "news butch" on the Grand Trunk Railway, which ran sixty-three miles between Port Huron and Detroit.[33]

Being a news butch was hard work that required spending a great deal of time away from home. A typical day had Edison on the 7:00 A.M. train bound for Detroit, returning to Port Huron around 9:00 that evening.[34] Young Edison wandered up and down the aisle of the train, hawking newspapers and magazines, plus candy, fruit, and anything else he thought would sell.

Edison rapidly became a successful entrepreneur. He figured he could make more money with both on-train and station-based stores, and he "started up two stores in Port Huron—one for periodicals and the other for vegetables, butter, and berries in the season."[35] He hired two boys to run the stores in return for a share of the profits. With these mobile and land-based establishments in place, he started buying produce at wholesale prices from local farmers at the many stops along the way. Edison became a supplier to railroad staff who received discounted sales of produce for their wives in exchange for not complaining about Edison's

Above*: Printing *The Grand Trunk Herald

growing need for storage on the train (they admired his "industriousness").[36] Not satisfied with selling newspapers on one train, he hired boys to sell them on other trains as well.

After a few years of peddling newspapers on the Grand Trunk, Edison decided he could make more money if he published his own, and he purchased an old printing press. He had gained the trust and forbearance of the engineers and conductors, and they let him set up his newspaper business in the baggage car—a kind of itinerant news-production center. The Civil War had begun in 1861, and readers devoured news from the front, even though the action was well south of where Edison plied his trade.[37] In addition to war reports, Edison focused on "local news, train schedules, birth announcements, advertisements, and egg, butter, and vegetable prices," all for the low subscription price of eight cents a month.[38] Growing to more than 400 copies an issue, the sheet was both well written and well received; not bad for a teenage "compositor, pressman, editor, publisher, and newsdealer."[39]

As his business grew, Edison started asking stationmasters to telegraph provocative headlines up the line so eager patrons would be waiting on the platform for a copy of his *Weekly Herald*.[40] Telegraphy stimulated a boon beyond belief. At a station where he normally sold two copies, he suddenly was able to sell thirty-five, even at

Above: **Edison on the train platform waiting to peddle his wares**
Following: **Edison at age twelve, hawking newspapers, cigarettes, and fruit**

Above and opposite: **Young Edison brisky selling newspapers**

increasing rates. At another where his sales were usually six to eight papers, he raised the price from five cents to ten cents per copy; he sold out his stocks in minutes.[41]

Edison saw a market for at least 1,000 papers but had only enough money to produce 300 copies. He decided he needed investors, so he walked into the offices of the *Detroit Free Press* and asked for credit. One newsman declined, but Wilbur F. Storey (who would go on to found the *Chicago Times*) decided to fund the teenager.[42] Soon Edison was selling out every day. His operation was mentioned in the London *Times* as the first—and most successful—mobile publishing press.[43] Demand was so high that Edison took to hopping off the train a quarter mile before the Port Huron station, where another boy with a wagon met him. Racing to the outskirts of town, they would be met by a large crowd, to whom Edison would yell:

> "Twenty-five cents apiece, Gentlemen! I haven't enough to go around!" He would instantly sell out and make what for him at the time was "an immense sum of money."[44]

Not one to sit idle, Edison also used his time on the train to continue his chemical experiments. Like his home basement enterprise, Edison stored a variety of chemicals alongside his printing press in the unused baggage car. Soon afterward he took over the car with a great variety of experimental apparatuses and transferred much of his basement laboratory to this traveling platform. The Grand Trunk arrived in Detroit around 10:00 A.M. and did not depart for the trip back to Port Huron until late afternoon, so Edison had plenty of time to work in his lab between runs.[45] George Pullman, later of Pullman sleeping car fame, even made him some wooden holders for his chemicals. All was going well for the teenage chemist-in-training.

And then disaster struck. An unexpected jolt rattled the train as it hit some misaligned track, sending bottles of chemicals flying off the tables and shelves. A "stick of phosphorus was jarred from its shelf, fell to the floor, and burst into flame."[46] Despite Edison's efforts, the fire spread, and the car was saved only by the arrival of "a quick-tempered Scotchman" doing double-duty as both conductor and baggage-master. He put out the fire, but for Edison all was not saved:

> On arrival at Mount Clemens station, its next stop, Edison and his entire outfit, laboratory, printing-plant, and all, were promptly ejected by the enraged conductor, and the train then moved off, leaving him on the platform, tearful and indignant in the midst of his beloved but ruined possessions.[47]

Edison resumed his chemistry experiments in his parents' basement laboratory—although, in light of previous incidents, he had to promise not to bring anything dangerous into the house. He also set up his newspaper printing shop there, continuing with the *Weekly Herald* before eventually switching to a gossip rag format called *Paul Pry*. An unfortunate incident involving the subject of a gossip piece eventually convinced Edison to forgo his budding journalist career, but he did not stop writing.[48]

Edison's time on the Grand Trunk Railway offered him amazing opportunities to develop his entrepreneurial skills and earn significant income. It also gave him exposure to the technology that would start his life as an inventor. The telegraph had already helped him sell newspapers on the train, and it would become an integral part of his future.

Learning the Telegraph

During the Civil War, the telegraph had become a critical means of communication, both to get news from the front and to relay

Above: **Young Edison's fiery mishap and subsequent ejection from the train**

strategies and orders from President Lincoln and Secretary of War Stanton.[49] A popular song of the era captured the essence of the power of the telegraph:

> For our mountains, lakes and rivers, are all a blaze of fire
> And we send our news by lightning, on the telegraphic wire.[50]

It was not long before Edison (at fifteen, he now preferred to be called Tom, not Little Al)[51] had subcontracted much of his news butch business, cleverly keeping the Port Huron to Mount Clemens section for himself so he could spend part of each day learning telegraph operation from James MacKenzie. Edison already had a good start.[52] He had picked up the basics of Morse code, the system of dots and dashes used to transmit messages by telegraph.[53] He even brought to the fore his own rudimentary telegraph instruments, which he made by hand in a Detroit gun shop.[54]

Above: **The Cat Battery, one of young Edison's less rewarding experiments**

Great Route to the West!
1857.
1857.
GRAND TRUNK
VICTORIA RAIL ROAD BRIDGE.
ENTIRE LENGTH 7000ft. BEING THE LONGEST BRIDGE IN THE WORLD.
RAIL ROAD
55 Miles Saved between Maine & the West.
AN EXPRESS TRAIN LEAVES PORTLAND & DANVILLE JUNCTION, FOR
Montreal, Quebec & Toronto
EVERY MORNING, making a Direct Connection (at Toronto,) with the GREAT WESTERN RAILROAD, and forming the MOST EXPEDITIOUS, PLEASANT AND ECONOMICAL ROUTE TO
HAMILTON, LONDON, BUFFALO
DETROIT, TOLEDO, CLEVELAND
PITTSBURG, CINCINNATI, CAIRO,
ST. LOUIS, CHICAGO
MILWAUKEE, DUNLEITH, ST. PAUL,
Madison, Iowa City, Burlington, Peoria, Quincy,
AND ALL PARTS IN THE WEST AND SOUTH.

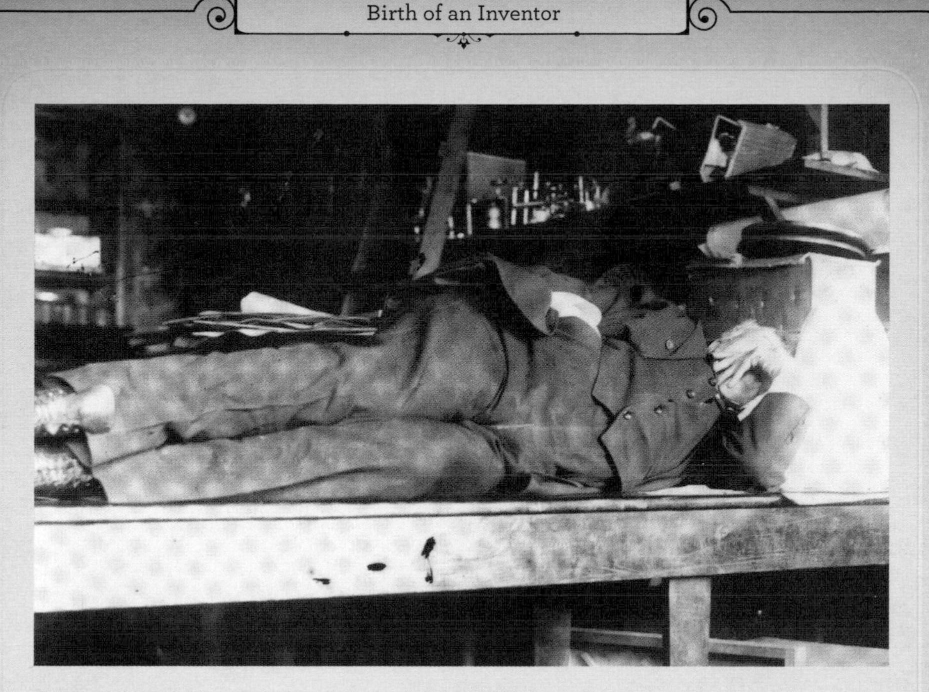

***Above:* Edison taking one of his famous "cat naps"**

After several months of intense study, often working eighteen hours a day, Edison set up his own telegraph line running from the station to a drugstore in the village, a distance of about a mile. With the Civil War in need of telegraph operators, Edison took up duties as a telegraph assistant to Micah Walker in Port Huron.[55] Working day and night, often sleeping at the jewelry and newspaper store where the telegraph was based, Edison later noted:

> I became quite valuable to Mr. Walker. After working all day I worked at the office nights as well, for the reason that "press reports" came over the wires until 3 a.m., and I would cut in and copy it as well as I could, to become more rapidly proficient.[56]

Soon afterward, Edison was able to obtain a job working on the same Grand Trunk Railroad where he had originally been a news butch and budding entrepreneur. He secured his preferred shift at night, so he had all day to work on experiments. Edison was stationed in Stratford Junction, just over the border into Canada from the family home, where relatives could keep an eye on him if needed. Edison hardly needed watching over—or, at least, hardly heeded to it. While employed to take and send telegraph signals, Edison was

***Above:* Stratford Junction Station**

just as likely to be reading scientific journals, running off to buy chemicals, and disappearing while he did experiments to test out what he had read.[57] He often scavenged vital equipment and parts—and borrowed tools from watchmakers and others without asking—as he focused tirelessly on the task at hand.

This meant giving inadequate attention to his telegraph duties, for which he was being paid $25 a month, a hefty sum in 1863.[58] While the office was not particularly busy, messages commonly sat unrecorded or unsent while Edison was busy with his chemical and electrical experiments.[59] Sometimes, however, Edison could merge the two vocations with his inventive mind. It was the practice at Stratford Junction and elsewhere for the telegraph operators to check in every hour during their long night shift by sending the code for "6" to the dispatcher's office. Because Edison tended to work all day rather than sleep, he sometimes found it difficult to stay awake. But he soon concocted a solution:

> He constructed a small wheel with notches on the rim, and attached it to a clock in such a manner that the night-watchman could start it when the line was quiet, and each hour the wheel revolved and sent in the dots required for "sixing."[60]

The invention succeeded until someone figured out that even though Edison sent hourly signals, he did not respond to immediate queries. (He was, of course, sleeping.) Rebukes seemed to have no effect, and his tendency to nap in any nearby chair whenever possible

STOP
RAIN No.73
OTHER
TRAIN
COMING!
"73" IS ALREADY PASSING! THEY'L
CRASH!
STOP!
STOP!

GOSH! I **WOULD** HAVE TO TRIP! --JUST WHEN I CAUGHT UP TO IT!
I SAW THE OTHER TRAIN IN TIME, NO THANKS TO YOU!
BUT THE MESSAGE CAME TOO LATE!

led to the end of his train career. One day, roused out of a short sleep, he missed a call to hold a passing freight train, which raced unimpeded through his station on the single track available. After telegraphing ahead to stop the train coming the other direction proved unsuccessful, Edison raced off on foot, only to fall in a ditch and knock himself "senseless."[61] Only by luck and the attentiveness of the two train engineers was catastrophe averted.[62]

Called to the manager's office to hear his fate, Edison took advantage of a distraction to escape the room and hopped a freight train, then ferry, back to Port Huron. He had made a rather abrupt—and preemptive—resignation from the Grand Trunk Railway.[63]

AS A NIGHT TELEGRAPH OPERATOR, THOMAS A. EDISON'S PROPENSITY TO SLEEP WAS THE MOTHER OF HIS FIRST INVENTION.

This was by no means the end of Edison's railroad telegraphy career. From 1864 to 1867 he became one of many young, single men who traveled around the Midwest working temporary positions in telegraph offices in Michigan, Indiana, Pennsylvania, Kentucky, and Tennessee.[64] These highly skilled workers were in great demand, so Edison worked continuously during this period.[65] He had already built up an understanding of how to maintain, repair, and adjust the equipment (in addition to sending and receiving messages), and he was one of the rare few who also worked hard to improve telegraph design.[66]

The skill of telegraphy has two prongs: receiving messages and sending messages. Edison was much better at the former, and so he liked to work the night shift when "press services transmitted long newspaper copy."[67] Always thinking ahead, by 1867 Edison had

sketched in one of his notebooks "designs for new relays that would increase the strength of incoming telegraph messages; repeaters that would allow the transmission of messages over long distances; and multiple telegraph circuits, designed to send more than one message over the same wire." These designs would serve him well in the not-too-distant future.

After traveling the telegraphy circuit for several years, Edison was invited to Boston for an interview with Western Union. He jumped at the opportunity, although he almost failed to make it there. In early 1868 he boarded a Grand Trunk Railway car for the long journey from Michigan to Boston, but a raging snowstorm stopped the train completely. Stranded for four days, Edison eventually made it to Boston with just the clothes on his back. He arrived at his

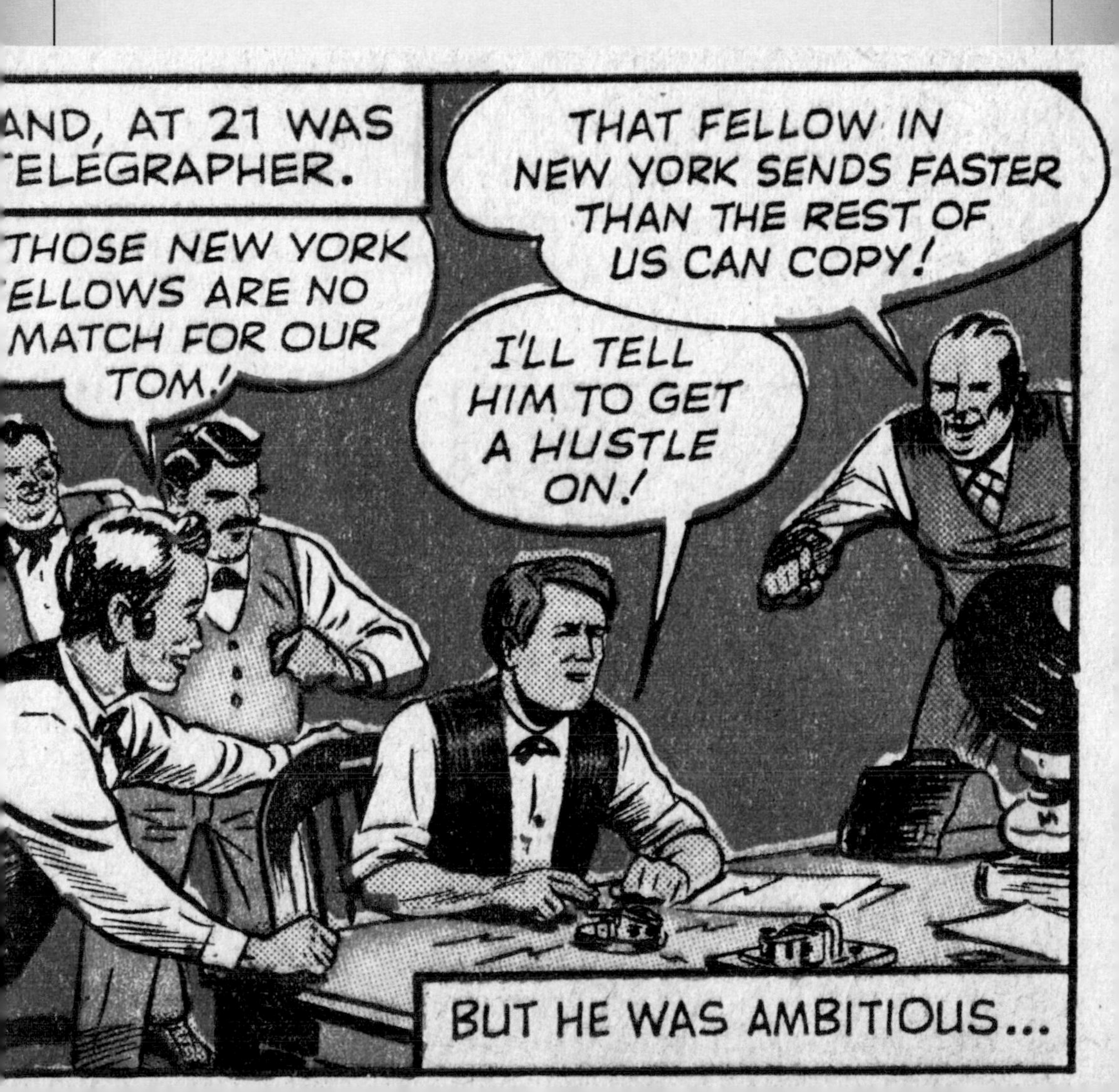

Cable Address "Edison, New York"

From the Laboratory of Thomas A. Edison,

Orange, N.J.

T. A. EDISON.

Electric Vote-Recorder.

No. 90,646. Patented June 1, 1869.

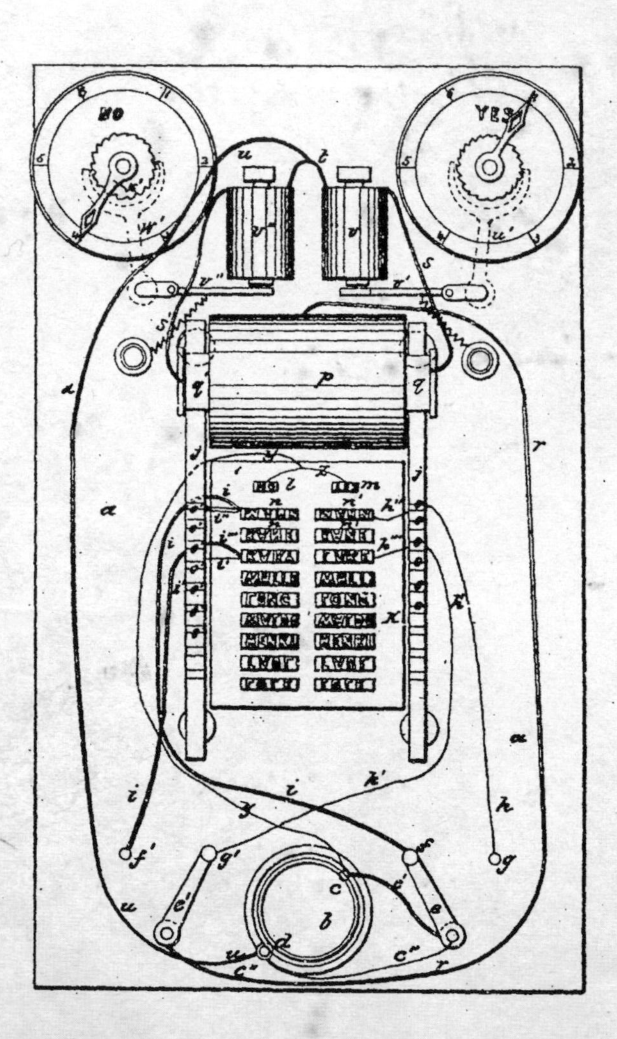

Witnesses.

Carroll D. Wright

De Witt C Roberts

Inventor.

Thomas A Edison.

Above: **Edison as a telegraph operator at age sixteen**

interview looking nothing like the professional the company was expecting.[68] But his reputation and skills were enough for him to get his preferred night shift job "as a receiver on the prestigious 'Number One' press wire from New York City."[69] Edison worked for Western Union in Boston for only a year, but during that time his ambitious experiments presaged the inventor he would become.

CHAPTER 2

THE BEGINNINGS OF INVENTION

Disheveled as he was when he showed up on the doorstep of the venerable Western Union Company, Edison was confident that management would see through the rough exterior into his insightful mind.[1] The company had made a name for itself before the Civil War, but the widespread use of telegraphy during the conflict enabled Western Union to grow immensely, swallowing up its nearest competitors and becoming a force in the industry.[2] This was just the opportunity Edison was looking for. During his initial interview, office manager George Milliken was so impressed that he hired the twenty-one-year-old immediately. Milliken asked how soon Edison would be ready to work, to which Edison replied "Now." He was put to work that day at 5:30 P.M.[3]

The more professionally attired and traditionally educated eastern men thought the ill-dressed "westerner" was somewhat of a rube, so they devised a way to put him to the test. Edison recalls:

> I was given a pen and assigned to the New York No. 1 wire. After waiting an hour, I was told to come over to a special table and take a special report for the Boston Herald, the conspirators having arranged to have one of the faster senders in New York send the despatch and "salt" the new man. I sat down unsuspiciously at the table, and the New York man started slowly. Soon he increased his speed, to which I easily adapted my pace. This put my rival on his mettle, and he put on his best powers, which, however, were soon reached. At this point I happened to

Opposite: **Edison as shown in a French chocolate confection trade card, 1900**

TRAVELLER BUILDING.
DAILY EVENING
WESTERN UNION TELEGRAPH Co.
WESTERN UNION TELEGRAPH COMPANY
31
WILLIAM W. LOWE
AND
WILLIAM R. GRAY
REAL ESTATE
KANSAS
MORTGAGE & INVESTMENT
COMPANY
W. W. LOWE
REAL ESTATE
MORTGAGES
INVESTMENTS.
STATE STREET
TRAVELLER OFFICE.
SOVEREIGNS.
MONEY EXCHANGE.
MONEY
EXCHANGE.
COIN BOOKS
FOR SALE HERE.
TRADE.
MEXICAN
SPANISH
CANADA BILLS
SOVEREIGNS
CANADA BILLS

> look up, and saw the operators all looking over my shoulder, with their faces shining with fun and excitement. I knew then that they were trying to put up a job on me, but I kept my own counsel. The New York man commenced to slur over his words, running them together and sticking the signals; but I had been used to this style of telegraphy in taking report, and was not in the least discomfited. Finally, when I thought the fun had gone far enough, and having about completed the special, I quietly opened the key and remarked, telegraphically, to my New York friend: "Say, young man, change off and send with your other foot." This broke the New York man all up and he turned the job over to another man to finish.[4]

And just like that, he had won over the new office.

Edison earned $125 per month at Western Union, but more importantly, the job gave him considerable flexibility and many opportunities to access equipment to continue his independent research. While in Boston he bought copies of the works of Michael Faraday, one of the foremost experimenters in electricity and the father of electromagnetic induction.[5] At the time, "the only people who did anything with electricity were the telegraphers and the opticians making simple school apparatus to demonstrate the principles."[6] Edison experimented with telegraphy equipment and electricity and "had an unflagging desire and belief in his own ability to improve the apparatus he handled daily."[7] He worked all day long in his own makeshift laboratory before heading into Western Union for his night shift duties.

After a year on the job, Edison found it increasingly difficult to juggle his telegraph operator responsibilities with his more interesting extracurricular activities. On January 30, 1869, he published a notice in *The Telegrapher*:

> Mr. T.A. Edison has resigned his situation at the Western Union office, Boston, Mass., and will devote his time to bringing out his inventions.[8]

He was only twenty-two years old.

Opposite: **Boston office of the Western Union Telegraph Company**

Above: **Edison's first patented invention, the electromagnetic vote recorder**

While he experimented with methods for improving the telegraph, including ways to convert the Morse code into English printouts, Edison designed and built an operating model of what would become his first patented invention—a vote recorder.[9] During all his years receiving press briefings by telegraph and "taking miles of Congressional proceedings," Edison noticed that the process wasted an "enormous amount of time... foolishly calling the members' names and recording and then adding their votes." Vote counting often took hours to complete, but Edison saw it could be accomplished in just moments.[10] He created an apparatus derived from telegraph technology that allowed each member to vote on any legislation by "merely pressing a particular button at each desk."[11] The presiding office of the House could thus sit in the Speaker's chair and watch "twin dials displaying running totals for 'aye' and 'nay.'"[12] The machine would then transmit the votes to a central recorder that would quickly provide a complete list of members voting on either side of any question.[13] The machine was fast and accurate.

It was also an utter failure.

When Edison's colleagues presented it to the necessary House committee in Washington, D.C., the device worked perfectly. But instead of being impressed, the chairman of the committee was aghast:

> Young man, if there is any invention on earth that we don't want down here, it is this. One of the greatest weapons in the hands of the minority to prevent bad legislation is filibustering on votes, and this invention would prevent it.[14]

Edison learned a valuable lesson. He determined that he would invent things only if there was "a real, genuine demand, something that subserved the actual necessities of humanity."[15] He may not always have followed his own edict, but he did come to understand the importance of knowing the market for new products.[16]

Stock Ticker

When Edison's vote-counting machine was soundly rejected, he became more intently focused on how to improve telegraph systems.[17] His working arrangement with Western Union allowed him considerable leeway to do his own experimenting; today this flexibility would be seen as a conflict of interest. By the time Edison published his resignation on January 30, 1869, he had already signed an agreement with two Boston investors to fund his development of an improved printing telegraph.[18] Printing telegraphs, which were more commonly known as stock tickers, already existed, but

Above: **Edison's universal stock printer**
Following: **North-facing view up Broadway from Western Union's New York Building**

Edison's machine turned out to be much simpler and faster. He was in business.

In fact, he hastily set up a stock quotation business in which subscribers would receive stock prices transmitted by telegraphy but delivered in printed form on a continuous stream of paper tape.[19] While he claimed to have lined up between thirty and forty subscribers,[20] Edison determined he would never be able to make substantial money in Boston. He then set off for New York City.

On to New York City

When Edison moved to New York, he was in considerable debt. He had already made great strides in developing a duplex telegraph in which two separate messages could be sent over the same wire simultaneously,[21] but he needed funding in order to make a success of it—and himself.

His first step was to get a job. He applied for a telegraph operator position with Western Union in Manhattan. The company took a few days to get back to him, and Edison passed the time in the battery room of the Laws Reporting Telegraph Company,[22] where he was able to study the complicated apparatus by which the company collected and transmitted stock prices to subscribers.[23] Then, as today, stock trading was a wild, hectic affair where instant communication of prices and trends kept the office humming along at a frantic pace.

And then the machine broke.[24]

> The complicated general instrument for sending on all the lines, and which made a very great noise, suddenly came to a stop with a crash. Within two minutes over three hundred boys – a boy for every broker in the street – rushed upstairs all yelling that such and such a broker's wire was out of order and to fix it at once.[25]

Not surprisingly, the office devolved into pandemonium and panic. Edison, who was not actually employed at the shop, knew exactly where to look for the problem. "One of the innumerable contact springs

Opposite: **Western Union Telegraph Building, New York**
Following: **Main operating room of Western Union's New York office, including the pneumatic system for transmitting messages**

Western Union Telegraph Building West Broadway

had broken off and had fallen down between the two gear wheels and stopped the instrument." At this point, Samuel Laws, owner of the company, came onto the floor. When Edison said he knew what to do, Laws replied, "Fix it! Fix it! Be quick!"[26]

Edison made the needed repairs in just a few hours, and the company—and Wall Street—was able to go back to the business of making and breaking fortunes. Edison saw his fortunes rise as well: Laws officially hired him and put him in charge of operations for the entire plant at a salary of $300 a month, more than twice anything he had ever been paid.[27] Suddenly he had a great start at a new life in New York. Unfortunately, the job lasted only four weeks, ending when the company merged with a competitor.[28]

Collaboration with Pope

Edison looked for ways to continue his own invention business. The panic of Black Friday[29] had made financiers and companies skittish about investing in unknown inventors, but Edison had made the acquaintance of Franklin L. Pope while at the Laws Company. Pope was an influential telegraph engineer whose skills complemented Edison's.[30] On October 1, 1869, Pope and Edison, along with *Telegrapher* editor James Ashley,[31] formed an engineering and consulting business to create and manufacture improved telegraph systems.[32] Edison worked out of a small machine shop in Jersey City, New Jersey, and boarded at the Pope residence in Elizabeth.[33]

Edison and Pope kept in close contact with and often consulted to Western Union and other telegraph companies, and their highly productive collaboration grew in value.[34] After developing a single-wire telegraphic printer, they started a system devoted to recording gold quotations and silver exchanges. They offered the service at a discount to the standard indicator services, and soon they prospered. Then they began engaging subscribers for private telegraph lines. Wealthy patrons paid up to $100 for

Above: **Franklin Pope**

rental of an instrument, plus $25 weekly to receive instant stock prices and information. These early inventions and services not only made Edison and Pope a great deal of money, but the rights were also bought outright and absorbed into the growing Gold & Stock Telegraph Company. Thus, the inventors received routine cash infusions that enabled continued development of new products.[35] The relationship later soured, however, as Pope and Ashley found Edison to be increasingly unreliable, often setting up side arrangements they felt conflicted with company goals.[36]

Edison shrugged off this falling out and continued to pursue his dealings with outside benefactors. Aside from providing much-needed capital, Marshall Lefferts, head of the Gold & Stock Telegraph Company, hoped to use Edison to expand his company's dominance of the printing telegraph technology, which was the mainstay of the stock reporting business.[37] Edison willingly contributed his expertise, and in early 1870 received two lucrative contracts from Lefferts for

GOLD AND STOCK TELEGRAPH COMPANY.

DIRECTORS.

TRACY R. EDSON, WILLIAM ORTON, GEORGE B. PRESCOTT, MARSHALL LEFFERTS, JAMES H. BANKER, ALONZO B. CORNELL, JOSEPH M. COOK.

This Company furnish

GOLD AND STOCK QUOTATIONS, COTTON AND PRODUCE EXCHANGE, and GENERAL COMMERCIAL NEWS REPORTS,

To its Subscribers, by

TELEGRAPHIC PRINTING INSTRUMENTS,

At their respective places of business; and also erect and maintain

PRIVATE TELEGRAPH LINES

For Corporations and Individuals, operated with

PRINTING INSTRUMENTS.

As manufacturers of all the *perfect* Telegraphic Printing Instruments in use, and owners of a large number of Patents, we are prepared, under the facilities of our contracts with the Western Union Telegraph Co., to extend our system of Commercial Reports and Private Lines to all parts of the United States.

General Offices, No. 61 Broadway, New York.

MARSHALL LEFFERTS, Pres't.
HENRY H. WARD, Sec. and Treas.
GEORGE B. PRESCOTT, Vice-Pres't.
GEORGE B. SCOTT, Sup't.

improving stock printers, plus a significant stipend to cover rental of space for a laboratory and the required equipment. With this financial backing, Edison moved to Newark, New Jersey, and, along with machinist William Unger, opened up a laboratory under the name of Newark Telegraph Works.[38]

During this time Edison had been diligently working on a "special ticker," which would become the ubiquitous "Universal Stock Printer" used in New York, London, and other major financial centers.[39] Lefferts, who was called General to honor his Civil War service, had been funding development and wanted Edison to wrap it up. After calling the twenty-three-year-old Edison into his office, Lefferts asked, "Now, young man, I want to close up the matter of your inventions. How much do you think you should receive?" Edison considered, and estimated about $5,000 based on his time and effort, but figured he could accept $3,000. Fortunately, he lost his nerve at suggesting this seemingly huge sum of money, and said, "Well, General, suppose you make me an offer."

"How would $40,000 strike you?" Lefferts asked.[40]

Edison nearly fainted. He had always based his consulting service on the amount of time needed to develop a new product, but now he realized that a price based on the *value* of the product to the buyer was more important. He had learned a valuable business lesson that would help him considerably in the future.[41]

Going Big

This new influx of cash, and the substantial loyalty from old employers and new companies alike, led Edison into an expanded realm of invention.[42] Rather than stash his money in the bank for safekeeping, Edison moved to a larger laboratory on Ward Street in Newark.[43] After convincing Lefferts to give him a huge order for new stock stickers, he hired fifty men to help manufacture them.[44] The business grew enough to add a night shift, and in keeping with his history of working constantly, Edison assigned himself as foreman of both shifts.[45]

Over the next five years, Edison and his various companies used Newark as a base for developing dozens of new patent applications.[46] Several of these were for improvements to an automatic telegraph system, originally invented by an Englishman named George Little.[47] Unlike hand-keyed telegraphs that require an operator to send the message, messages could be prepared in advance by coding strips of paper with punched holes corresponding to the dots and dashes of standard Morse code. Once prepared, the strips could be read automatically by the telegraph; "electrical contact wherever there is a perforation, permitting the current from the battery to flow into the line and thus transmit signals correspondingly."[48] Little's original design did not always work well, so Lefferts called in Edison to improve it.

Edison's main focus was improving the perforator, the device used to make the holes in the strips of paper.[49] Aside from his impressive fee, Edison also received stock in the National Telegraph Company (NTC) that was worth $3,500 at the time.[50] Meanwhile, Daniel Craig, already a general agent for the NTC, helped create the Automatic Telegraph Company (ATC) to promote automatic telegraphy. While Edison was working on improvements to the perforator for the NTC, the ATC hired him to design his own automatic system. This led to a Craig-Edison partnership called the American Telegraph Works, which Edison ran alongside his already busy Newark Telegraph Works.[51] If that was not complicated enough, Craig enlisted the help of George Harrington, who had been assistant secretary of the treasury under Abraham Lincoln during the Civil War, to negotiate yet another partnership with Edison for automatic telegraph systems.[52]

The results of Edison's efforts were astounding. He "succeeded in transmitting and recording one thousand words per minute between New York and Washington, and thirty-five hundred words per minute to Philadelphia."[53] This far surpassed the usual rate of

Above: **Edison's telegraph perforator, 1915**
Following: **Edison's stock ticker**

T.A.EDI
MAK
NEWAR

SON.
ER.
K, N. J.

Above: **Edison's automatic telegraph**

forty to fifty words per minute possible with manual telegraph transmission.[54] The investors were ecstatic over the success, and gave Edison additional funds to set up yet another shop in Newark. This time he developed an automatic telegraph receiving system to convert the dots and dashes of the received Morse code into bold Roman letters to be read without the need for a trained operator hand transcribing into English.[55] The system worked so well that more than 3,000 words could be received between New York and Philadelphia.[56] Craig especially liked the idea that skilled operators could be eliminated: "You captivate my whole heart when you speak of making machines which will require 'No Intelligence.' That's the thing for Telegraphers."[57]

From Duplex to Quadruplex

Edison, not yet thirty years old, had already established himself as the go-to guy for improving telegraph technology. His duplex and printing telegraph systems had sped up transmission, and his automatic telegraphs allowed messages to more easily reach business leaders otherwise unskilled in telegraphy operation. Still, he was not finished with his telegraphic inventiveness.

Around this time, Edison found himself embroiled in some industrial intrigue. His long relationship with Western Union had been extremely fruitful, with the company a regular contractor of invention and manufacturing services from Edison's various laboratories. He routinely turned out new telegraph-related patents—thirty-eight in 1872 and twenty-five in 1873. But the costs of invention were high, and a recession in 1873 had left Edison with a cash-flow problem.[58] Western Union had strongly supported Edison's duplex work, and now wanted him to develop a quadruplex system.[59] He was happy to oblige, although both parties neglected to construct an ironclad contract for the work.

Quadruplex telegraphs could send four messages on a single wire simultaneously, two in each direction.[60] While duplex telegraphs (two messages going in opposite directions) and diplex telegraphs (two messages going in the same direction) were relatively easy to develop, combining them into a quadruplex system proved to be a technical challenge.[61] With the financial and technical support of Western Union, Edison was able to meet that challenge, and by the summer of 1874 was putting initial quadruplex systems into service.[62] All was good, at least for the moment.

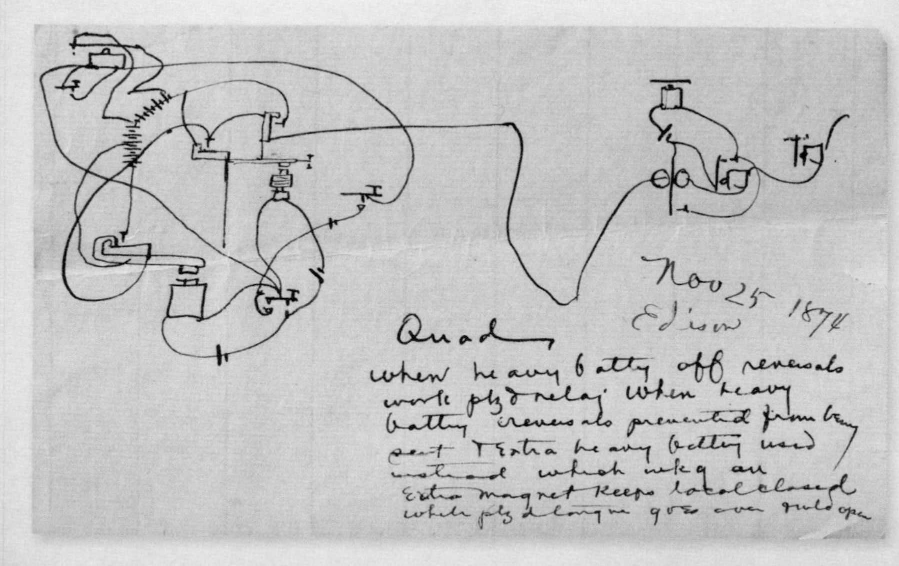

Above: **Edison's sketch of a quadruplex telegraph circuit**

ONLY ANTI-MONOPOLISTS CARRIED
BRIMSTONE
HADES & WORLD LIGHTNING TRANSPORTATION LINE
CRASHER
TERMINUS
PRESIDEN
JAY GOU
SULPHURIC TELEGRAPH CO. GOULD PRES
ANY IMP WHO ATTEMPTS TO STRIKE WILL BE TRANSFERRED TO THE WESTERN UNION COMPANY
OFFICE JAY GOU SUCCESS TO SATA
TO THE HELLEVATOR
THE BOTTOMLESS PIT ROASTING CO. JAY GOULD PRES
MAJORITY OF STOCK
ANTI-MONOPOLY EDITOR IN EFFIGY
PUCK IN EFFIGY
THURBER IN EFFIGY
KEROSENE
SATAN. JANITOR
F. Opper

While all of this was happening, however, wealthy financier Jay Gould was quietly seeking to gain control of the burgeoning telegraphy business. Gould owned the Atlantic & Pacific Telegraph Company, a staunch competitor of Western Union, and he was looking for an advantage.[63] Gould had been secretly negotiating with Western Union Superintendent Thomas T. Eckert to take over the competing company. Eckert had been assistant secretary of war in the Lincoln administration during the Civil War and had learned a trick or two about manipulation from Secretary of War Stanton.[64] When Western Union President William Orton took a long overseas trip, Eckert and Gould approached Edison and convinced him to sell quadruplex telegraph rights to Atlantic & Pacific Telegraph Company.[65]

It was not a hard sell. Gould had recently purchased Edison's Automatic Telegraph Company, which came with all of Edison's previous telegraph patents "and his services as an electrical expert."[66] Meanwhile, Orton had left town just as Edison had run out of the seed money Orton had provided. There was no firm contract for the quadruplex, so Gould offered Edison $30,000. Not surprisingly, Edison said yes.[67]

Above: **Pope-Edison telegraph printer**
Opposite: **Frederick Opper cartoon for *Puck* showing Jay Gould as the Devil presiding over Hell**

EDISON'S
ELECTRIC PEN and PRESS
5000
COPIES FROM A SINGLE WRITING.

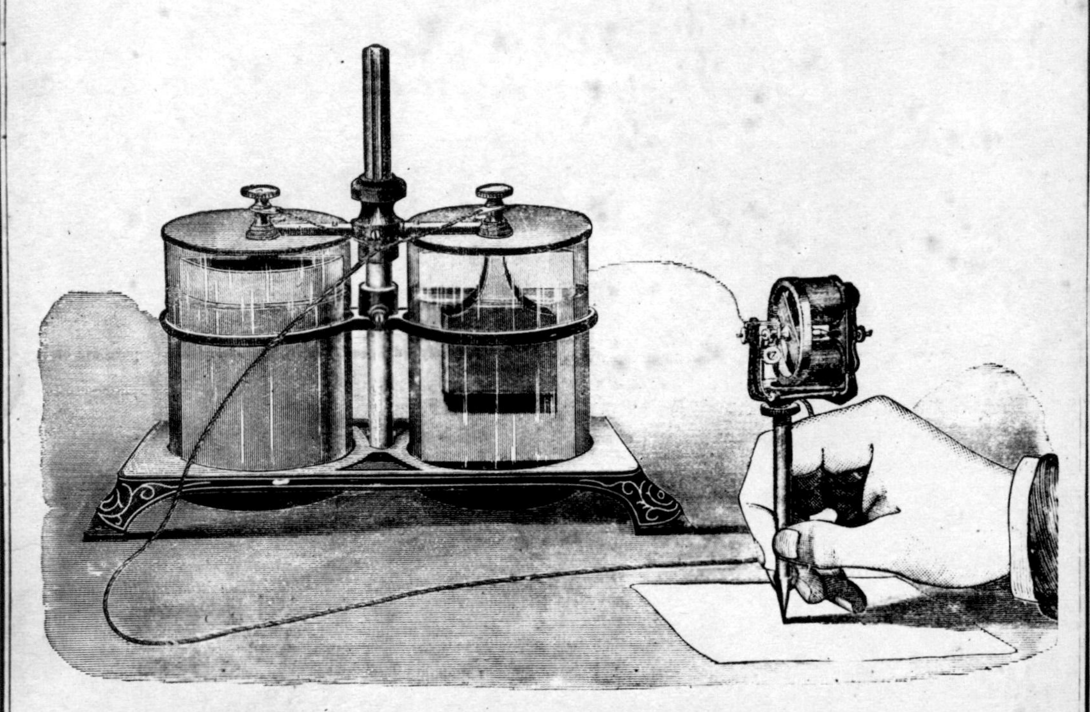

THE ELECTRIC PEN AND DUPLICATING PRESS

Was invented three years ago. Many thousands are now in use in the United States, Canada, Great Britain, France, Germany, Russia, Australia, New Zealand, Cuba, Brazil, China, Japan, and other countries.

Stencils can be made with the Electric Pen nearly as fast as writing can be done with an ordinary Pen. From 1,000 to 15,000 impressions can be taken from each stencil, by means of the Duplicating Press, at the speed of five to fifteen per minute.

The apparatus is used by the United States, City and State Governments, Railroad, Steamboat and Express Companies, Insurance and other Corporations, Colleges and Schools, Churches, Sabbath Schools, Societies, Bankers, Real Estate Dealers, Lawyers, Architects, Engineers, Accountants, Printers, and Business Firms in every department of trade.

It is especially valuable for the cheap and rapid production of all matter requiring duplication, such as Circulars, Price Lists, Market Quotations, Business Cards, Autographic Circular Letters and Postal Cards, Pamphlets, Catalogues, Ruled and Blank Forms, Lawyers' Briefs, Contracts, Abstracts, Legal Documents, Freight Tariffs, Time Tables, Invoices, Labels, Letter, Bill and Envelope Heads, Maps, Tracings, Architectural and Mechanical Drawings, Plans and Specifications, Bills of Fare, Music, Insurance Policies, Cypher Books, Cable and Telegraphic Codes, Financial Exhibits, Property Lists, Manifests, Inventories, Schedules, Shipping Lists, College and School Documents, Rolls, Examination Questions, Examples, Illustrations, Scholars' Reports, Lecture Notes, Regulations, Blanks, Official Notices, Mailing Lists, Committee Reports, Sermons, Lectures, Pastoral Information, Manuscripts, Journals, Fac-Similies of Papers, Drawings, Hieroglyphics, Programmes, Designs, etc.

Circulars prepared with the Electric Pen pass through the mails as third class matter at one cent per ounce or fraction thereof. Additional information and samples of work furnished on application.

PRICES—No. 1 Outfit, with 7×11 Press, $40.00.
" 2 " " 9×11 " 50.00.
" 3 " " 9×14 " 60.00.

Sent C.O.D., or on Receipt of Price.

GEO. H. BLISS. GENERAL MANAGER, 220 TO 232 KINZIE STREET, CHICAGO.

LOCAL AGENCY, 142 La Salle Street, Chicago. | PHILADELPHIA AGENCY, 628 Chestnut St., Philadelphia.

DOMINION AGENCY, 44 Church Street, Toronto, Ont. | GEN'L EASTERN AGENCY, 20 New Church St., New York.

Also not surprisingly, Orton was not happy when he learned of the news. Western Union sued Edison and Gould and became "involved in an intense legal conflict that involved the company's political allies at the highest levels of government in Washington."[68] The "big fight" would go for many months, damaging Edison's relationship with his long-time benefactor.[69]

Going Acoustic and More

As it turns out, the damage was temporary. Seeing the benefit of continued access to his expertise, Western Union approached Edison in the summer of 1875 about the next big breakthrough in telegraphy—acoustic telegraphs.[70] Unlike the Morse code of early telegraphs or the paper strips of printing ones, acoustic telegraphs could transmit "multiple messages by sending acoustic signals of different tones."[71] By December, Edison had made enough progress that he and Orton signed an agreement to settle the ongoing lawsuits regarding the quadruplex telegraph, plus finance Edison's new research into acoustic telegraphy.[72] This groundbreaking work not only paved the way for what would eventually be telephones, but also provided the funding that allowed for Edison to move to Menlo Park and make a huge expansion in laboratory space and management.[73]

During the early years at the various Newark shops, Edison and his team worked on no fewer than forty-five different inventions at a single time and received dozens of patents.[74] Most of these patents were related to improvements in telegraphy. Edison built a reputation as someone who could work independently and provide services and manufacturing to the big telegraph companies.

Other inventions also came out of the Newark years, including the inductorium, a set of battery-powered induction coils for inducing electric shocks.[75] Developed with a partner, Joseph Murray, the inductorium was touted as a cure for rheumatism, and less medically, "as an inexhaustible fount of amusement."[76] It was marketed directly to the public and "sold well enough" that Edison got the feeling that "marketing to the masses was not particularly difficult."[77]

Above: **Edison's electric pen**

Cable Address "Edison, New York"

From the Laboratory of Thomas A. Edison,

Orange, N.J.

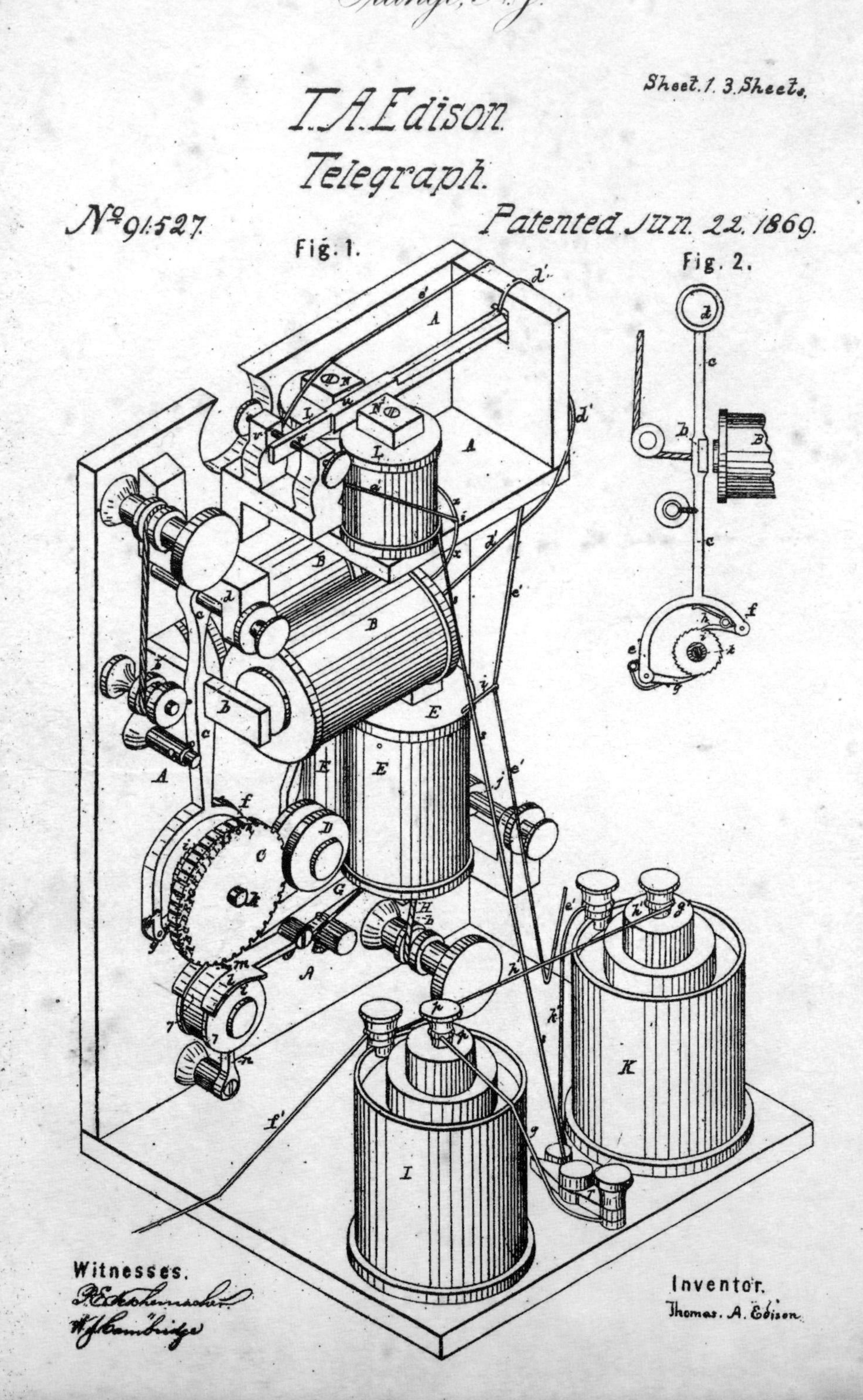

***Above*: The electric pen in action**

Another invention was the electric pen, which would eventually be sold to A. B. Dick and become the basis for the mimeograph machine (and later supplanted by modern copier machines).[78] Essentially, a stylus "is moved over a kind of tough prepared paper placed on a finely grooved steel plate. The writing is thus traced by means of a series of tiny perforations in the sheet, by which, as a stencil, hundreds of copies can be made."[79] An advanced form was electrified, "in essence, a reciprocating motor," and inside:

> the barrel of the electric pen a little plunger, carrying the stylus, travels to and fro at a very high rate of speed, due to the attraction and repulsion of the solenoid coils of wire surrounding it; and as the hand of the writer guides it the pen thus makes its record in a series of very minute perforations in the paper.

A small battery was sufficient to supply the current needed to run the electric pen.[80] If this gadget seems familiar, it is because Edison had inadvertently invented the precursor to the modern-day tattoo pen.

CHAPTER 3

INVENTING THE ART OF INVENTION

Today when people think of Thomas Edison, it is almost always with the sobriquet "The Wizard of Menlo Park."[1] Certainly Menlo Park was where he first made a name for himself, even though he worked there only about ten years of more than seven decades as an inventor. Still, Menlo Park epitomizes what may be Edison's most lasting contribution: a system for invention.[2]

Long before Menlo Park, Edison began to establish a new strategy for the independent inventor. Early on he set up a laboratory in his parents' basement in Port Huron.[3] He collected every kind of chemical he could get his hands on—borrowing when he could, taking excess from the local pharmacists, and using his hard-earned money to buy supplies.[4] He worked alone, often late at night after putting in a full day on the Grand Trunk Railroad.[5] Before long, the teenage Edison had started his next laboratory on the railroad car itself. These early experiences typified the standard of inventiveness at the time—the loner genius toiling for hours in a grungy basement in hopes of coming up with the next big thing.

Becoming R&D

This practice started to change after Edison moved to Boston. Western Union offered him a great deal of flexibility to work on his own, and the many machine shops around town gave him access to both equipment and skilled artisans. Before long he had set up his own manufacturing shop and laboratory, combining resources

Opposite: **Edison (center) with his experimenters on the porch of the Menlo Park lab, 1880**

with two young men to improve telegraphy and develop other inventions.[6] Edison realized he needed financing if he was going to expand his inventing potential.

Not long after he arrived in Boston, Edison lined up financial support from Dewitt C. Roberts, a telegrapher with an interest in manufacturing stock printers.[7] Roberts provided "sufficient money to patent and manufacture one or more of [Edison's proposed] Stockbroker Printing Instrument."[8] Ebenezer B. Welch, a wealthy merchant, financed fire alarm telegraphs and double transmitting telegraphs. In January 1869, Edison signed an agreement with two additional merchants, Joel Hills and William E. Plummer, to develop an improved printing telegraph.[9] Ten days later he resigned from Western Union to set up his own consulting laboratory. In his later years he advised young inventors to follow his example and find corporate financial backing.[10]

In a relatively short time, Edison developed a strong reputation for solving problems, and he became a contracted external research-and-development department for the growing corporate world. One of his first customers was Western Union, despite his recent departure from the firm. He was building a loyal clientele contracting work to him on a regular basis.[11]

Edison picked up partners when necessary. In most cases, these were people who could supply financial contracts or specific expertise. He collaborated with Franklin Pope because of Pope's telegraph engineering ability.[12] He worked with Joseph Murray because of his electrician skills.[13] His strategy of picking up complementary associates evolved into more permanent relationships as Edison's workload increased and broadened into new areas. The trend of creating a more organized inventive process continued after Edison left Boston and set up shop in the greater New York City area.

A contract for printing telegraphs from the Gold & Stock Telegraph Company helped Edison set up much larger lab space in Newark, New Jersey, to manufacture telegraphs and invent ways of improving them.[14] Edison was developing into a shrewd businessman, and he insisted not only on start-up funds, but also continuing stipends to allow him to hire additional workers. In short order he had more than four dozen men working for him in several buildings in Newark. Edison was no longer just an inventor; he was managing an invention factory.[15]

Menlo Park

Before long Edison's companies outgrew the space in Newark. A contract dispute with the landlord helped spur his decision to look elsewhere, and he settled on Menlo Park, the lab in which he would reside from 1876 to 1886 and that would spawn his nickname and celebrity.[16] At the time, Menlo Park was nothing more than a tiny hamlet with "only about seven houses"[17] and was probably best known simply as "a stop on the Pennsylvania Railroad."[18]

Because the railway line connected Philadelphia and New York City,[19] Menlo Park offered access to clients and financiers, but was far enough away to limit distractions for his workers. Outside of a small saloon by the railway station, "there was very little social life of any kind possible under the strenuous conditions prevailing at the laboratory."[20] Edison always felt that Menlo Park was his first real laboratory.[21] It certainly set the standard of what laboratories were to become.

The lab's basic structure was simple. The main building was made of wood and had two large floors. At one-hundred feet long by thirty feet wide it was gloriously spacious.[22] Nine lightning rods stretched

Above: **Menlo Park lab, 1880**
Following: **Edison and his staff on the lab's second floor**

skyward from its roof, while twelve telegraph lines spidered out from its side.[23] The ground floor contained offices and a large central table full of equipment for testing various inventions.[24] The rear of this floor was originally the machine shop, "completely equipped, and run with, a ten-horsepower engine."[25] Wires ran all over the building to allow testing of experiments in different areas. Also on the ground floor was the chemical laboratory and other specialized testing labs. But, according to one former employee, "It was on the upper story of this laboratory that the most important experiments were executed."[26] This second floor consisted of a single large room filled with several long tables "upon which could be found all the various instruments, scientific and chemical apparatus that the arts of that time could produce."[27]

> Books lay promiscuously about, while here and there long lines of bichromate-of-potash cells could be seen, together with experimental models of ideas that Edison or his assistants were engaged upon. The side walls of this hall were lined with shelves filled with bottles, phials, and other receptacles containing every imaginable chemical and other material that could be obtained.[28]

More than 2,500 bottles of chemicals were on hand at any given time.[29] A large glass case held the world's most precious metals in sheet and wire form, together with very rare and costly chemicals."[30] Oddly enough, the second floor also contained a large organ that played an important role in laboratory operations.

A second large building made of sturdy brick was added for the machine shop after it became clear the constant noise and vibrations were adversely impacting the experiments. Outfitted with a boiler and engine room to run the equipment, the brick edifice contained many "light and heavy lathes, boring and drilling machines, all kinds of planing machines," and just about every tool needed to build whatever equipment necessary to meet the needs of Edison and his assistants.[31] Other small buildings served as a carpentry shop, a gasoline plant, and a place to make crude lampblack cakes for use in carbon transmitters.[32]

Opposite and following: **Edison's lab as it looks today**

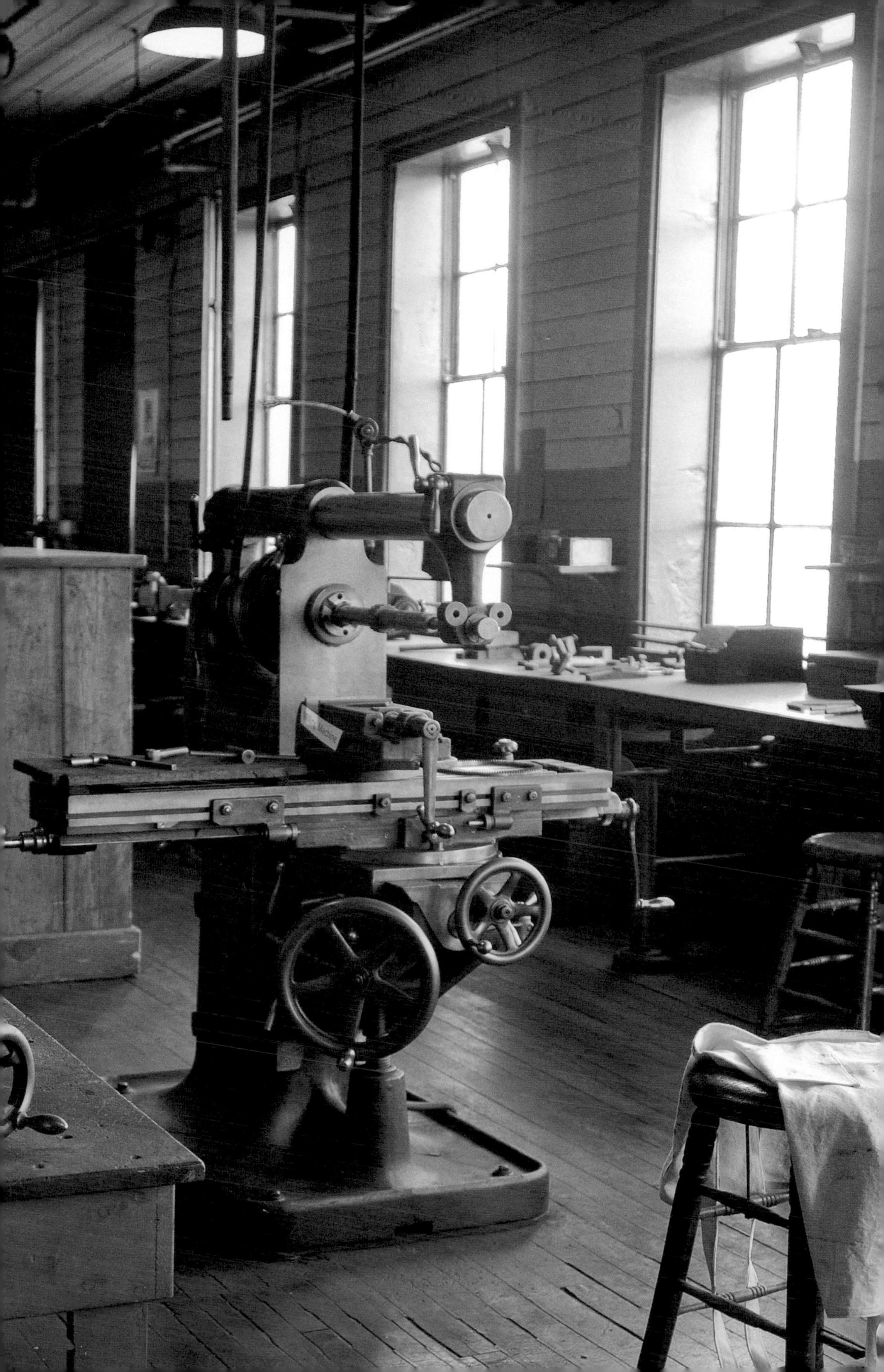
Machine

Hiring the Cream of the Crop

The Menlo Park facilities represented the ultimate in laboratory design for end of the nineteenth century. In essence, this first industrial research laboratory provided not only a place for Edison to meet the manufacturing and R&D needs of his clients, but also the freedom to experiment on completely new inventions.[33]

Above: **Edison's assistant Charles Batchelor**

Menlo Park also offered a place to collect talent. Unlike normal factories, where largely unskilled workers were employed to grind out simple tasks, Menlo Park hired skilled machinists who were more artisans than employees.[34] They generally brought their own tools and had more flexibility to solve whatever problems were tossed their way. Even though Edison often referred to his employees as "muckers,"[35] his real talent was in bringing in the cream of the crop. He did not tell his team how to accomplish their goals, but expected them to think for themselves.[36] This inspired a sense of accomplishment and loyalty.

> I generally instructed them on the general idea of what I wanted carried out, and when I came across an assistant who was in any way ingenious, I sometimes refused to help him out in his experiments, telling him to see if he could work it out himself, so as to encourage him.[37]

However, Edison did not simply let his employees do what they wanted. As Leonard DeGraaf notes, "Edison's ability to motivate experimenters to pursue a common agenda was key to his success."[38] He was able to direct his teams of experimenters to pursue *his* ideas and work toward *his* goals. Edison also knew where to find other great leaders to assist him and take charge of key projects, a skill that compensated for his own inability to focus on single products through to commercialization.

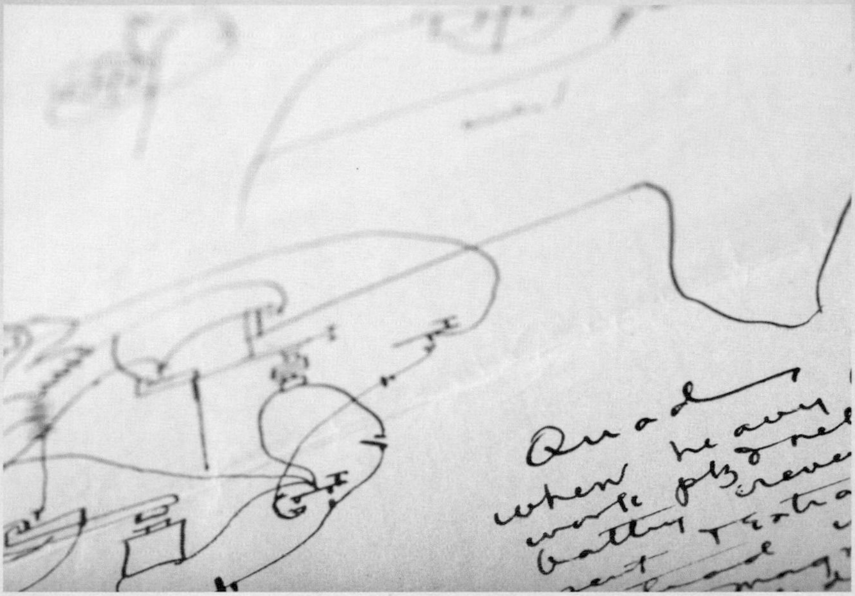

Above: **Edison's scribbled notes**
Following: **A General Electric brochure illustrating Edison and his team hard at work on the lightbulb**

One of the first assistants to become critical in Edison's organization was Charles Batchelor. "Batch" was an Englishman who had originally come to the United States to set up thread-weaving machinery for the Clark Thread Works. As another colleague later recalled, "he was a most intelligent, patient, competent, and loyal assistant to Mr. Edison."[39] But Batchelor was much more than an assistant. He became Edison's right-hand man, usually holding the coveted position beside Edison on the lab bench during their long hours working through the night.[40] They worked particularly closely on developing a better lightbulb. Batchelor painstakingly tried hundreds of different materials as filaments before he finally located the substance that would provide adequate light and last for a sufficient period of time.[41] Later, Batchelor moved to Paris at Edison's behest and set up the Continental Edison lamp works at Ivry-sur-Seine.[42] Batchelor was with Edison for twenty-five years, beginning in Newark and following him through Menlo Park, West Orange, and even ore mining work at Ogden.[43] Without Batch, Edison may not have achieved many of his most famous inventions.

Above: **Francis R. Upton**

Above: **John Kreusi**

Around the same time, John Kruesi, another key contributor to Edison's fortunes, joined the team. Born and apprenticed to a clockmaker in Switzerland before moving to Paris, where he worked for the Singer Sewing Machine Company, Kruesi spent twenty years employed with Edison.[44] Eventually he became the superintendent of the Menlo Park laboratory. Like Batchelor, Kruesi was an excellent mechanic and a tireless worker, and he could inspire other employees to labor as hard as he did.[45] He was also adept in reading Edison's scrawls and rough drawings and turning them into wood, brass, and tin models.[46] "It was an ideal combination, that of Edison, Batchelor, and Kruesi."[47]

Yet another important player was Francis R. Upton, who had been hired as a mathematician—one of Edison's weaker spots—and became part of the core team that kept inventions coming out of the Menlo Park laboratory. Upton describes the dynamics of the group:

> Mr. Edison, with his wonderful flow of ideas which were sharply defined in his mind, as can be seen by any of the sketches that he made, as he evidently always thinks in three dimensions; Mr. Kruesi, willing to take the ideas, and capable of comprehending them, would distribute the work so as to get it done with marvelous quickness and great accuracy. Mr. Batchelor was always ready for any special fine experimenting or observation, and could hold to whatever he was at for as long as Mr. Edison wished; and always brought to bear on what he was at the greatest skill.[48]

Other skilled workers and businessmen who devoted themselves to Edison include Ezra Gilliland, Samuel Insull, Francis Jehl, William J. Hammer, Martin Force, Ludwig K. Boehm, and John W. Lawson.[49] Each played a critical role in developing the inventions that Edison made famous. Many started in Newark, moved to Menlo Park, and continued on (sometimes without Edison) to create some of Edison's most iconic inventions. They often accomplished their goals despite Edison's tendency to "flit from project to project,"[50] often opting to "strike off from the main path, follow an interest, then branch off from that path, and then from that one, too."[51]

Whatever the challenges to his colleagues, Edison's methods worked. Many of these men, although they may have remained unknown to the public while Edison was becoming more and more famous, became rich.[52] All told, Edison and his teams made Menlo Park

> the birthplace of the carbon transmitter, the phonograph, the incandescent lamp, and the spot where Edison also worked out his systems of electrical distribution, his commercial dynamo, his electric railway, his megaphone, his tasimeter, and many other inventions of greater or lesser degree.[53]

Work all Day, Work all Night

Edison desperately needed the organization and skills of people like Batchelor, Kruesi, and others. Samuel Insull described the early Menlo Park days as "storm and stress," noting that Edison's workaholic ways would "upset the system of any office."[54] When one new employee asked what the procedures were, Edison reportedly answered, "Hell, there are no rules here—we're trying to accomplish something."[55] He simply had no sense of day and night, and was as likely to work at midnight as at noon. If he felt exhausted, he slept. These naps were more likely to occur "in the middle of the day than in the middle of the night" because Edison maintained his preference for working at night most of his life.[56] One long-time employee noted:

> It often happened that when Edison had been working up to three or four o'clock in the morning, he would lie down on one of the laboratory tables, and with nothing but a couple of books for a pillow, would fall into a sound sleep.[57]

These extended hours and constant pressure to perform were transferred to every employee in Menlo Park. Staff "typically worked

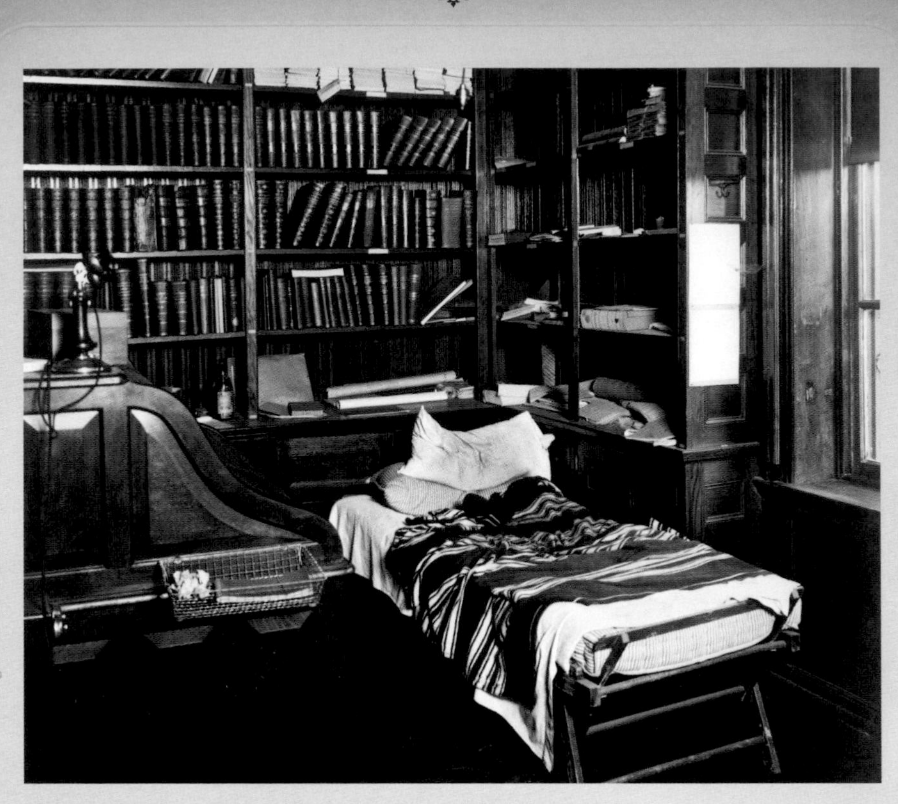

Above: **Thomas Edison's desk and sleeping cot in his lab in East Orange**

six days a week, ten hours a day."[58] Some could not take the strain and left; others learned as much as they could and became successful in their own right. Francis Upton, who knew Edison for more than three decades, noted that he "often felt that Mr. Edison never could comprehend the limitations of the strength of other men, as his own physical and mental strength have always seemed to be without limit."[59]

At times Edison seemed to grasp his workers' basic human needs:

> Many a time during the long, weary nights of experimenting Edison would call a halt for refreshments, which he had ordered always to be sent in when night-work was in progress. Everything would be dropped, all present would join in the meal, and the last good story or joke would pass around.[60]

These refreshments were not merely cold sandwiches, but "a hot dinner of flesh or fowl with vegetables, dessert and coffee."[61] Often the midnight break included a good cigar while the laboratory's massive second-floor organ—manned by one of the tired but still enthusiastic workers—would be put to good use for a round of rousing songs and irrepressible good humor.[62]

Francis Jehl may have best summed up the relationship between Edison and his "invention factory" colleagues many years later:

> Those who were gathered around him in the old Menlo Park laboratory enjoyed his confidence, and he theirs. Nor was this confidence ever abused. He was respected with a respect that only great men can obtain, and he never showed by any word or act that he was their employer in the sense that would hurt the feelings, as is often the case in the ordinary course of business life. He conversed, argued, and disputed with us all as if he were a colleague on the same footing. It was his winning ways and manners that attached us all so loyally to his side, and made us ever ready with a boundless devotion to execute any request or desire.[63]

Above: **Edison and his "Insomnia Squad" who averaged only three-and-a-half hours of sleep each day. Left to right: (seated) John Lamont, Wm. Fulton, S. Moore, Thomas Edison; (standing) Edward McGlynn, Robert Spahle, and Al Hoffman**

On to West Orange

By 1887, Edison had outgrown Menlo Park. He and his staff moved into larger facilities in West Orange, New Jersey, where he and his new wife had purchased Glenmont, a large estate on thirteen acres of exclusive country land in Llewellyn Park.[64]

The breakneck pace of inventing not only continued, it also expanded. "We have got 54 different things on the carpet & some we have been on for 4 or 5 years," Batchelor wrote to his brother.[65] Edison predicted that in West Orange "a man could produce 10 times as much" as he did at Menlo Park.[66] Edison, Batchelor, Upton, and much of the rest of his team continued to work ungodly hours meeting the needs of their corporate funders. His team-oriented approach and corporate financing of research helped him build a "brand" that continues to elicit nods of recognition to this day.[67]

Where Menlo Park was large, West Orange was massive. The site was originally designed as a three-story brick building with 37,500 square feet of work space, but Edison determined it was not going to be enough. Four one-story brick buildings, "each 100 feet by twenty-

Above**: The West Orange lab, 1890s**

***Above*: An aerial view of the West Orange lab in the 1920s**

five feet," were added to the two-acre property.[68] By now Edison had become famous and was in great demand from a variety of industries, so he designed the West Orange laboratory to allow him to invent and manufacture a wide variety of products. Now equipped "with every modern appliance for cheap and rapid experimenting," he built up "a great industrial works" to meet every need.[69]

The main site, Building 5, "housed a large research library, a stock room, two machine shops, a photography studio and darkroom, a lecture hall, and several experimental rooms."[70] The library portion was spectacular, with thousands of books dramatically shelved on two open tiers above the main floor.[71] The library also had a large fireplace and wooden clock that Edison's staff had given him.[72] Each of the four smaller buildings had specific functions. Building 1 focused on electrical research and testing, Building 2 was the chemical laboratory, and Building 3 was for chemical storage and a carpentry shop where workers made wood patterns to cast metal parts. Building 4 "contained a forge, blacksmith's shop, and metallurgical laboratory."[73] Later a temporary building was added to film motion pictures.[74]

In the library Edison began using what has become iconic of his genius, a large rolltop desk with two dozen pigeonholes crammed with papers and notes related to his many ongoing inventions.[75] Located just steps from experimentation labs, Edison had designated pigeonholes for broad categories like chemistry, electricity, and the phonograph, but also more specific labeled spaces like "diamond points-johns." There was also a pigeonhole for "New Things."[76]

And Even More Labs

While West Orange was Edison's focal point for many decades and where he most fully demonstrated his new way of inventing, it was not his last laboratory. Around the same time he moved into Glenmont, he also bought a house in Fort Myers, Florida, where he went to "relax."[77] Of course, he had a laboratory built on the property so he could work all night after the strain of enjoying the calm sea air. As projects dictated, he also set up labs in New York City; Schenectady, New York; and Ogden, New Jersey.

Throughout all of these labs, Edison, Batchelor, Upton, and others kept meticulous notes in a series of lab books.[78] Since he was

***Above*: Edison's Glenmont house**
***Previous*: The West Orange lab's heavy machine shop**

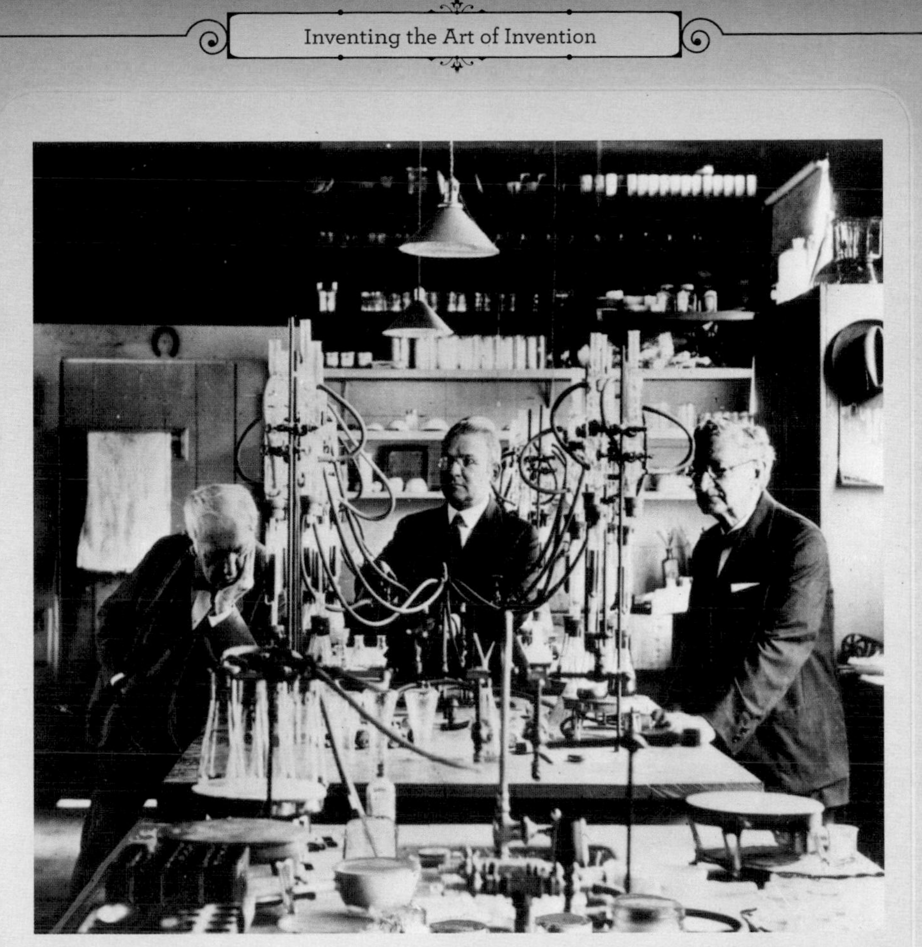

Above: **Edison and assistants Schumarica and Ott at work in the Fort Myers laboratory, 1912**
Following: **The West Orange lab's heavy machine shop, at rest**

a teenager, Edison had kept pocket notebooks where he scribbled ideas as new inventions and improvements popped into his head.[79] He had learned that keeping accurate drawings and descriptions would protect him from patent thieves, a common problem in the early days of invention.[80] In 1870 he scrawled on the inside back cover of one of his pocket notebooks: "All new inventions I will hereafter keep a full record."[81]

All 3,500 of these notebooks show that "raw ideas for each future project sprang rough and fully formed from Edison's brain."[82] His annotations reflected both his hurried thinking and his desire to make sure his inventions could be protected in courts of law. It was common to find hastily scrawled, "I claim…I believe myself the first one to use this method…Another idea has just occurred to me…This is a novel affair… Try this…Test this," and more. Both Edison and Batchelor (or whomever

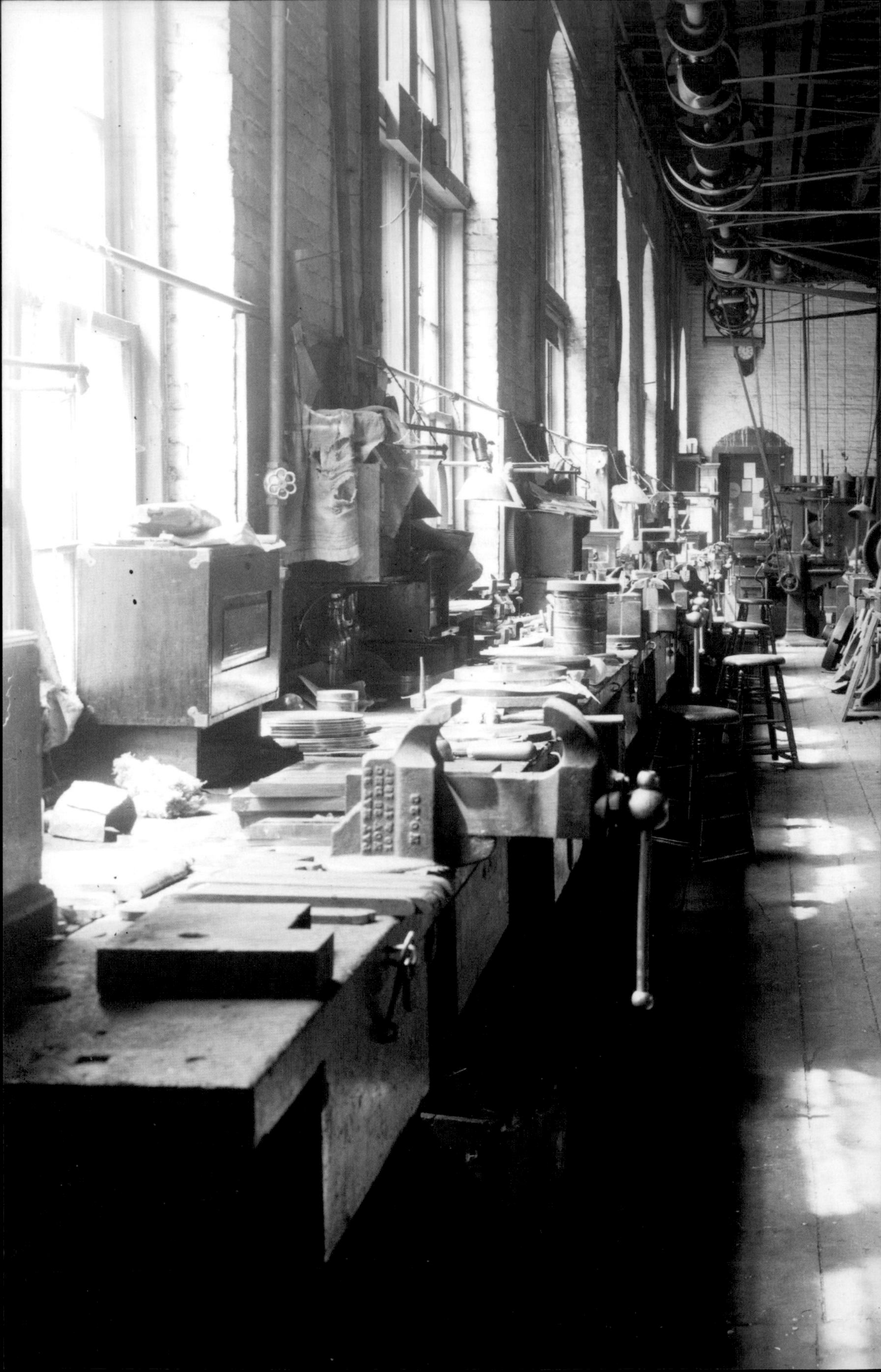
No.20

Cable Address "Edison, New York"

From the Laboratory of Thomas A. Edison,
Orange, N.J.

T. A. EDISON.
Stencil-Pen.

No. 196,747. Patented Nov. 6, 1877.

Fig. 1.

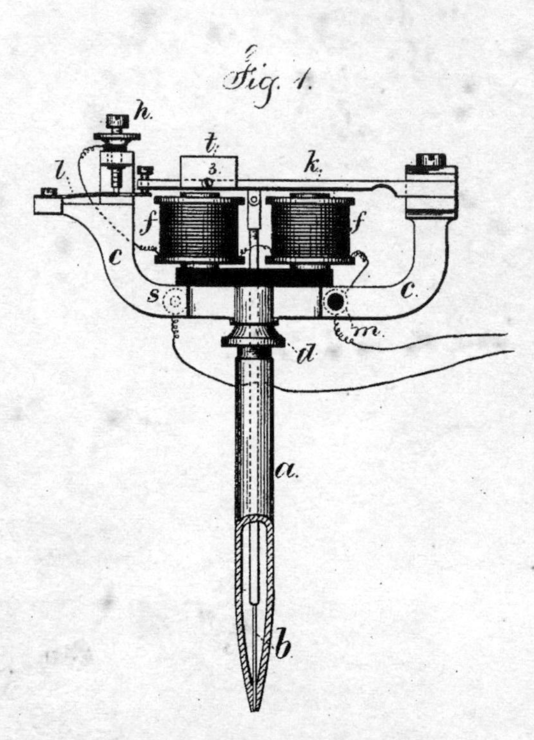

Fig. 2.

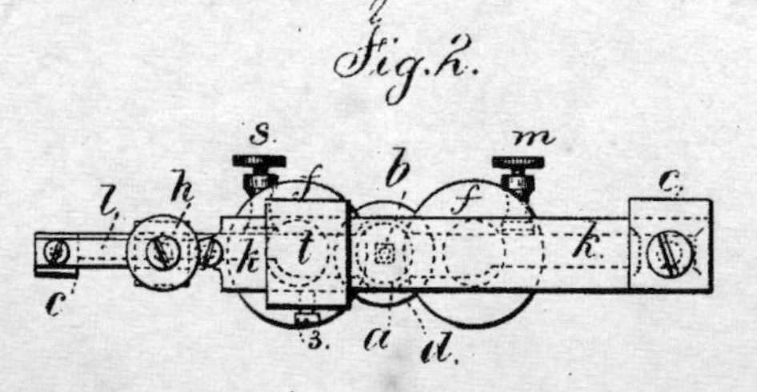

Witnesses
Chas. H. Smith
Geo. T. Pinckney

Inventor
Thomas A. Edison.
per Lemuel W. Serrell
att'y.

else was working with him) initialed and dated the annotations and drawings. Sometimes future records contradicted earlier ones as projects became more refined, or Edison forgot that he had "solved" the problem earlier. It was Batchelor's job to make sure the correct final version was passed downthe line to assisting mechanics.[83]

As many of his colleagues noted, Edison was often considered "just one of the guys," arguing with other mechanics over the best way to do a certain task and singing along during the late-night breaks. Key people like Batchelor, Upton, and Insull took over management of certain development and production projects. However, Edison never ceded control to his collaborators. In fact, his reticence to delegate often held back development of products, even ones for which he would essentially become famous for fathering.[84]

A good example is the phonograph.

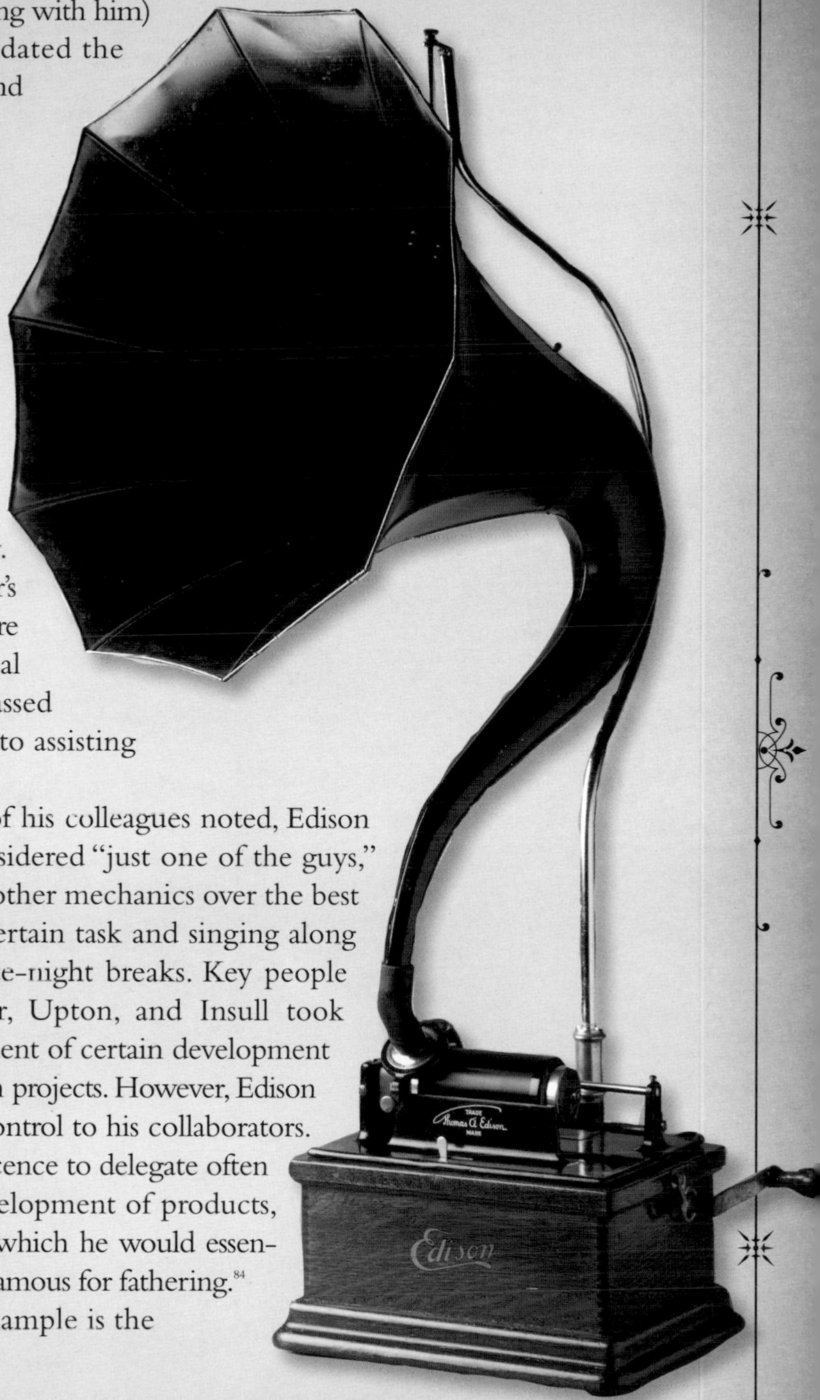

Above: **An Edison Standard Model D phonograph with the unusually large Cygnet horn, ca. 1905**

CHAPTER 4

OF PHONOGRAPHS AND CELEBRITY

The phonograph was discovered almost by accident, but its development nearly ended by choice. Telegraphs had always been the main focus of Edison's work, and most of his inventions were improvements to telegraphy or some derivative of it. One of his many improvements was acoustic telegraphy, but in 1875 Alexander Graham Bell discovered that acoustic telegraphy could be expanded to convey actual human sound. The race to develop telephones was on.

Building a Better Telephone

Bell was initially way ahead in the race. With "ear pressed against a vibrating reed, [Bell] could hear the faint blurry sound of [assistant] Thomas Watson's voice."[1] A year later, after building a prototype and filing a patent, a more famous exchange would be heard: "Mr. Watson, come here, I want to see you."[2] Because Edison had already made major strides with acoustic telegraphy, he joined the competition to make a better telephone.

Collaborating with Elisha Gray—an electrical engineer and ex-Bell collaborator on acoustic telegraphy[3]—and with financial support from old friend William Orton at Western Union, Edison made it a priority to produce a telephone that

Opposite: **Thomas Edison examining a disc phonograph record at the West Orange lab, 1921**
Right: **Elisha Gray**

could compete with Bell's.[4] On "the very day that Bell's application for a patent went into the United States Patent Office," Gray filed a caveat[5] for the work he was doing with Edison "for the specific idea of transmitting speech and reproducing it in a telegraphic circuit 'through an instrument vibrating responsively to all the tones of the human voice, and by which they are rendered audible.'"[6] The "extraordinary coincidence" of this same-day filing led to many years of lawsuits over who invented the telephone.[7] To add even more intrigue, more than a month before the fateful "same-day" patent filing, Edison had filed a caveat for a device "crudely capable of use as a magneto telephone."[8]

Edison's main focus in telephony was improving the transmitter.[9] Bell had developed "a metal diaphragm and a wire-wrapped magnet to transmit speech."[10] Speaking into the transmitter caused vibrations at the receiving end that could be understood as speech,[11] but the signal in Bell's version was incredibly weak. Edison strengthened the signal by inventing a carbon transmitter that varied the current's resistance.[12] He also increased the complexity of the circuits and invented an induction coil that allowed the signal to be sent over much longer distances.[13] Edison's system turned out to be better than Bell's, and Edison sold the rights to his telephone system to Western Union for $100,000, a fortune in those days.[14] To avoid spending it all at once, Edison stipulated that this would be paid to him at $6,000 a year for the seventeen years of the patent protection.[15]

Opposite: **Woman on Edison Carbon Telephone with Blake Transmitter, 1882**
Above: **Alexander Graham Bell**
Following**: Edison seated at desk, dictaphone to his left, 1914**

After making a better telephone using Edison's carbon transmitter and other improvements, Western Union sued American Bell Telephone Company for patent infringement. In a supreme act of irony, Western Union lost the lawsuit and Edison's telephone patents were transferred back to Bell in exchange for royalties.[16] Just as quickly as it began, Edison was out of the telephone business (at least in the United States),[17] and Bell was on its way to becoming a monopoly.

An Accidental Discovery

While the telephone work resulted in some spin-off products, including the motograph[18] and microphone,[19] the most fortuitous result was the almost serendipitous invention of the phonograph. "Eureka" moments frequently build on the work of existing inventions. Such is the case with the phonograph, although the inspiration for invention is firmly established as July 18, 1877.[20]

Edison, as usual, was working late at night with Charles Batchelor and others testing different types of diaphragms for the telephone. At one point during the midnight dinner, Edison was toying with a diaphragm and discovered if he held his finger on the back while speaking into the front, he could feel the vibrations. "Batch," he mused, "if we had a point on this we could make a record on some material which we could afterwards pull under the point, and it would give us the speech back."[21]

Edison later suggests that "invention of the phonograph was the result of pure reason,"[22] but that was probably a wishful rewriting of history. On this night, as with many of the ideas that flashed through Edison's head, he and his staff were quick to give it a test. John Kruesi soldered a needle onto the middle of a diaphragm and "attached the diaphragm to a stand holding one of the wheels used in the automatic telegraph."[23] Edison reasoned that if a strip of paper could be "imprinted with elevations and depressions representative of sound waves," the diaphragm should be able to "reproduce the corresponding sounds."[24]

Strips of waxed paper were then attached to the wheel, and Edison spoke into the mouthpiece as the paper was pulled through. His first words to be recorded and replayed were "Mary had a little lamb."[25] Batchelor noted that after the first pass to record on the waxed paper, "on pulling the paper through a second time, we both of us recognized that we had recorded speech."[26]

Of course, "speech" is an optimistic description of what they heard when they tried to replay the inscribed paper—in actuality it was more like "ary ad ell am."[27] It was not great, but it was recorded sound. Further attempts during that first night resulted in enough improvement to hear the actual words.[28] The phonograph, in its most primitive sense, was born.

However, it appears Edison and Batchelor did not instantly recognize the significance of this observation. As was company practice, Edison diligently recorded in his laboratory notebook for that night:

> Just tried experiment with a diaphragm having an embossing point & held against paraffin paper moving rapidly the spkg vibrations are indented nicely & theres [sic] no doubt that I shall be able to store up & reproduce automatically at any future time the human voice perfectly.[29]

Edison wrote "Speaking Telegraph" at the top of the page, which also included notations on other unrelated experiments, and Charles Batchelor and James Adams dated and countersigned it.[30] Then all three returned to their more important work on the telephone.

From Accident to Icon—the Tinfoil Phonograph

A few days after the initial discovery, Edison tried switching to a ridged tape and added a stylus connected to a telephone receiver diaphragm to create "voice-impressions."[31] This basic concept remained the standard over at least the next few months, although he also pursued other refinements.[32] One of the main areas of interest was the contact point of the stylus needle with the receiving media. The initial use of waxed paper was insufficient and the tracings could not be played back with dependable coherence.[33] The ridged tape was better, but still unsatisfactory. Edison even tried recording on the edge of papers of different thicknesses. He played with the size and shape of the styluses and tested different ways to hold the paper, "including spools of paper tape and spirally grooved paper discs."[34]

Edison felt the linear method of scratching a strip of treated paper under the stylus and then collecting it on a spool was not an efficient means of producing sounds for reliable playback.[35] Not long into the process he had started to think in terms of a cylindrical machine, and shortly afterward he decided on a sheet of tinfoil wrapped around a metal cylinder.[36] Edison's laboratory notebooks show that on November 29, 1877, he sketched out the basics of what would become his first phonograph.[37] It showed "a spiral-grooved, solid brass cylinder three and one-half inches in diameter and mounted on a feed-screw

Above: **The first tinfoil phonograph**

operated with a hand crank."[38] Metal points (the styluses) connected to diaphragms, were held firm against the cylinder with watch springs. As an operator turned the hand crank, which rotated the tinfoil-covered cylinder underneath the metal stylus, the speaker would speak into "a funnel-like mouthpiece made from a telephone transmitter."[39]

This early phonograph, as one might expect, was rather basic. Edison envisioned this system could "indent about 200 spoken words & reproduce them from the same cylinder."[40] Once etched with the recording, the tinfoil sheet could be played back or, at least in theory, removed for storage or transit.[41] Edison described the sheet as "a matrix of words and voice," although the matrix was fragile and the voice was faint.[42]

Two other impediments remained. The early tinfoil phonograph required adept hand-eye coordination to operate. The crank had to be turned evenly to get a coherent recording, then had to be turned just as evenly—and at the same speed—to get a coherent playback, all while the foil was maintaining at "just the right amount of tension" and the stylus held its connection smoothly.[43] This was easier said than done.

And then there was the yelling.

While all this mechanical stuff was going on, the speaker had to speak quite loudly into the small mouthpiece funnel that focused sound vibrations onto the recording apparatus. The funnel did not amplify the sound so much as merely focus it toward the device. So yelling "Mary had a little lamb" was the best that could be achieved. Still, despite the yelling, the words were barely perceptible on playback.[44] Clearly the tinfoil phonograph needed more work before it was ready to market.

Instead it got publicity. A lot of publicity.

Off to the Races

Edison, always one to boast about his accomplishments, was quick to let the press know of his new invention.[45] The fact that it was not ready for commercialization did not stop him from suggesting it was, a precedent he repeated many times during his career. As early as August 1877, Edison associate Edward Johnson, with a wink and a nod, let the *Philadelphia Record* know that Edison had invented a device "by which a speech can be recorded while it is being delivered on prepared paper."[46] Spurred on by rumors of work by French n that will shorten the process of extracting the metals educe the cost, so as to enable poor ores, which are so ant, to be worked at a profit. Millions of tons of the ial are technically known as "tailings" (that is, ores which has been taken all the gold and silver that, by t processes, can be profitably extracted, but which still n an appreciable quantity of the precious metals) ex- all the auriferous districts. For the treatment of these arious methods have been suggested. The principal lty that has been encountered is that of bringing mer- nto contact with the gold where the latter exists in mall quantities, or from the flouring of the mercury vapors of mercury are employed, entailing loss of am and mercury in the subsequent treatment.

srs. Forster and Firmin, of Norristown, Pennsylvania, recently devised a novel method of treating ores with ry, for which letters patent have been granted them in nited States, Canada, Australia, and other countries. ulverized ore containing free gold or silver is fed from opper, shown in the illustrations, with a horizontal A, Fig. 2. While in the act of falling it is impinged

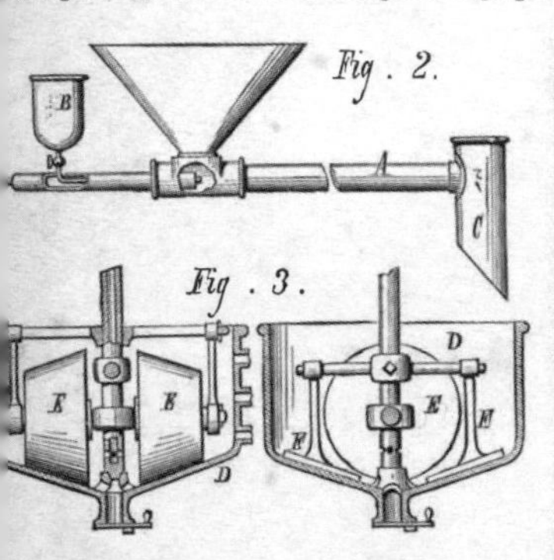

by a stream of mercury, which escapes from the recep- B, through the inner pipe shown. The flow is broken carried forward by steam or air pressure, after the r of the well known principle of the sand blast. The ntal tube connects with a vertical tube, C, upon which e and the atomized mercury are together forcibly pro- grain by grain, in a continuous stream, and fall, by wn gravity, into the washer or receiver, D. It is d that an almost unlimited quantity of ore may be l by this process, as the attendants have only to feed ppers and remove the deposit. The inventors state that only a three inch tube from three to five tons of ore treated per hour."

onnection with this amalgamator an improved washer, in detail in Fig. 3, is used. This consists of a vessel, a conical bottom, in which rollers, E, and also with rs or mullers, F, are placed. The feed water is injected h the shaft or near the bottom of the vessel, and the d current carries off the waste ore, while the amal- nd surplus mercury collect in the dead water space in nical bottom, whence they are drawn off through the rge cock.

advantages claimed for this invention are: 1st. The continuous process of amalgamating, thus treating arge quantities of ore. 2d. The thorough impregna- the metals with the mercury, giving larger results. e profitable working of poor ores or tailings, which w valueless. 4th. The simplicity of the apparatus, no parts to get out of repair. 5th. The cheapness rtability of the apparatus, and the ease and economy hich it can be operated wherever there is a steam

e improved washer the amalgam and mercury are re- l rapidly with a comparatively small flow of water, t the danger of carrying off a portion of either the am or mercury. For further information, address the ors as above.

CONSTRUCTING ICE HOUSES.

ple who do not own ice houses generally find that the summer is over, they have paid a very high figure ir ice and that the sum so expended would have gone ward the construction of a suitable storage building. n be gathered near almost any country place, and it sily be moulded into blocks even if obtained only in m of a thin layer. The question is how to build a ce house that will preserve it, and on this point there en much discussion. Mr. R. G. Hatfield, one of the rominent architects of this city, points out the best, st and simplest way in SCIENTIFIC AMERICAN SUP- NTS Nos. 55 and 59. There he gives working draw- an admirable ice house which he has constructed hich has been found to answer its purpose in every ilar. If the reader retained an architect to prepare a plan the cost would probably be at least fifty dollars; SUPPLEMENT, plans, specifications, and descriptions

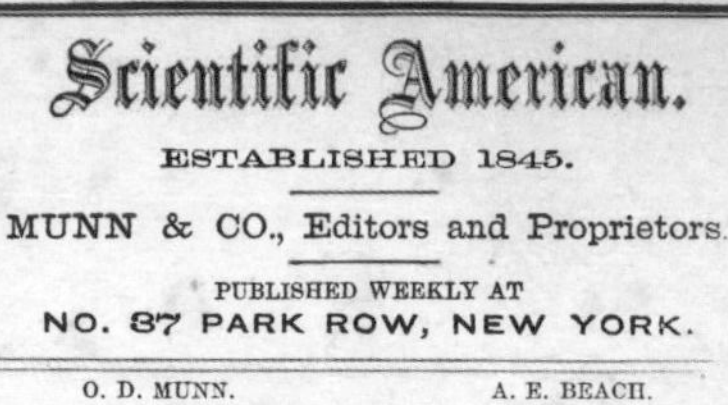

ESTABLISHED 1845.

MUNN & CO., Editors and Proprietors.

PUBLISHED WEEKLY AT
NO. 37 PARK ROW, NEW YORK.

O. D. MUNN. A. E. BEACH.

TERMS FOR THE SCIENTIFIC AMERICAN.

One copy, one year, postage included........ $3 20
One copy, six months, postage included 1 60

Clubs.—One extra copy of THE SCIENTIFIC AMERICAN will be supplied gratis for every club of five subscribers at $3.20 each; additional copies at same proportionate rate. Postage prepaid.

The Scientific American Supplement

is a distinct paper from the SCIENTIFIC AMERICAN. THE SUPPLEMENT is issued weekly; every number contains 16 octavo pages, with handsome cover, uniform in size with SCIENTIFIC AMERICAN. Terms of subscription for SUPPLEMENT, $5.00 a year, postage paid, to subscribers. Single copies 10 cents. Sold by all news dealers throughout the country.

Combined Rates.—The SCIENTIFIC AMERICAN and SUPPLEMENT will be sent for one year, postage free, on receipt of *seven dollars*. Both papers to one address or different addresses, as desired.

The safest way to remit is by draft, postal order, or registered letter.

Address MUNN & CO., 37 Park Row, N. Y.

☞ Subscriptions received and single copies of either paper sold by all the news agents.

Publishers' Notice to Mail Subscribers.

Mail subscribers will observe on the printed address of each paper the time for which they have prepaid. Before the time indicated expires, to insure a continuity of numbers, subscribers should remit for another year For the convenience of the mail clerks, they will please also state when their subscriptions expire.

New subscriptions will be entered from the time the order is received; but the back numbers of either the SCIENTIFIC AMERICAN or the SCIENTIFIC AMERICAN SUPPLEMENT will be sent from January when desired. In this case, the subscription will date from the commencement of the volume, and the latter will be complete for preservation or binding.

VOL. XXXVII., No. 25. [NEW SERIES.] *Thirty-second Year.*

NEW YORK, SATURDAY, DECEMBER 22, 1877.

Contents.

(Illustrated articles are marked with an asterisk.)

TABLE OF CONTENTS OF
THE SCIENTIFIC AMERICAN SUPPLEMENT
No. 108,
For the Week ending December 22, 1877.

Price 10 cents. To be had at this office and of all newsdealers.

THE TALKING PHONOGRAPH.

Mr. Thomas A. Edison recently came into this office, plac a little machine on our desk, turned a crank, and the m chine inquired as to our health, asked how we liked t phonograph, informed us that *it* was very well, and bid u cordial good night. These remarks were not only perfec audible to ourselves, but to a dozen or more persons gather around, and they were produced by the aid of no oth mechanism than the simple little contrivance explained a illustrated below.

The principle on which the machine operates we recent explained quite fully in announcing the discovery. Th is, first, a mouth piece, A, Fig. 1, across the inner orifice which is a metal diaphragm, and to the center of this d phragm is attached a point, also of metal. B is a brass cyl der supported on a shaft which is screw-threaded and tur in a nut for a bearing, so that when the cylinder is caused revolve by the crank, C, it also has a horizontal travel front of the mouthpiece, A. It will be clear that the poi

Fig. 1.

on the metal diaphragm must, therefore, describe a spi trace over the surface of the cylinder. On the latter is cu spiral groove of like pitch to that on the shaft, and arou the cylinder is attached a strip of tinfoil. When sounds a uttered in the mouthpiece, A, the diaphragm is caused vibrate and the point thereon is caused to make contacts wi the tinfoil at the portion where the latter crosses the spi groove. Hence, the foil, not being there backed by the so metal of the cylinder, becomes indented, and these inden tions are necessarily an exact record of the sounds which pr duced them.

It might be said that at this point the machine has alrea become a complete phonograph or sound writer, but it y remains to translate the remarks made. It should be remer bered that the Marey and Rosapelly, the Scott, or the Bark apparatus, which we recently described, proceed no furth than this. Each has its own system of caligraphy, and aft it has inscribed its peculiar sinuous lines it is still necessa to decipher them. Perhaps the best device of this kind ev contrived was the preparation of the human ear made by D Clarence J. Blake, of Boston, for Professor Bell, the inve tor of the telephone. This was simply the ear from an actu subject, suitably mounted and having attached to its drum straw, which made traces on a blackened rotating cylinde The difference in the traces of the sounds uttered in the e was very clearly shown. Now there is no doubt that b practice, and the aid of a magnifier, it would be possible read phonetically Mr. Edison's record of dots and dashe but he saves us that trouble by literally making it read itsel The distinction is the same as if, instead of perusing a boo ourselves, we drop it into a machine, set the latter in motio and behold! the voice of the author is heard repeating h own composition.

The reading mechanism is nothing but another diaphrag held in the tube, D, on the opposite side of the machine, ar a point of metal which is held against the tinfoil on the cylinder by a delicate spring. It makes no difference as to the vibrations produced, whether a nail moves over a file or a file moves over a nail, and in the present instance it is the file or indented foil strip which moves, and the metal point is caused to vibrate as it is affected by the passage of the indentations. The vibrations, ho ever, of this point must be precisely the same as those of t other point which made the indentations, and these vib

Fig. 2

researchers to reproduce recorded speech, in November Edison had Johnson write a letter to *Scientific American* touting his own success in such an endeavor.[47]

Scientific American was extremely excited about the phonograph and begged for a demonstration. On December 7, Edison and Batchelor carefully transported their tinfoil phonograph into New York City.[48] The unveiling must have gone well, because *Scientific American* noted:

> Mr. Thomas A. Edison recently came into this office, placed a little machine on our desk, turned a crank, and the machine inquired as to our health, asked how we liked the phonograph, informed us that it was very well, and bid us a cordial good night.[49]

While the earlier story in the *Philadelphia Record* got little attention, the press fell over themselves to get the scoop after the *Scientific American* presentation.[50] Batchelor helped the cause by writing to friends at the *English Mechanic* that "Mr. Thos. A. Edison of New York, the well-known electrician has just developed a method of recording and reproducing the human voice."[51]

Despite Batchelor's assertion, Edison was not particularly well known. He and his men toiled within the narrow corporate confines

Opposite: **The December 22, 1877, *Scientific American* describes the invention of the phonograph**
Above: **Edison with his Business Phonograph, 1912**

of telegraph executives and manufacturers, and he was essentially invisible to the general public. This was about to change.

As though a switch had been flipped, Edison's name was splashed across all the major newspapers in New York, Boston, Philadelphia, and elsewhere. Edison had opened up the Menlo Park laboratory to any journalist that wanted to visit, and now that accessibility was starting to pay off. In April 1878, Edison's longtime friend William Croffut wrote a glowing profile of Edison for the *New York Sun* in which he coined the nickname "the Wizard of Menlo Park."[52] Others picked up the mantra and began referring to Edison as the world's most famous inventor. So many people flocked to the Menlo Park laboratory to see the wizard that "the Pennsylvania railroad ran special trains."[53]

Tinfoil or Bust

Notwithstanding the attention, the tinfoil phonograph was still not ready for anything more than simple demonstrations of principle. During the first few months of 1878, Edison and Batchelor spent a great deal of time dragging tinfoil phonographs around a series of eastern cities to demonstrate the product.[54] Edward Johnson, an

Above: **Edison's first phonograph**
Opposite: **The *Daily Graphic*'s fanciful rendering of Edison as "The Wizard of Menlo Park," in April, 1878**

July 9 '79

avid marketer, and took one early unit to Rhode Island and several upstate New York towns to regale curious crowds.[55] Generally these presentations went very well, and even though Edison lacked a viable commercial product, he set up contracts with various associates to market phonographs for specialized applications. None of them amounted to anything.[56]

April 1878 was a big month for the phonograph: Edison took it to Washington, D.C., for a visit to the prestigious National Academy of Sciences. Congress had created the Academy and Abraham Lincoln signed it into law in 1863.[57] In only fifteen years it had become the preeminent and influential scientific body it remains today. Edison arrived on the morning of April 18, and his first stop was with famed Civil War photographer Mathew Brady, who took an iconic photo of the somewhat bored-looking inventor sitting alongside his tinfoil phonograph.[58] By this time the phonograph had been outfitted with a heavy flywheel to smooth out the turning of the cylinder, although it still needed to be cranked by hand.[59] Afterward Edison met with Joseph Henry, who was doing double duty as the first secretary of the Smithsonian Institution and president of the National Academy of Sciences.[60]

In the famed "Castle," the red brick headquarters of the Smithsonian Institution, Edison touted the glories of the phonograph. He was introduced as "a man of deeds, not words"; because of his deafness, Edison rarely spoke publicly. "I can talk to two or three persons," Edison once said, "but when there are more they radiate some unknown form of influence which paralyzes my vocal cords."[61] Batchelor did the actual presentation, "singing, shouting, 'crowing,' and crooning 'Old Uncle Ned'" into the speaker funnel. The demonstration went well and the attending scientists crammed into the tiny room were duly impressed.

Word reached President Rutherford B. Hayes, and Edison was summoned up to the White House at 11:00 P.M. to give a private audience to the first of many presidents he would come to know over his career.[62] He arrived to find the President and several others being entertained by multitalented Secretary of the Interior Carl Schurz, who was playing a lively tune on the piano. Edison set up

***Right:* Photo by Mathew Brady of Edison alongside his tinfoil phonograph**

the phonograph and repeated his oft-yelled "Mary had a little lamb" and other ditties until 12:30 A.M., at which point Mrs. Hayes "and other ladies who had been induced to get up and dress, appeared." He then continued the show until 3:30 A.M.[63]

When Edison returned from Washington he was even more famous. Before the tinfoil phonograph he was known only to the business world, but after this he was a public celebrity. He "had arrived."[64] The press began the process of creating the "Edison myth," which included breathless accounts of his exploits and inventions regardless of whether or not those inventions were commercially viable.[65] Collaborators rushed to get the new tinfoil phonograph on the market even though it was not much more than a working prototype. It did have "exhibition qualities," and for a short time that was enough to bring in thousands of dollars in royalties.[66]

Edison then ignored it for ten years.

Distracted

Edison was easily distracted. When he had a technical problem he threw himself into it with abandon, working night and day until he had found a solution. But his mind was constantly coming up with new ideas, and sometimes one drew him away from the project at hand.

One problem with pursuing the phonograph was that in 1878 it lacked a clearly defined application.[67] This lack of focus was not the result of a lack of effort. With characteristic assurance, Edison compiled a list of "many uses to which the phonograph will be applied" for the summer issue of *North American Review*. They included letter writing and dictation without the need of a stenographer, phonographic books for the blind, "the teaching of elocution," reproduction of music, compiling an audio family history and the last words of the dying, music boxes and toys, self-speaking clocks, preservation of languages, myriad educational uses (e.g., preserving lectures for later review), and what could best be described as an automatic recording device attached to telephones.[68] All of these seemed plausible,

Above: **Edison wax cylinder record**

but continuing efforts in 1878 to improve the mechanism simply never expanded the device to a wider market. The tinfoil phonograph was either a public novelty or a technical machine for scientists doing acoustic research.[69] To become a moneymaker it needed Edison's attention, and "during this period of arrested development" Edison was distracted by the electrical lighting projects that would keep him busy for a decade.[70]

Perfecting the Phonograph

After ten years of dormancy, and with both demand and competition heating up, in 1887 Edison once again returned his attention to the phonograph.[71] Over the next few years he discarded the idea of a tinfoil-covered cylinder and "substituted a wax-like material, in which the record was cut by a minute chisel-like gouging tool."[72] The "wax-like material" was the result of "more than 700 experiments on waxes, soaps, and fatty acids to produce a cylinder soft enough to take a recording yet durable enough to withstand repeated reproduction."[73] Edison and his associates also got rid of the hand crank, replacing it with a battery-operated electric motor to turn the cylinder under

Above: **The Edison Business Phonograph was marketed as an early dictation device.**

R. F. SCHABELITZ

Every Member of Your Family

and your friends who come to see you will enjoy

The Edison Phonograph

They'll love it, every one of them—because it plays every kind of music, just the kind that each one likes best and in the purest, truest, most lifelike rendering. Perhaps you like rag-time best; one member of your family may prefer Grand Opera; another, band, orchestra or vaudeville monologue. All right, here they are—the Edison Phonograph plays them all—and plays them as no other instrument can because it is the only instrument which plays both Standard and Amberol Records.

Amberol Records

are the longest playing records made—and that means that only on Amberol Records, and only in the Edison Phonograph, can you get all of the best of all kinds of music, played as originally composed and as meant to be played without hurrying or cutting out important parts.

Have you ever heard the Edison Phonograph play? You can hear the Edison in your own town any day you wish, on just the music you like best, or *all* the music you like best—on both Standard and Amberol Records.

The more you know about music the more you will appreciate the Edison Phonograph—for the Edison is the ***universal*** musician—it is the one instrument that plays all the kinds of music that no one musician could master in a lifetime. AND IT IS THE HEART OF YOUR HOME CIRCLE

Edison Phonographs . .	$12.50 to $[illegible]
Edison Standard Records	
Edison Amberol Records (play twice as long	
Edison Grand Opera Records .	.75 an[illegible]

There are Edison dealers everywhere. Go to the nearest and hear the Edison Phonograph play both Edison Standard and Amberol Records. Get complete catalogs from your dealer or from us.

National Phonograph Co.
97 Lakeside Avenue
Orange, N. J.

TRADE MA[illegible]

the new shaving tool (which replaced the stylus).[74] The cylinder itself could be removed and stored.[75] A large horn-shaped attachment was added to amplify the playback sound. By early spring 1888 Edison had started up yet another company, the Edison Phonograph Works, and by summer he released his "perfected" phonograph.[76]

Initial plans were to market the phonograph to offices as a substitute for stenographers.[77] This turned out to be easier said than done because of technical problems both with the machines and the people using them. Changes in temperature and humidity "warped and cracked" the recording cylinders, and the shavings from recycled cylinders clogged the machines.[78] Although office workers received substantial training, many complained that the machine was too heavy and too difficult to use. Worse, the chemical battery that powered the electric motor had a limited charge life, and sometimes drained almost as soon as it was put into use. The high cost and messy maintenance schedule (chemical cells had to be refilled periodically) made the batteries both inefficient and dangerous.[79]

Despite these technical problems, the public was clamoring for phonographs as sources of entertainment. Late in 1889, entrepreneur Louis Glass figured out how to make the phonograph into a coin-operated machine.[80] He then set up an emporium in San Francisco where, for a nickel, customers "could hear a recorded song, short comedy skit, or dramatic reading."[81] Within two years the growing number of phonograph-entertainment companies had installed 704 coin-operated machines around the country. These machines were highly profitable, bringing in thousands of dollars to the businessmen who exploited the public's demand for musical entertainment.[82]

In a bit of fancy, Edison and Batchelor made a reproducing mechanism small enough to fit into the torso of a child's doll. Pulling a string would engage "a small phonograph…with an automatic return motion so that you simply turn always in one direction and it always says the same thing over and over again."[83] Unfortunately, the mini-phonographs were easily damaged in transit and rarely remained in working order. This was perhaps for the best, as the high-pitched, tinny voice, when it worked, shrieked out creepy versions of child's nursery rhymes.[84]

EDISON'S TALKING DOLL.

No. 3.

This Doll Recites:

There was a little girl,
And she had a little curl,
Right in the middle of her fore
head;
And when she was good,
She was very, very good,
But when she was bad she wa
horrid.

G

[OVER.]

The entertainment value of phonographs was not what Edison had expected. Noting his own commercial failure of dictating phonographs, he later admitted, "Our experience here shows that a very large number of machines got into private houses for amusement purposes—that such persons do not attempt to record nor desire it for that purpose."[85]

The Home Entertainment Market

During the last decade of the nineteenth century, Edison further refined his phonograph machines for the home market.[86] He eliminated some of the more complicated recording controls and focused on providing

Previous: Manufacture of Edison talking dolls at the Edison Phonograph Works, near the Edison Laboratory, in West Orange, New Jersey
Above: Coin-operated phonograph emporium
Opposite: Enrico Caruso with a Victrola

units that would be used solely for playback.[87] At first Edison had the market to himself, but by the beginning of the twentieth century he started getting competitors, some of whom came up with ideas he vehemently resisted.

The biggest competitor was the Victor Talking Machine Company, which produced a gramophone that was encased in beautiful wooden cabinets, designed for living rooms, with enclosed speaker horns that fit inside.[88] Called the Victrola, it also featured a flat disk instead of a cylinder. The disk was easier to handle and store, and played for between four and seven minutes compared to Edison's two-minute cylinders. The buying public overwhelmingly preferred this format.[89]

Edison initially refused to switch to the more popular long-playing disks.[90] It would be another decade, in 1912, before he was finally convinced to develop and market the Diamond Disc phonograph. The new machine lived up to its name: It featured a diamond-pointed reproducer and a flat disk record made of a material called condensate.[91] But even then Edison refused to give up on his cylinder format, issuing a celluloid version with higher sound quality during the very same year.[92]

Edison's obstinacy also created problems with music selection. Victor's strategy was to feature well-known popular singers like Enrico

Caruso and put their names on the records to attract fans.[93] Edison refused to pay for celebrities; his focus was on ensuring that "the voice shall be as perfect as possible." He wanted quality, both in the voice and the recording, and saw no reason to put the name of the artist on the record at all. In 1911 he explained, "There are, of course, many people who will buy a distorted, ill-recorded scratchy record if the singer has a great reputation, but there are infinitely more who will buy for the beauty of the record, with fine voices, well instrumented, and no scratch."[94]

Edison insisted that only he was qualified to determine which singers and musicians were good enough to be included on his recorded disks and cylinders—an ironic assertion, given that he was essentially deaf. His hearing loss had gotten progressively worse, and in order to hear the music he had to sit right next to the singer, often with an ear horn to catch the sound. He could be found literally biting the cabinetry of a piano as a song was being played.

Cable Address "Edison, New York"

From the Laboratory of Thomas A. Edison,
Orange, N.J.

No. 607,588. **Patented July 19, 1898.**

T. A. EDISON.
PHONOGRAPH.

(Application filed Jan. 27, 1897.)

(No Model.)

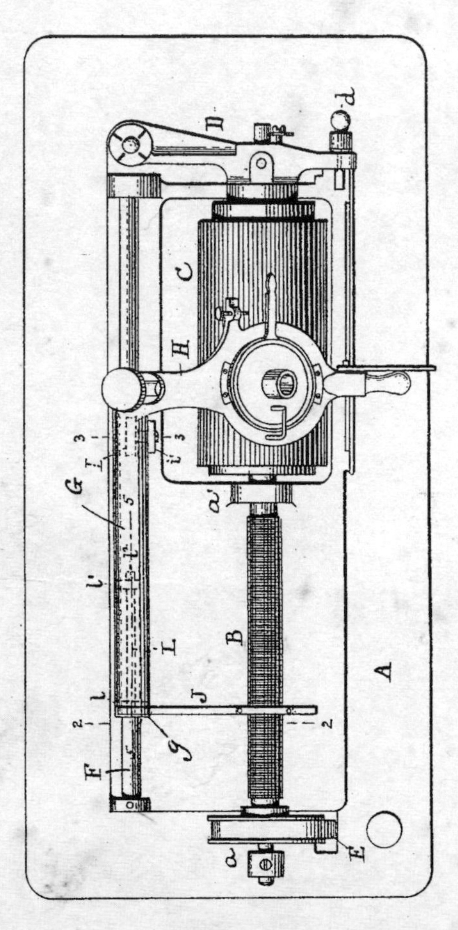

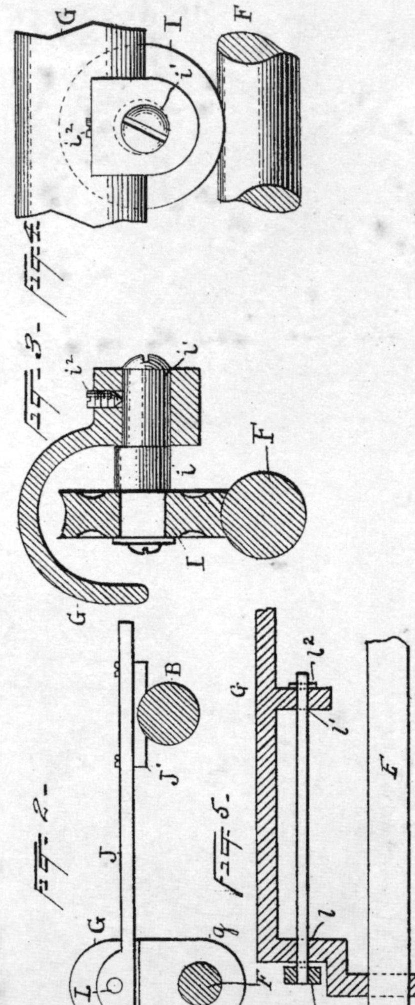

Witnesses
Norris A. Clark
W. Pelzer

Inventor
Thomas A. Edison
By his Attorneys
Dyer & Driscoll.

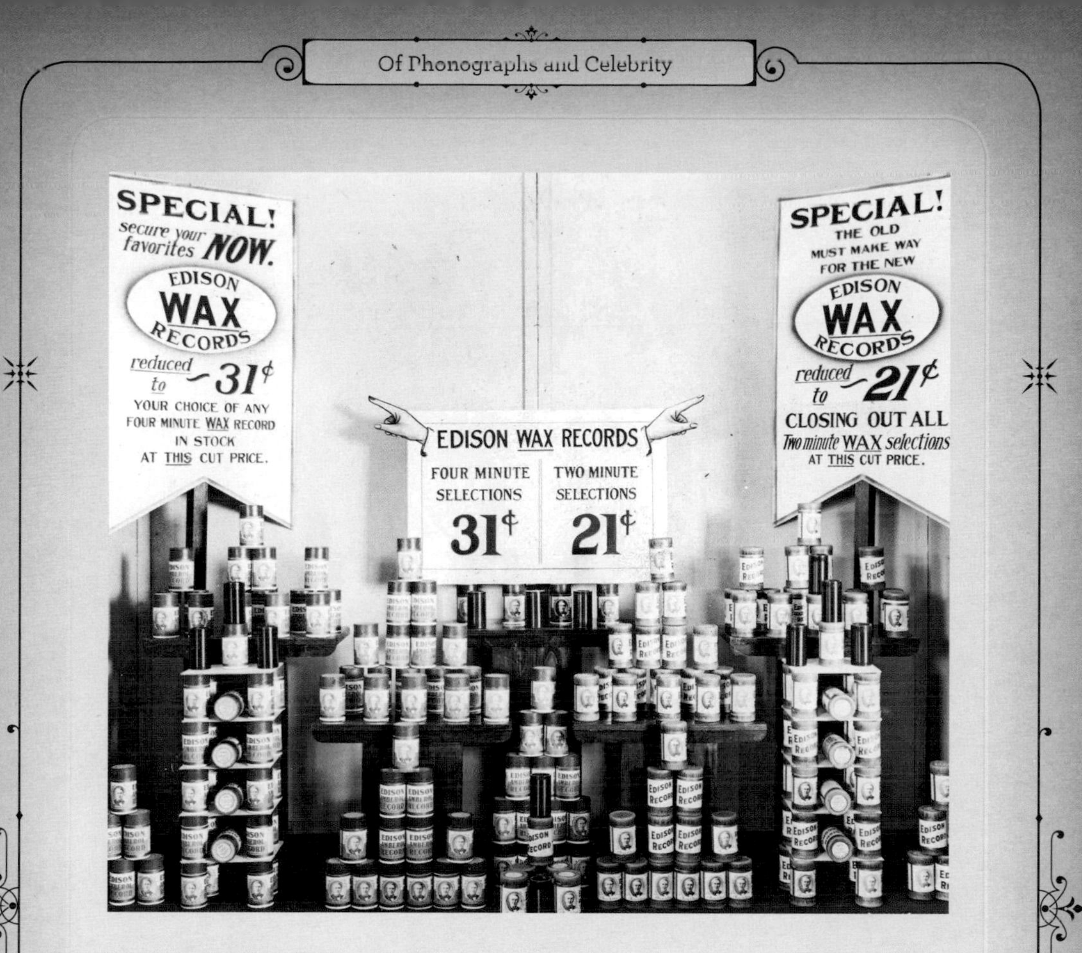

His emphasis on "quality" music also kept him away from popular dance music, jazz, and other forms that arose with changing musical tastes. As the Victor and Columbia companies adapted to new crazes, Edison tried hard to dictate the kind of music he believed the public should listen to. Although he was eventually convinced to be more flexible and tried several new ideas, it was too late; the Victrola and other phonographs were surging in popularity.

Edison was wrong in predicting the market. Victrola became the brand of phonograph most people remember today, although Edison often received credit for the machine that effectively knocked him out of the phonograph business.[95]

CHAPTER 5

FAMILY AND FRIENDS

Thomas Edison was a workaholic. He regularly worked eighteen hours a day and actually preferred to work late at night, taking catnaps on any nearby laboratory bench when he was tired. As might be expected, this routine was not particularly conducive to a healthy family life. And yet he managed to marry two wives (not at the same time) and sire six children. Clearly the man kept busy even when he was home from the laboratory.

Meeting Mary Stilwell

By 1870 Edison was making substantial money as an inventor. Business was so good that by the time he moved his Newark laboratory into the much larger quarters on Ward Street, he was on pace to produce 600 stock printers by the end of the year.[1] While not yet "in possession of a good fortune," Edison did start thinking that he was in want of a wife.[2] It did not take him long to find one.

In October 1871, he started up the News Reporting Telegraph Company, a subscription company that promised to deliver "all general news of the world…the moment such news is received in the main Telegraph Office in New York."[3] The company would install a private telegraph line and printer in homes for free, then for $3 a week would provide the news as it happened.[4]

Opposite: **Edison with his family in 1907**
Following: **Edison's Ward Street office in Newark, New Jersey, 1873**

It was a huge flop, closing within three months.[5]

All was not lost, however. Demand for skilled transmitters was high, so the company had started a trainee program for young girls. John Ott, who worked for Edison for the next fifty years[6] and was William Unger's cousin, had an acquaintance who had a sister, sixteen-year-old Mary Stilwell.[7]

Given his tireless focus on inventing, twenty-four-year-old Edison was not much of a ladies' man. He was not sure how to approach Mary Stilwell, but his nervous infatuation became apparent to her—and everyone else in the shop. After a while they began talking, and somewhat of a romance developed. He was already a successful inventor on the cusp of greatness and wealth; she was from a financially challenged but abundantly populated middle-class home.[8] Somehow they hit it off and enjoyed going to the music hall (although he disdained dancing), and many humorous stories passed between them.

Several early biographies recount an incident regarding Edison's proposal to Mary.[9] One version of the story goes as follows:

> While she was typing away on the telegraph transmitter one day, Edison hovered over her until she became so distracted she stopped and looked up at him.
>
> "Mr. Edison," she said, swinging around suddenly, "I can always tell when you are behind me or near me."
>
> "How do you account for that?"
>
> "I don't know, I am sure," she answered, "but I seem to feel when you are near me."
>
> "Miss Stilwell," said Edison, "I've been thinking considerably of you of late, and if you are willing to have me, I'd like to marry you."
>
> "You astonish me," she protested, "I–I never–."
>
> "I know you never thought I would be your wooer," interrupted Mr. Edison, "but think over my proposal, Miss Stilwell, and talk it over with your mother."[10]

Whether this exchange happened the way it was reported is open to question. A variation of the story has Edison telling her, "Don't be in a rush, though. Think it over; talk to your mother about it and let me know as soon as convenient. Say Tuesday."[11] In any event, Mary said yes the next day. A week later, on Christmas Day, 1871, they were married.[12]

Family Life

Edison and Mary took a week off to honeymoon in Boston,[13] then settled back into a new home he rented in Newark, complete with servants and filled with furnishings.[14] Soon Edison was back in the laboratory and working night and day. Initially he assumed that his new wife would continue to work alongside him in the invention business. That idea was quickly scrapped. One night he wrote in his laboratory notebook, alongside sketches of telegraph circuits:

> Mrs. Mary Edison My Wife Dearly Beloved Cannot invent worth a Damn!![15]

Another, on Valentine's Day, 1872, more whimsically noted,

> My Wife Popsy Wopsy Can't Invent.[16]

Above: **Edison's first wife, Mary Stilwell**

Before long Mary was dismissed from the lab and relegated to managing household duties. She tried hard over the years to be a good wife, but never grew accustomed to her husband's long days and nights in the lab. While she took pains to make improvements to the house, he was rarely there to see them, and never seemed to take notice. Edison had been "attendant, entertaining, theater-going" during their brief courtship, but as a husband he was, at best, inattentive,[17] bordering on neglectful.[18] Mary was so starved for companionship that she talked Edison into letting her sister Alice move into the house to keep her

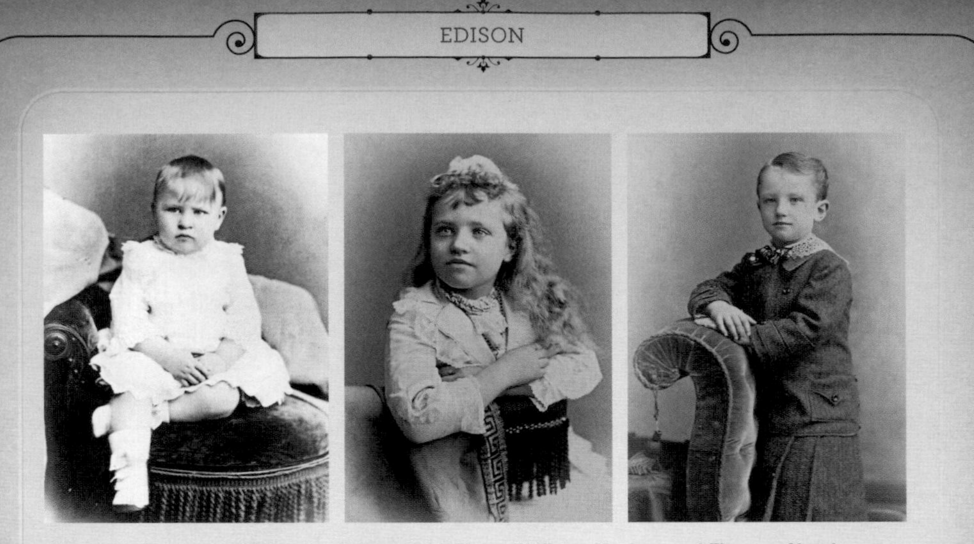

Above (left to right): **Edison's children with Mary: William, Marion, and Thomas Alva Jr.**

company. Edison gladly acquiesced, since Alice kept Mary occupied while he focused on inventing. Mary, who had grown up in a house full of people, frequently threw dinner parties, and while they were usually great successes, Edison often did not make it home in time to attend.[19]

Still, they managed to find enough time together to have three children during their thirteen years of marriage. Marion Estelle was born about fourteen months after their wedding, on February 18, 1873. Fond of creating nicknames for everyone, and as an homage to his beginnings as a telegrapher, Edison called his firstborn "Dot." When his namesake son, Thomas Alva Edison, Jr., was born three years later, Edison called him "Dash." William Leslie completed the first family tree, arriving in 1878. Given the limitations of Morse code, one has to wonder if Edison called him "Stop."[20]

To compensate for his inattention, Edison provided plenty of money for Mary to entertain. She was not particularly good at managing the funds, and often splurged on "fancy clothes and feathered hats." She spent money at home like Edison spent it on his many businesses.[21]

Edison's inattentiveness extended to his sons and daughter. He was so busy with work on his automatic telegraph and making trips to Washington and Pittsburgh to deal with suppliers and financing that he barely noticed Marion's birth. Then he sailed to England and was gone for nearly four months.[22] His relationships with Tom Jr. and William were no closer, and the boys spent much of their childhood being shuttled among various nannies, Mary, Alice, and, later, boarding schools. Both had troubled lives and fell in and (mostly) out of favor with their father as they rebelled against his lack of interest, while still seeking his attention.[23]

Tom Jr. engaged in a short and tumultuous marriage to a local chorus girl while lamenting his inability to please his father. He tried and failed to become an inventor (in a somewhat fraudulent business deal, to his father's grave disapproval), struggled with alcoholism, and eventually fell into severe depression.[24] Edison was so angry at Tom Jr. that he asked his son to change his last name. Tom Jr. did, at least briefly, to Thomas Willard. "I never could get him to go to school or work in the laboratory," Edison once told a friend, mournful that "he is therefore absolutely illiterate scientifically and otherwise."[25] After his father's death, Tom Jr. was finally hired into the Edison business by his half-brother Charles, only to die shortly thereafter of heart disease.[26]

William had a similarly difficult time. Like Tom Jr. he was sent to boarding schools in New Hampshire and Staten Island.[27] He later managed to attend the Sheffield Scientific School at Yale, and while not a particularly adept student, he graduated in 1900 and attempted to make it as an inventor.[28] Again like Tom, his choice in a wife—Blanche Travers, daughter of a successful "gentleman farmer and wholesale produce man in Baltimore"—did not meet with Edison's approval.[29] Worse, Edison attacked William for "tarnishing his good name"[30] by trying to set up somewhat dubious invention companies. Furious, Edison stated, "I see no reason whatever why I should support my son. He has done me no honor and has brought the blush of shame to my cheeks many times."[31] Angry and resentful at his treatment, William settled down to farm life, and died in 1937.

These crises with his sons would come long after Mary passed away unexpectedly at the age of twenty-nine on August 9, 1884.[32] In 1876, Edison and Mary had moved from Newark to a more spacious home in Menlo Park near the new laboratory. Being closer to home did not solve their intimacy problems, as Edison continued to work (and catnap) all night in the lab even though it was only a short walk from his own bed. Mary's cause of death remains somewhat of a mystery.[33] The official cause was "congestion of the brain,"[34] although it could have been a brain tumor or even an overdose of morphine being used to treat her sickness.[35] Edison later considered this a blot on his family, and when Marion asked him eleven years later what killed her mother, he insisted, "Typhoid."[36] That is not to say he was not anguished; Marion later remembered her father "shaking with grief, weeping and sobbing."[37]

Meeting Mina Miller

After Mary's death, Edison was clearly lonely, and perhaps guilt-ridden, so he decided to keep eleven-year-old Marion at his side. She traveled with him for the next year.[38] Mary had been responsible for child rearing, so Edison struggled to keep Marion busy while he searched for the next big project on his horizon. Her education during this time consisted of reading ten pages a day from an encyclopedia and taking a pop quiz.[39]

Marion was also present for her father's search for a new wife. Edison often traveled with colleague Ezra Gilliland and his wife, Lillian. Gilliland was an old friend from their Civil War days as roaming telegraphers, and he had worked for Edison in Newark

***Above*: Edison's Menlo Park home**

before moving on to Bell Laboratories in Boston. Gilliland played matchmaker on a February 1885 trip to New Orleans for the World Industrial and Cotton Centennial, where several Edison telegraph inventions were on display in the Boston Bell Company booth.[40] While strolling the aisles of the Exposition, Marion in tow, Edison and Gilliland ran into Lewis Miller, an Ohio industrialist who made his fortune inventing a better reaper and mower.[41]

It is unclear how much this meeting was planned in advance—Miller was a friend of Gilliland and they had shared many family events—but Edison was instantly enamored of Miller's nineteen-year-old daughter, Mina, even though she was half his age.[42] Gilliland continued to play a role in the budding courtship after the exposition was over. Because of their continued business dealings, Edison frequently traveled to Boston, where Gilliland held frequent social events in his summer cottage, Woodside Villa, on the north shore of Boston Bay.[43] Mina Miller was a student at a Boston finishing school, and the Gillilands made sure to invite her to gatherings whenever Edison was in town.[44]

Mina was everything Mary was not. Whereas Mary had been "buxom and fair," Mina was "petite and dark," looking somewhat "like a gypsy" with her thick, dark hair, "liquid brown eyes and flawless olive skin."[45] She was also engaged to be married. Her betrothed was the son of the co-founder (with her father, Lewis Miller) of Chautauqua Assembly in upstate New York, a spiritual and nature retreat that later became synonymous with thoughtful introspection.[46] Edison had refused an invitation to speak there a few years earlier. When he got another opportunity, he used it to solidify his claim on Mina.

Whereas Edison approached his marriage with Mary as a contractual arrangement, he seemed altogether smitten with Mina. This became apparent in a diary he kept for

***Above and following*: Edison with wife Mina**

nine days during the summer of 1885, the only time he ever recorded his private thoughts. The journal was part of a game initiated by Ezra Gilliland, who had implored Edison to stay with him for a few weeks at Woodside Villa. The objective was to allow Edison and others to "survey social prospects at his leisure."[47] Edison wrote to his colleague Samuel Insull, also seeking female com-panionship, and suggested he should "come over here at Gill's there is lots of pretty girls here."[48] Edison began his diary entry with:

> Awakened at 5:15 am. Thought of Mina, Daisy, and Mamma G.

His first thoughts on the first day of the diary were of Mina. Although he was supposedly at the Villa for the chance to explore several young women as potential wives, his mind was already fixated on her. "Took Mina as a basis, tried to improve her beauty by discarding and adding certain features borrowed from Daisy [another guest] and Mamma G [Mrs. Gilliland] a sort of Raphaelized beauty, got into it too deep, mind flew away and I went to sleep again."[49] A few days later, amidst mentions of other girls at the retreat and many sidetracks into business, Edison again mentioned he was thinking of Mina:

> Slept so sound that even Mina didn't bother me as it would stagger the mind of Raphael in a dream to imagine a being as comparable to the Maid of Chataqua.

He also referenced twelve-year-old Marion, still known as Dot, who was tagging along on the trip. Dot had set her sights on a different woman to become her father's next wife. "I picked out the stepmother I wanted right away," she writes in her own account of the summer, "more because she was a blonde like my Mother than for any other reason." Alas, Dot "had the impression that my father was in love with the Ohio girl." In response to Dot's plan to write a novel whose "basis seems to be a marriage under duress," Edison suggested "in the case of marriage to put in bucketfulls of misery" (hardly what you might expect from a man looking for a mate). Still, this period of time is probably the closest Edison would be with any of his children."[50]

Second Family, More Attention

After a year of courtship, much of it from afar, Edison found his way up to Chautauqua and proposed to Mina. Again, myth has blended with reality, and there is no verified account. The most intriguing story has Edison teaching Mina how to "sign" with Morse code so they could communicate in private.[51] By this time Edison was extremely famous and often had reporters following him around for the latest news. Because of his ever-worsening deafness, conversations usually involved shouting at high volume into his one barely working ear. Tapping Morse code allowed Edison and Mina to "converse" without the whole world knowing what they were discussing.[52]

After visiting Chautauqua again in August, Edison invited Mina to join him, Marion, and the Gillilands for a trip through upstate New York and New Hampshire.[53] Riding in a carriage through the White Mountains with Mina, Edison "tapped out a marriage proposal in Morse code on Mina's hand." She tapped back, "Yes."[54] Unlike the week between proposal and vows with Mary, Edison and Mina waited six months before getting married on February 24, 1886, in the Miller family home in Akron, Ohio. Marion was split

Above: **Edison's Glenmont mansion, Orange, New Jersey**

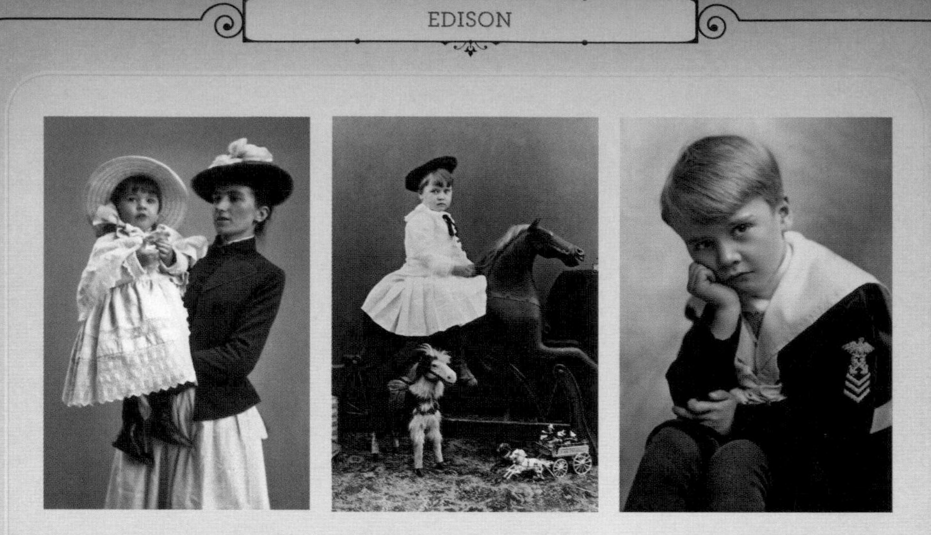

Above (left to right): **Edison's children with Mina, Madeline, Charles, and Theodore**

on the idea of Mina as a stepmother, who at only eight years older was "too young to be a mother to me but too old to be a chum."[55]

The new couple moved into an exquisite mansion called Glenmont in West Orange, New Jersey.[56] Edison had left the Menlo Park laboratory and was looking to start fresh with his new wife. Mina's upbringing in a wealthy family made her quite comfortable taking over the twenty-three-room Victorian mansion on thirteen acres near Edison's new lab. She became the perfect companion for the now-famous Edison, running the household staff while supporting her husband's expanding business dealings, wealth, and celebrity status.[57] She became a willing partner to Edison, often working at side-by-side desks in the upstairs living room at Glenmont. Mina became his protector, keeping him focused on his work, shielding him from distractions and the annoyances of the constant callers, and nurturing a creative environment. Without Billy, his oddly masculine pet name for Mina,[58] Edison may not have achieved all that he did.[59]

Two years after their marriage, on February 18, 1888, daughter Madeleine was born. Son Charles was born in 1890, and Theodore followed eight years later. While Edison was somewhat more attentive to his second family than his first, he was still consumed with long hours and work-related excursions. Unlike his older sons, Thomas Jr. and William, who never quite fit into their father's plans, both Charles and Theodore became key executives in the Thomas A. Edison Inc. brand.[60]

Some Friends are Out

Edison had few close friends. His work schedule left little room for deep relationships, so mostly he had close working acquaintances such as Charles Batchelor, John Kruesi, Samuel Insull, and Ezra Gilliland. During that initial trip to New Orleans in which Edison first met Mina, he and Gilliland extended their time to tour the Gulf Coast of Florida, where they found themselves in Fort Myers, then only a tiny village. Edison fell in love with the area, and he and Gilliland bought side-by-side properties and erected palatial summer homes. They even built a common dock stretching far out into the bay, where they enjoyed fishing and discussing important issues of the day.[61]

This friendship ended abruptly during the development of the phonograph. Gilliland played a major role in advising Edison in an arrangement with glassware magnate and financier Jesse Lippincott.[62] Without Edison's knowledge, however, Gilliland had also engaged in a side deal with Lippincott that would give Gilliland significant kickbacks once a deal was signed.[63] When Edison found out he had been duped, he unceremoniously cut all ties, and Gilliland never returned to Fort Myers.[64] Edison eventually bought up Gilliland's now-empty adjoining property.

Above: **Edison's Fort Myers, Florida home**

Some Friends are In

Edison was already a successful inventor and celebrity by the time he first met Henry Ford. In 1896, however, young Ford was merely an engineer in Edison's Illuminating Company in Detroit.[65] At a company convention at Coney Island, Ford was introduced to Edison and rather forwardly described his side project—a prototype for a car powered by a gasoline engine (rather than the electric cars that were already in existence). Edison was fascinated with the idea and, according to Ford, reportedly exclaimed while pounding his fist on the table, "Young man, that's the thing!" He encouraged Ford to "Keep at it." An inspired Ford decided to pursue his idea further.[66]

Despite Edison's apparent enthusiasm, it appears he quickly forgot about Henry Ford and the gasoline-powered car. The two did not cross paths again for eleven years, and only because Ford, now head of Ford Motors and successfully producing automobiles, asked Edison for a signed photo. Edison dismissed Ford without sending a photo. By 1912 the two agreed that Edison would work on an electric battery for use in Ford's cars.[67] While many attempts never quite achieved their goals, Edison and Ford became good friends, and Ford financed many of Edison's future endeavors.

And then they decided to go camping.

In 1916, sixty-nine-year-old Edison joined the sprightly forty-eight-year-old Harvey Firestone (of tire-manufacturing fame) and seventy-nine-year-old naturalist John Burroughs on the first of what would become annual camping trips.[68] The goal was to get away from the stress of running their respective businesses and the constant press of attention. In their first year, they traveled by car "through the Adirondacks and Green Mountains."[69] At the last minute, fifty-three-year-old Ford had to bow out, but joined them on all ensuing trips for nearly ten years.[70]

The members of "The Millionaires Club"[71] hardly roughed it in the wilderness.[72] Burroughs referred to the "Waldorf-Astoria on Wheels that followed us everywhere."[73] The group consisted of a party of up

***Opposite:* Henry Ford greeting Thomas Edison**
***Following:* (seated from left) Henry Ford, Thomas Edison, President Warren Harding, Harvey Firestone, and others on one of their celebrated camping trips**

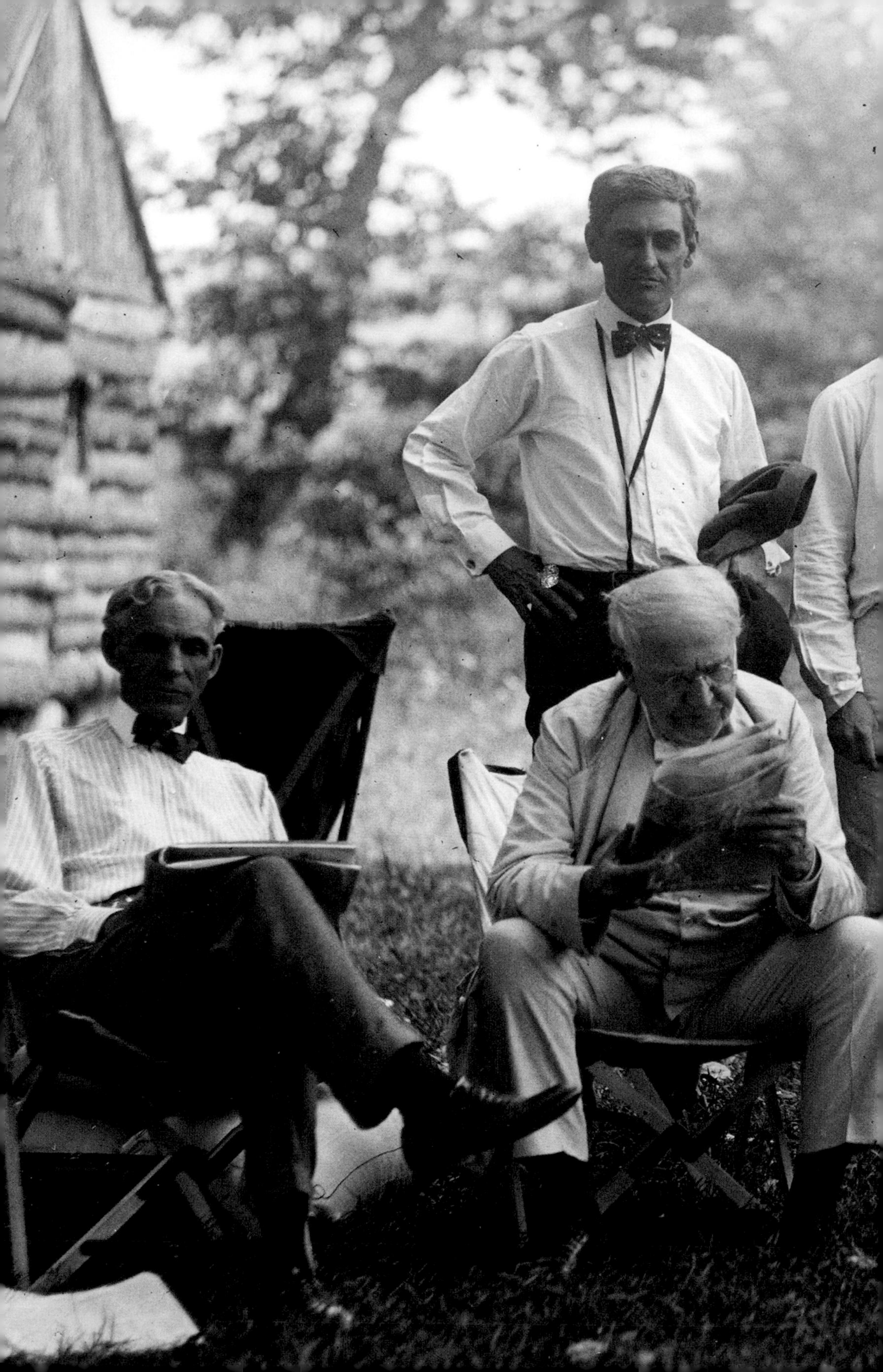

Cable Address "Edison, New York"

From the Laboratory of Thomas A. Edison,

Orange, N.J.

2 Sheets—Sheet 2.

T. A. EDISON.

Phonograph.

No. 227,679. **Patented May 18, 1880.**

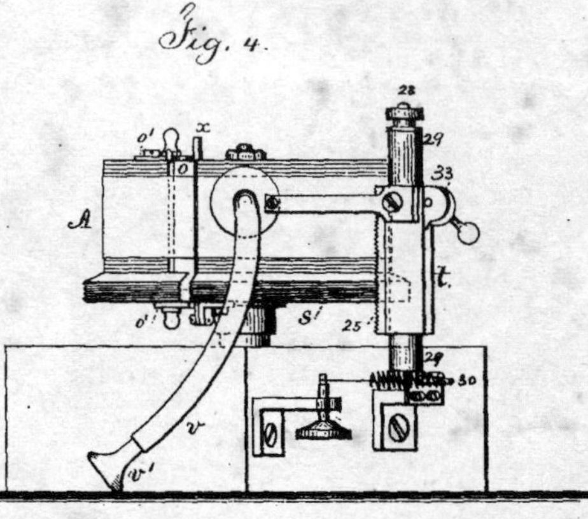

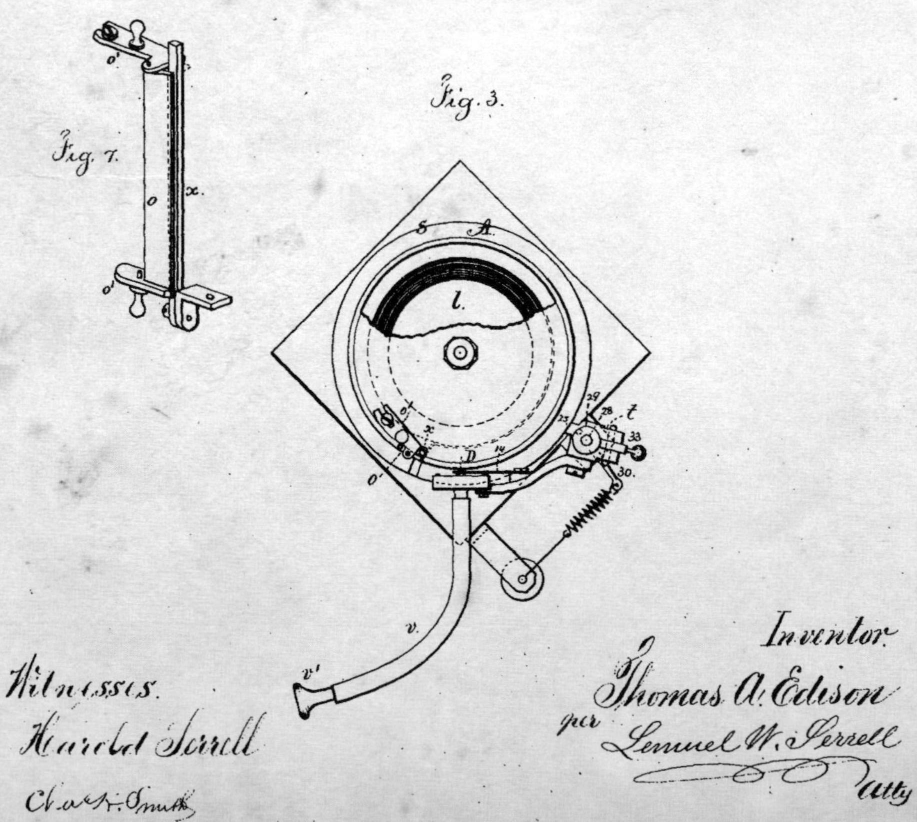

to fourteen, including "Firestone's son, Harvey Jr., three friends, a chef, and various assistants."[74] For their 1918 expedition, the group piled into at least three cars, followed by several trucks filled with camping equipment. An accompanying chef whipped up nightly banquets to be served *al fresco*. A professional "photographer was always on hand to take still photos for distribution to the press and movies for newsreels."[75] So much for going camping to get away from the paparazzi.

By 1919 the entourage had expanded to "fifty cars and trucks transformed into moving billboards carrying placards encouraging passersby to 'Buy Firestone Tires.'"[76] Trips included driving from San Francisco to Santa Rosa one year; through the Adirondacks and Green Mountains of Vermont another year; and caravans through the Great Smoky Mountains, the "trail of the Minute Men in Historic Old New England," and various jaunts around Ohio, Maryland, West Virginia, and Pennsylvania.[77] Each town was tipped off to their impending arrival, which led to grand events complete with autographs, speeches, and plenty of fodder for newsreels such as "Genius Sleep Under the Stars."[78] The trips had become less about "getting away" and more about a sleek marketing campaign. Edison's daughter Madeleine later admitted they were more of a "publicity stunt."[79] Given the pedigree of the campers—Ford, Edison, and Firestone continued after Burroughs died in 1921—other famous notables sometimes joined them. Not the least of these was President Warren G. Harding (a friend of Firestone) in 1920, followed by President Calvin Coolidge in 1924.

When not traveling, Edison and Mina opened up Glenmont to entertain celebrities such as Maria Montessori, General "Black Jack" Pershing, Helen Keller, Orville Wright, Charles Lindbergh, George Eastman, and of course, Ford, Firestone, and Burroughs. Presidents Hoover and Wilson were welcomed guests any time they wanted to get away. According to Edison, he also hosted the president of Mexico, Lord Kelvin, and "Sitting Bull and fifteen fteen Sioux Indians."[80] Whenever he traveled abroad, Edison was often an invited guest of royalty, presidents, and other notables. As he grew older and more financially secure, he relaxed and spent more time away from the laboratories, although he never actually stopped working completely.

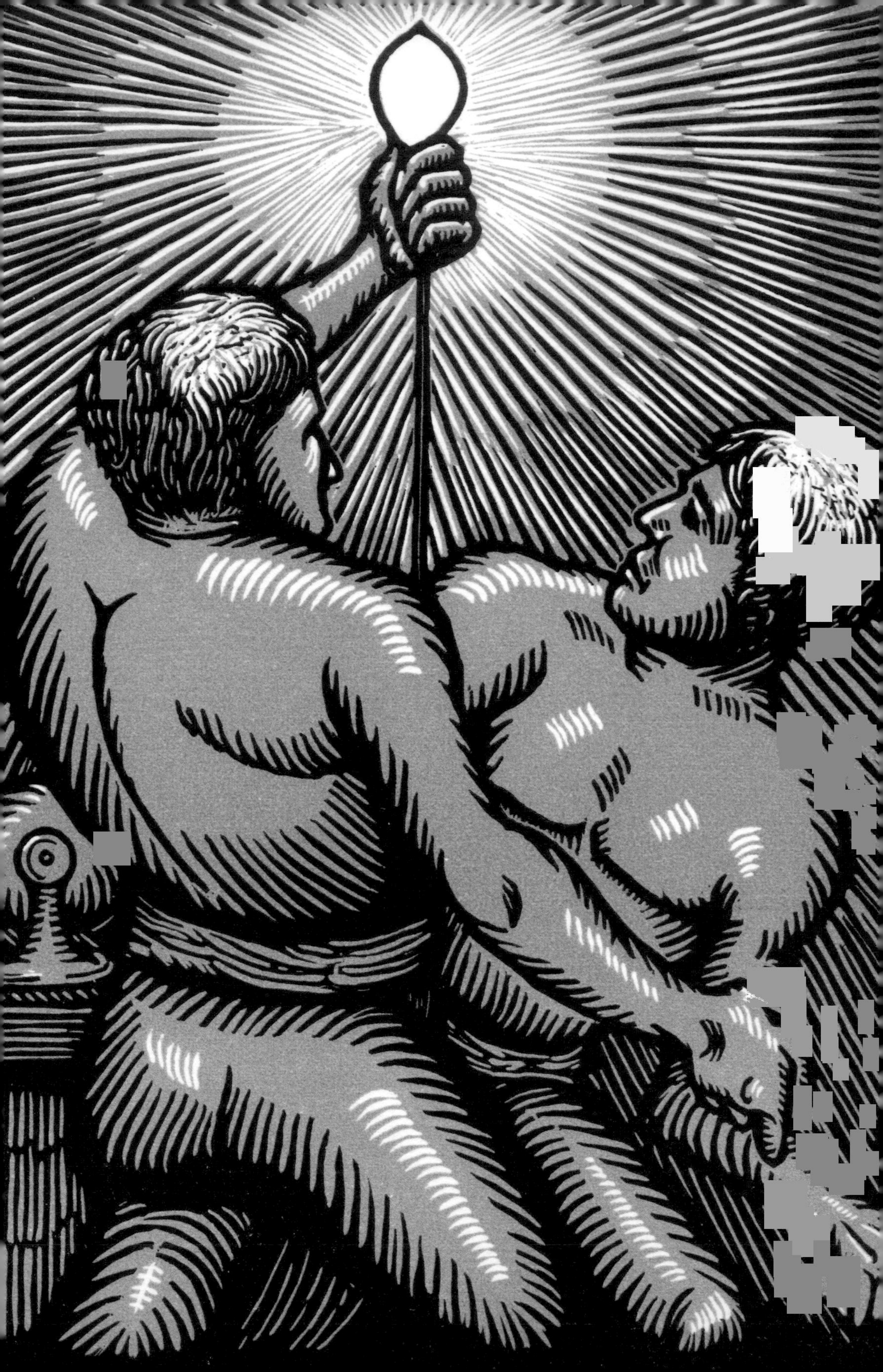

CHAPTER 6

BUILDING A BETTER LIGHTBULB

By mid-1878 Edison was deep into the development of the tinfoil phonograph. After many successful demonstrations, marketers were clamoring for a more refined version to sell to offices and the public. But Edison had grown bored, or at least distracted, and dropped all efforts on the phonograph while he pursued his next big invention—a better lightbulb.[1] More accurately called an incandescent lamp, these bulbs would offer light far different from the flaming brightness of the common arc lamps.[2]

The idea of producing a practical electric light was not new.[3] Until the middle of the nineteenth century, the focus had been "obtaining the illumination from the actual consumption of the light-giving material" (e.g., burning grease, wax, whale oil, or some other form of carbon).[4] Edison saw the future differently. He believed that the answer was not in consuming the source, but simply making it glow—otherwise known as incandescence—by passing an electric current through it.[5] There was one problem with this idea: "Almost the entire scientific world had pronounced such an idea as impossible of fulfillment."[6]

> The leading electricians, physicists, and experts of the period had been studying the subject for more than a quarter of a century, and but with one known exception had proven mathematically and by close reasoning that the "Subdivision of the Electric Light," as it was then termed, was practically beyond attainment.[7]

***Opposite**: The Invention of the Incandescent Light*, **woodcut by Walter Huxley**
Following: **Edison ponders the filament**

FRANK LESLIE'S ILLUSTRATED NEWSPAPER

No. 1,267—VOL. XLIX.] NEW YORK, JANUARY 10, 1880. [PRICE, WITH SUPPLEMENT, 10 CENTS. $4.00 YEARLY. 13 WEEKS, $1.00.

NEW JERSEY.—THE WIZARD OF ELECTRICITY—THOMAS A. EDISON EXPERIMENTING WITH CARBONIZED PAPER FOR HIS SYSTEM OF ELECTRIC LIGHT, AT HIS LABORATORY, MENLO PARK.—FROM SKETCHES BY OUR SPECIAL ARTIST.—SEE PAGE 353.

Never one to let the impossible stop him, Edison set out to prove everyone wrong. After telling colleagues to "hurry up" because he had "struck a big bonanza," Edison prematurely announced to the *New York Sun,* "I have it now!"[8] He did not actually yet have it, but to Edison the principle of incandescence was simple: Heat could be generated by passing electric current through wires of platinum and other metals, or through pieces of carbon, and this could produce the glowing white heat of incandescence. It would create light.[9]

The concept had been proven in a 1847 patent on "two forms of incandescent lamps, one having a burner made from platinum foil placed under a glass cover without excluding the air; and the other composed of a thin plate or pencil of carbon enclosed in a Torricellian vacuum."[10] Other experimenters developed a means to put a metallic cup on a glass globe, from which all the air could be removed.[11] These and other refinements created a "bulb" that could provide light, but only briefly. Two big problems remained: The carbon lamps burned out within seconds, and the expensive platinum lamps could burn a little longer but had to be heated to a point just short of melting—a point that was almost universally exceeded, resulting in these lamps also producing light for mere seconds.[12] A commercial product was not yet in the making, and as Edison later admitted, "it is very difficult to make a practical system and introduce it."[13]

Edison saw the solution of building a useful incandescent lamp as being able to achieve three critical features: "The burning of an indefinite number of lights on the same circuit; each light had to give a useful and economical degree of illumination; and each light had to be independent of all the others in regard to its operation and extinguishment."[14] In other words, one switch would turn on many lights; the lights would remain lit for a reasonable amount of time at an affordable cost; and if one light blew out, it would not take the others with it.

This was a lofty goal. Never shy about his capabilities, Edison felt he could achieve it via hard work and intellectual acumen. According to him, his breakthrough in developing the incandescent lamp was not simply improving on what others did, "it was the legitimate outcome of a series of exhaustive experiments founded upon logical

***Opposite:* Edison experimenting with carbonized paper as a potential lightbulb filament**

and original reasoning in a mind that had the courage and hardihood set at naught the confirmed opinions of the world." He would show them, Edison felt, despite "jeers and derision" from the learned masses.[15]

Finding a Filament

Because of his phonograph and telephone work, as well as the invention of the carbon transmitter, Edison's obvious starting point was some form of carbonized paper.[16] Others had proven that carbon paper did not last long enough to be useful, but Edison always had to do the experiments himself before believing anything he read. Back in 1877 he tried a "strip of carbonized paper about an inch long, one-sixteenth of an inch broad, and six or seven one-thousandths of an inch thick."[17] The ends were attached to clamps that formed the poles of a battery. As expected, the paper disintegrated when it was heated to incandescence. Edison then tried the same carbonized paper under a vacuum, which increased the lifespan up to about eight minutes,[18] although with a hand-operated pump they could only get a partial vacuum.[19] Several other experimental variations did nothing to improve performance, so Edison acknowledged the inadequacy of carbonized paper, at least for the time being.[20]

Setting aside the carbon, Edison tried the platinum others had used. In addition to the difficulty of finding the point of incandescence without melting, platinum was incredibly expensive. Edison also experimented with other metals with higher melting temperatures that were less likely to turn into a melted mess when heated, including "boron, ruthenium, chromium."[21] He tried them as bridges between two carbon points and by putting them directly into the circuit. He even tried powdered silicon.[22] These trials achieved some success, but the materials would not be sufficient for a marketable product. While others may have been fatally frustrated, Edison was the kind of scientist who tried thousands of options before giving up on a technical problem he thought he could solve. He once told a colleague: "Results? Why, man, I have gotten a lot of results! I know several thousand things that won't work."[23]

Opposite: **Edison's first incandescent bulb, 1879**

Above: **Moses G. Farmer, a fellow inventor who was key in the development of the lightbulb**

Around this time he and some colleagues made a fateful trip to Connecticut to visit with William Wallace, who had been experimenting with arc lighting.[24] Not long after the visit Edison filed an application for his first lighting patent, "Improvement in Electric Lights,"[25] which suggests he may have "borrowed" some ideas from Wallace. Edison himself later gave Wallace credit for being "one of the earliest pioneers in electrical matters."[26] He added:

> [Wallace] has done a great deal of good work, for which others have received the credit; and the work which he did in the early days of electric lighting others have benefitted by largely, and he has been crowded to one side and forgotten.[27]

It may have been Edison who benefitted the most.

In any case, Edison was also aided by Moses G. Farmer, another of Wallace's associates he knew from his duplex telegraph days.[28] Edison was familiar with Farmer's work, which included getting short-lived incandescence from small pieces of platinum and iridium wire. Returning home to Menlo Park, Edison put renewed effort into developing a commercial incandescent lamp. Once again returning to the idea of a carbon burner, he and Batchelor famously went through many trials of different materials.[29] Among them were carbonized paper strips, tissue paper coated with tar and lampblack and rolled into thin sticks, hard carbons, wood carbons, "and almost every conceivable variety of paper carbon."[30] All of these trials were done in a glass globe hand-pumped to create a vacuum, but none of the trials produced a bulb that lit up for more than ten or fifteen minutes before disintegrating.

Other Problems

Even Edison needed a break. He and Batchelor had not been able to find a material that would create incandescence for a commercially feasible time period. So he turned to other technical challenges in need of attention.

To be viable, Edison felt that the incandescent material needed to have high resistance combined with a small radiating surface. The bulb also must be capable of working in a "multiple arc" system such that each bulb could be turned on or off without interfering with other bulbs.[31]

These were significant challenges, and the reasons others had not been able to produce a reliable incandescent system.[32] "The crucial point was the production of a hairlike carbon filament, capable of withstanding mechanical shock, and susceptible of being maintained at a temperature of over two thousand degrees for a thousand hours or more before breaking."[33] Furthermore, the filament needed to be supported in a vacuum chamber "so perfectly formed" that it would withstand thousands of hours of use in which "not a particle of air should enter to disintegrate the filament."[34] All of this needed to be manufactured at low cost and large quantities.

With his trademark confidence, Edison acknowledged that only he, "in the enormous mass of patiently worked-out details," could have solved the problem. With Batchelor's help, of course.[35]

While toggling between platinum-iridium and carbonized-paper filaments, Edison managed to improve the vacuum process enough to extend the time of incandescence. He also improved the quality of the glass bulb.[36] On October 21, 1879, Edison had a major breakthrough. By carbonizing a piece of cotton sewing-thread bent into a loop or horseshoe form and sealing it in a vacuum bulb, Edison was able to light up the lamp to incandescent brilliance for more than forty hours, "and lo! the practical incandescent lamp was born."[37]

But What About That Filament?

Edison was ecstatic, and as had become his habit, he announced his great discovery to the press. The *New York Herald* published an aggrandizing

Following: **Edison's lighting display at the Paris Exhibition, 1889**

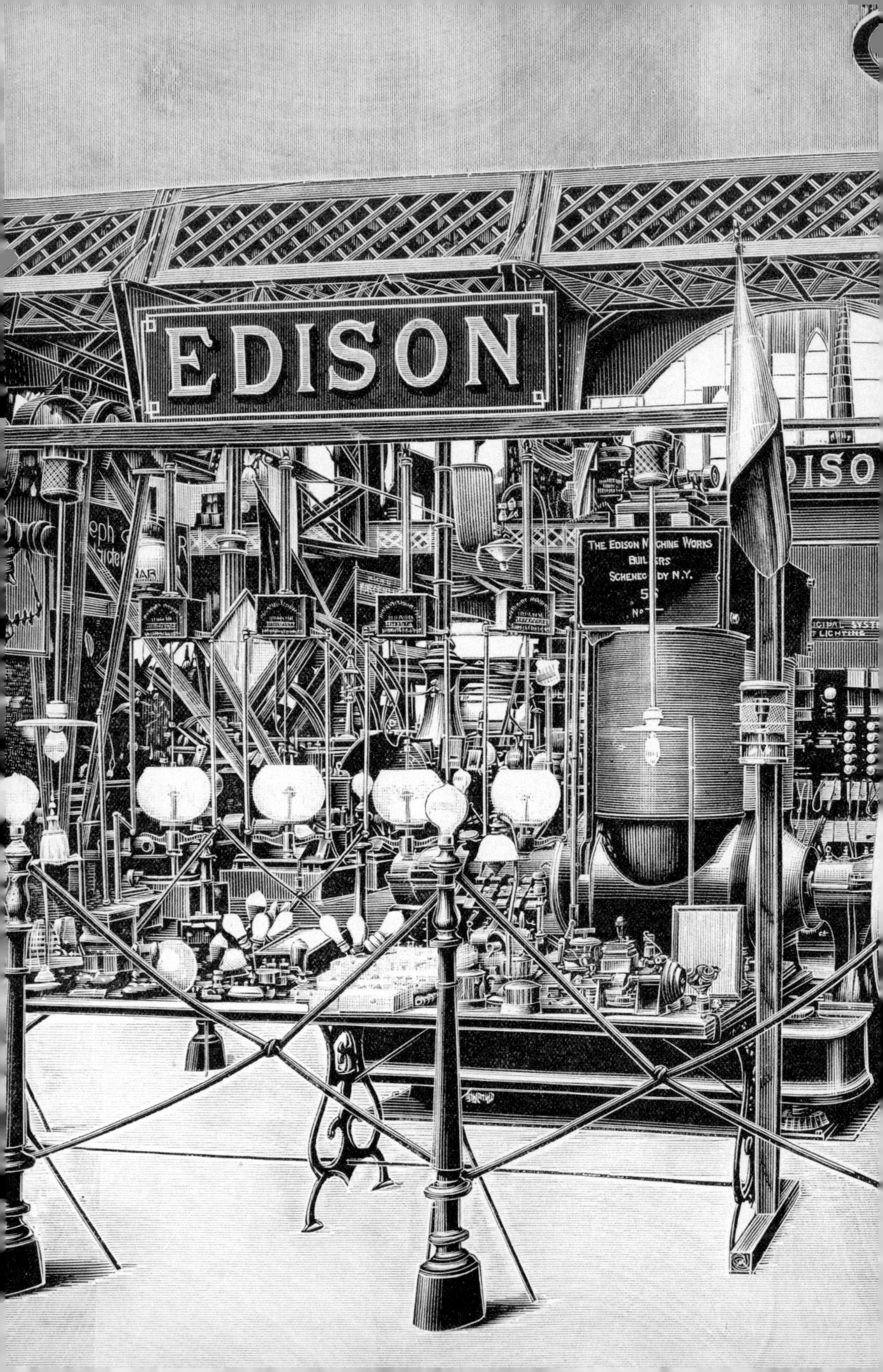
EDISON

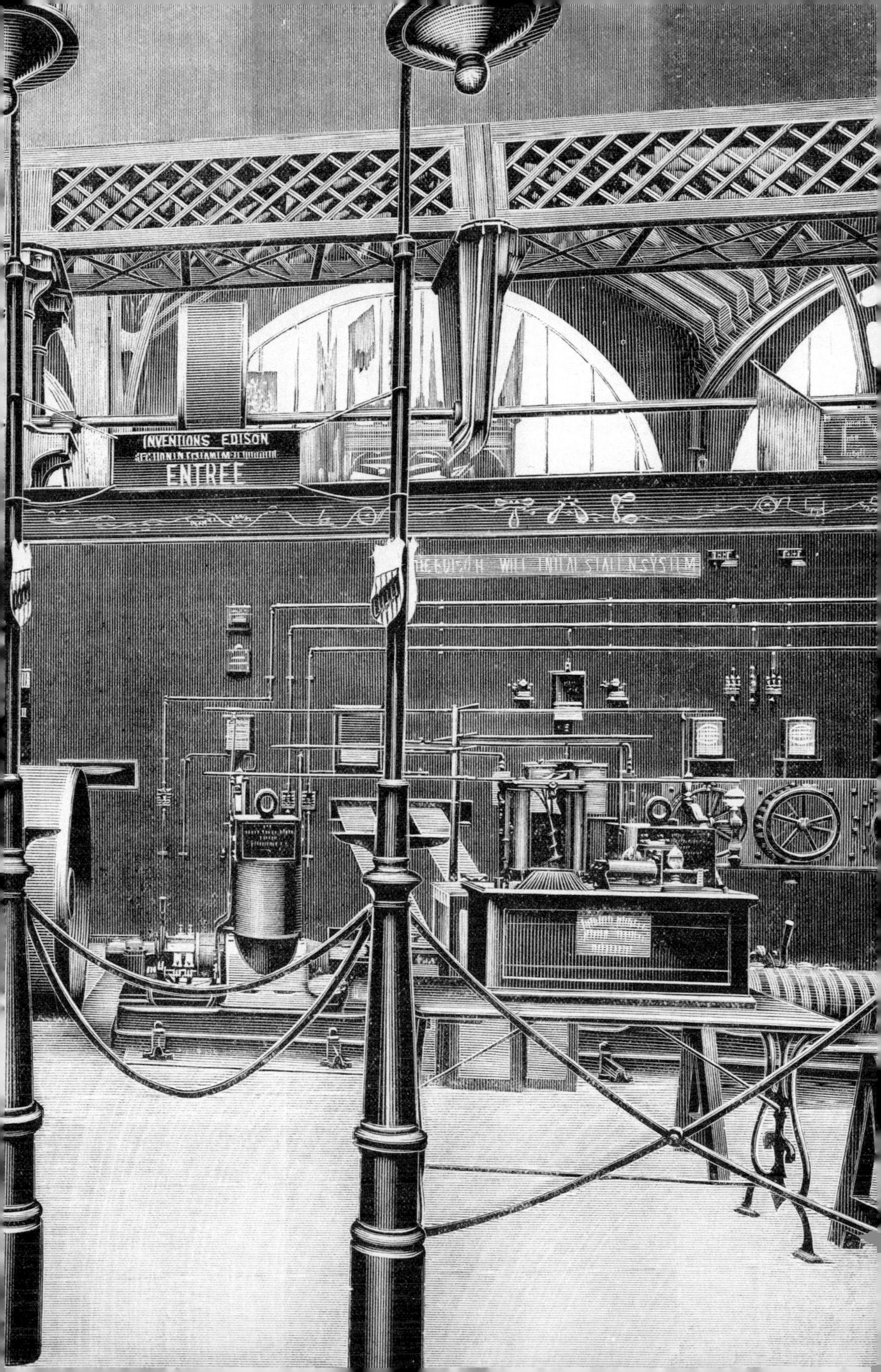
INVENTIONS EDISON
ENTREE

article on December 21, 1879, and Edison rushed to install a display to entice interest. "The laboratory was brilliantly illuminated with twenty-five electric lamps, the office and counting room with eight, and twenty others were distributed in the street leading to the depot and in some of the adjoining houses."[38] Soon he had long lines of gawkers crowding the laboratory for a look. On New Year's Eve, "special trains were run to Menlo Park by the Pennsylvania Railroad, and over three thousand persons took advantage of the opportunity to go there and witness this demonstration for themselves."[39]

Despite the throngs of admirers, Edison's work was not even close to being complete. Promises of usable electric lights were grossly premature, to the point where once again people started to think of Edison as the guy who promised more than he delivered.[40] The cotton sewing-thread filament was clearly a breakthrough, but even forty hours of use was simply not going to be sufficient at the cost each bulb would take to produce.

While Edison fended off visitors and set up production companies, Batchelor and others in the lab were frantically searching for an even better material for the filament. Upton later noted the unsung

Above: **Charles Batchelor reading by Edison's first lamps**

contributions of Batchelor to the development of a filament for the new lighting system: "As a mechanic, Batchelor was second-to-none, 'the control he had of his fingers was marvelous, and his eyesight was sharp. Mr. Batchelor's judgment and good sense were always in evidence.'"[41] It was the "deft and cautious" Batchelor who put pains to testing "as one fragile filament after another refused to stay intact until it could be sealed into its crystal prison and there glow with light that never was before on land or sea."[42]

So with Batchelor leading the team, the staff carbonized "everything in nature that he could lay his hands on," including "tissue paper, soft paper, cardboards, drawing paper of all grades, paper saturated with tar, all kinds of threads, fish-line, threads rubbed with tarred lampblack, fine threads plaited together in strands, cotton soaked in boiling tar, lamp-wick, twine, tar and lampblack mixed with a proportion of lime, vulcanized fibre, celluloid, boxwood, cocoanut hair and shell, spruce, hickory, baywood, cedar and maple shavings, rosewood, punk, cork, bagging, flax, and a host of other things."[43] And he did not stop there; he also delved into the suitability of various grasses, canes, and other plants. Overall, Edison "tested no fewer than six thousand different species of vegetable growths," all in an attempt to find a better filament material.[44]

At some point during this trial-and-error, test-anything-and-everything endeavor, Edison noticed a common palm-leaf fan with a binding rim made out of bamboo. Edison had an assistant cut a strip of bamboo, carbonize it, and test it in the lightbulb apparatus. The results were "far better than with anything thus far used."[45] Bamboo had "long, uniform fibers that would make sturdy, long-lasting filaments."[46] Edison had finally found the perfect material for his electric lightbulb.

In Search of Bamboo

Edison's next challenge was securing massive amounts of bamboo. Not just any bamboo would do; further experiments suggested some worked better than others. And so began a worldwide search for adequate supplies of the most effective bamboo.

Following: **Edison stands in New Jersey and leans across the Hudson to join hands with Charles F. Brush, inventor of the arc light, who stands with one foot in Brooklyn and the other in Manhattan.**

PUBLISHED BY CURRIER & IVES
NEW JERSEY
COPYRIGHT 1880,
NEW YOR
THE ELEC

RIER & IVES, N. Y.
115 NASSAU ST. NEW YORK
BROOKLYN

RIC LIGHT.

Edison was renowned for stocking everything he thought he might one day need in his lab. While he was able to acquire some bamboo, he knew from experience with other plants that the quality would vary depending on the environment in which it was grown. He sent a series of emissaries to distant lands.[47]

First out was William H. Moore, who in the summer of 1880 left New York City by boat for China and Japan, the two countries most likely to have ample supplies of many different species of bamboo.[48] Bushwhacking into the remote interiors of both countries, the adventurous Moore studied the bamboo as he collected it, "testing the relative value of its fibre in canes of one, two, three, four, and five year growths."[49] "Great bales of samples" were shipped to Edison for more detailed testing, who decided a particular species and growth of bamboo from Japan provided the best filaments for his lamps. Word was sent to Moore, and he made arrangements with a local farmer to grow and ship bamboo to the states.[50] As luck would have it, the Japanese farmer was adept at cross-fertilizing such that the bamboo was "constantly improved" and used in Edison lamps for many years.

But Edison was not finished. Not satisfied with one source, he continued his research into other possible materials that would work as filaments. One man, John Segredor, was sent to the swamps of Florida, where he wrote back "what makes this job extremely interesting is the strong possibility of getting bitten by a snake." He need not have worried; a month later he was in Cuba and died from yellow fever. Edison wired to his contacts in Cuba: "bury him at my expense."[51]

With Moore still collecting bamboo in China and Japan, Edison engaged John C. Brauner, an expert on various plants who had become familiar with many species of palms during an expedition for the Brazilian government. In December 1880 Brauner was sent to Brazil in search of whatever palms, fibers, grasses, and canes he felt would be suitable for Edison's purposes. On foot and by canoe Brauner covered nearly 2,000 miles of the largely unexplored Amazon and Southern Brazil. Once again, many tons of fibrous plant samples were shipped back to Menlo Park, each variety of which was tested as potential filament material. Despite Brauner's exhaustive collection, however, none of the materials he sent proved superior to the Japanese bamboo already in use. The same conclusion was reached for materials sent from Jamaica and Cuba, where Edison had also sent out explorers in search of bamboo or some other material.[52]

For several years Edison had to live with the Japanese bamboo, which worked but did not give him the satisfaction he was looking for. He was constantly seeking other materials, and in 1887 he again sent out emissaries to Brazil.[53] Frank McGowan and C. F. Hanington, both longtime employees of the Edison Electric Light Company, left New York in September. Before long the pair had managed to traverse 2,300 miles up the Amazon River to Iquitos, where they became separated. Hanington decided to head back down the Amazon and caught a steamer to Uruguay, up the Rio de la Plata through Argentina and Paraguay back to the southern border of Brazil, "collecting a large number of specimens of palms and grasses" along the way.[54]

As adventurous as that journey sounds, McGowan had an even more exciting time. On foot and by canoe he worked his way west through Peru, Ecuador, and Columbia. After leaving Hanington, McGowan braved somewhat unappreciative natives as he paddled his way along the Napo River to Quito in eighty-seven days, then to Guayaquil, where he caught a steamer to Buenaventura, from which he set off on foot to explore the Cauca Valley of Colombia.[55] His efforts for fifteen months were the stuff they make movies out of, as the May 2, 1889, issue of the *Evening Sun* reported:

> In pursuit of a substance that should meet the requirements of the Edison incandescent lamp, Mr. McGowan penetrated the wilderness of the Amazon, and for a year defied its fevers, beasts, reptiles, and deadly insects in his quest of a material so precious that jealous Nature has hidden it in her most secret fastnesses.[56]

And if that was not thrilling enough, they added:

> No hero of mythology or fable ever dared such dragons to rescue some captive goddess as did this dauntless champion of civilization. Theseus, or Siegfried, or any knight of the fairy books might envy the victories of Edison's irresistible lieutenant.[57]

The result of this "glorious" expedition? McGowan discovered "the mysterious bamboo" and shipped large quantities of it back to "the Wizard's laboratory, there to suffer another wondrous change and then to light up our pleasure-haunts and homes with a gentle radiance."[58] Success!

Not long after, McGowan vanished. After trading stories of his many adventures with friends in his favorite French restaurant on Fulton Street one evening, McGowan made plans to write out the narrative for future use, bid adieu, and was never to be seen again. His abrupt disappearance remains an unsolved mystery. This unexpected event put Edison at a loss. He had waited patiently for McGowan to return home with the bamboo, and then, without warning, he was gone without telling Edison exactly where he got it. Faced with this dilemma, Edison called upon James Ricalton, a school principal and avid world traveler. Ricalton recalled Edison telling him: "I sent a man to South America to find what I want; he found it; but lost the place where he found it, so he might as well have never found it at all."[59]

Ricalton was sent to Asia, where he was tasked with finding a suitable bamboo that at least equaled the usefulness and quality of the sample Edison had from McGowan. Trusting Ricalton's word that he would be as frugal as possible on his journey, Edison ordered a line of credit for Ricalton's use, with a second order ready in case it was needed.[60] Ricalton first set sail for England, then through the Suez Canal to Ceylon (now Sri Lanka), "that fair isle to which Sinbad the Sailor made his sixth voyage, picturesquely referred to in history as 'the brightest gem in the British Colonial Crown.'"[61]

In Ceylon, and again in Burma, Ricalton discovered the giant bamboo, up to twelve inches across and 150 feet high. It tested as the highest-quality carbon and would be his prize possession from the trip. But he did not stop there. From Ceylon he traveled to India and worked his way steadily north through its vast expanse, testing bamboos and other plants as potential filament materials. After getting up to the sub-Himalayas he backtracked to Calcutta, where he sailed on to Burma, then the Malay Peninsula (present-day Thailand and Malaysia). By this time he was satisfied that he had

Opposite: **James Ricalton in India crossing the rapid Jehlum River on a single rope bridge**

Cable Address "Edison, New York"

From the Laboratory of Thomas A. Edison,

Orange, N.J.

T. A. EDISON.

Electric-Lamp.

No. 223,898. Patented Jan. 27, 1880.

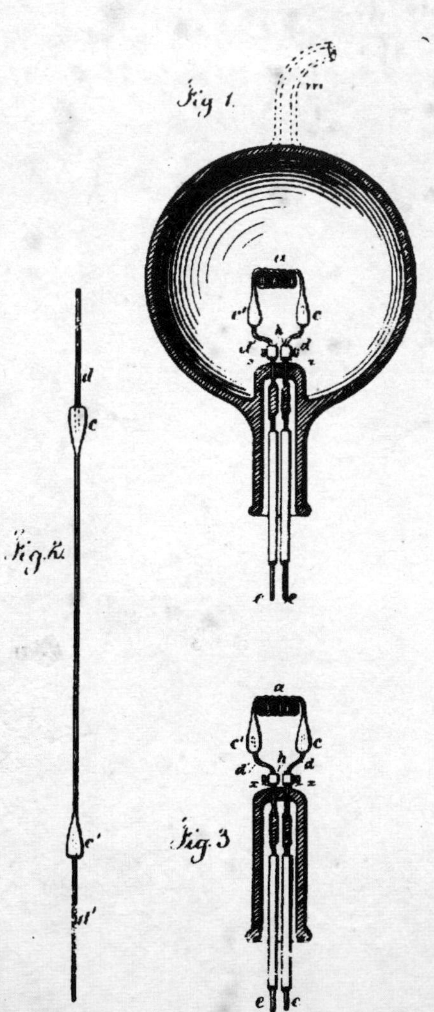

Witnesses

Chas H Smith

Geo T Pinckney

Inventor

Thomas A. Edison

for Lemuel W. Serrell

atty.

superior bamboo to meet Edison's needs, so he began his trip back home, stopping in various places in China and Japan along the way, just to make sure.[62]

He had spent exactly one year making a complete circuit of the globe, arriving "on the same day, at the same hour, at the same minute, one year to a second" back in New Jersey. He was greeted by cheers and celebrations at the Maplewood boys and girls school from which he had disembarked. Once he could extract himself from his adoring students and teachers, Ricalton made his way to West Orange to consult with Edison, who after Ricalton's year of around-the-world travel greeted him with, "Did you get it?"

Floored by Edison's nonchalance, Ricalton learned that during his long travels abroad Edison had "succeeded in making an artificial carbon which was meeting the requirements satisfactorily."[63] The bamboo Ricalton and others had spent years traveling the world to find would not be needed after all.

Still, it was a grand adventure, smiled Ricalton.

Finishing the Lightbulb

Edison had not been idle during these years of exploration looking for natural fibers. After much experiment he had devised a "squirted" filament using the artificial compound, and while many millions of lamps still retained the bamboo filament for another decade, the manufacturing plants would be retooled to use the artificial compound. In the early 1900s lamps would largely switch over to tantalum- and tungsten-based filaments. Other modifications, including various gases instead of a vacuum inside the glass bulb, would come much later. For now, Edison's lightbulb was essentially finished.

But Edison himself was not done. After all, lightbulbs need a source of electricity for them to incandesce. So Edison set himself the task of creating an entire direct current electric lighting system to produce, transmit, and incorporate electricity into homes and places of business. Doing so would solidify Edison as the greatest inventor of his time, except that it would not be that easy. In fact, it would lead to the "war of the currents."

THOMAS
EDISON

WAR OF THE CURRENTS

While the new lightbulb was getting all the press despite the fact that it was not ready for use, Edison and his team were busy creating the system that would provide the electricity for those bulbs.[1] This was no small order. Edison's achievement was in "conceiving and executing in all its details an art and an industry absolutely new to the world."[2] While it was one thing to produce enough electrical energy in a small laboratory to power a few lightbulbs, it was yet another to generate sufficient electricity to power an entire city block, and ultimately, an entire city—an "altogether prodigious undertaking."[3]

First up was the development of the dynamo to generate electricity. Dynamos produce direct current, also called DC.[4] Originally developed by Michael Faraday (and before him, Joseph Henry),[5] DC dynamos consisted of copper or iron conductors passing through the fields between opposite poles (positive and negative) of magnets.[6] The DC dynamos produced alternating current, which could not drive motors. A commutator, the added brush that gives off telltale sparks, was needed to convert it to direct current. Power production was low on these dynamos, and Edison set his laboratory colleagues on a path to improving them.[7] Batchelor, Kruesi, and Upton were kept busy building and testing various options.[8] As usual, they attempted many refinements, including different metals and forms of iron, placing motors in circuit with multiple arcs and fixed resistance, and various degrees of windings (wire coiled around the armatures).[9]

***Opposite*: Nineteenth-century tobacco card of Edison**
***Following:* Thomas Rowlandson's humorous caricature of reactions to the installation of the gas-burning street lighting in London in 1807**

PALL MALL
The Coals being steam'd produces tar or paint for outside of Houses – the Smoke passing thro' water is deprived of substance and burns as you see
Arrah honey if this man bring fire thro water nr have the Thames and burnt down – and all the Herrings & Whales. burnt to

Aye Friend but it is all Vanity. what is this to the inward light
If this light is not put a stop too - we must give up our business We may as well shut up shop
Wauns what a main pretty light it be. we have nothing like it in our Country

THE EDISON ELECTRIC LIGHT COMPANY

These improvements in dynamos were "of a radical nature" and put Edison in the position to fight three battles he would need to win to pursue his dream to electrify the world.[10]

Battle #1: DC Electricity vs. Gas

Armed with a brand-new dynamo design and his longer-lasting incandescent lamps, Edison was ready to move from the laboratory into the real world. His first problem was that an infrastructure for gas was already in place to provide lighting to homes and factories.[11] Gas lighting had become the standard in the nineteenth century, and most cities had laid gas mains down streets. Gas lights were in most households by the late 1800s, and people were used to them.

Gas, however, had some significant drawbacks. Production was somewhat complicated, with manufactured fuel gas requiring the gasification of combustible materials, most notably coal but also wood and oil.[12] Heating the source generated fumes that were mixtures of several chemicals, including hydrogen, methane, carbon monoxide, and ethylene. Depending on the source, the mixture could also include sulfur, ammonia, and heavy hydrocarbons, all of which needed to be removed during a purification process.[13] Later, after Edison had begun to establish his electricity potential, pipelines from natural gas fields in Texas and Oklahoma started flowing a cleaner gas to northern and eastern cities. Eventually, natural gas replaced manufactured gas.

Luckily for Edison, gas lighting sometimes led to buildings being burned to the ground. Occasionally there were explosions that accomplished the same destruction in an instant.[14] Gas also "silently poisoned the ground, and water wells and cisterns, leaking out from the mains through which it invisibly traveled."[15] Even when the gas fixtures worked as designed, they left a hydrocarbon residue on wallpaper and ceilings.[16] There was clearly room for improvement, and Edison took the gas companies to task.

The Edison Electric Light Company was formed in 1882, and wasted no time attacking the use of gas for lighting. Every example of "devastation and death caused by gas" was exploited and documented in the company's *Bulletin*.[17] Reports included a man found dead in

***Opposite*: Headquarters of the Edison Electric Light Co. at 65 Fifth Avenue, New York City**

his hotel room, young girls found dead in bed, explosions blowing out plate glass windows in office buildings, and many other frightful incidents resulting from gas leaks.[18] Electric lights, Edison argued, were not only safer, but also clean, would not leave sooty residues on walls and furniture.

Edison also had to look at the costs of designing and installing a completely new system of wiring, lamps, and switches for his new electrical system—and doing so at a cost that could beat the low price of gas lighting.[19] He sent out "a large battalion of canvassers to go house to house in the Pearl Street district [of lower Manhattan], noting the number of gas jets, the usual hours of use, and their cost."[20] He was eventually able to convince the city and several key decision-makers to give him a chance.

Battle #2: DC Electricity vs. Arc Lighting

In some ways a simpler battle was fought in competition with another form of electricity—arc lighting. While Edison's *Bulletin* highlighted the dangers of gas and the safety of electricity, it conveniently ignored the very real shocks, and sometimes electrocutions, occurring in the electrical business. In one celebrated case, a visitor touring the Brush Electric Light Company's arc lighting plant in Buffalo grabbed hold of two hanging wires and dropped dead.[21] Fatal electrocutions, while relatively rare, usually got front-page coverage and spurred one British newspaper to note "the electric Frankenstein turns now and then upon the magician who has raised him."[22] All of these were arc lighting.

These incidents were especially problematic for Edison not so much because of shocks using his direct current system, but because the public could not tell the difference between his direct current systems and the existing arc lighting systems based on alternating current.[23] Direct current was not entirely safe, either, as the stunned horses that had the misfortune of passing near "leaking" direct current would attest.[24] Edison's staff had to defend not only their own systems, but also their competitors'.

Opposite: **An 1830 cartoon by Thomas Rowlandson about the dangers of gaslight**

his Carbonin Hydrogen
afswill kill as many as Boney
O-We shall all be Poisened
Oh o what a Stink

Eventually, however, Edison found that his system was not actually in direct competition with arc lighting. While arc lighting was the first practical electrical lighting, it produced a brilliant light that was too intense for most indoor uses. The Brush Company had begun to sell it for interior lighting for some businesses, but was hindered by "a shortage of machinery needed to expand its generating capacity."[25] Brush could not keep up with demand, so his arc lighting was largely limited to a few large industrial factories and street lighting, functions for which Edison's soft incandescent glow were not entirely suitable.[26] Edison's lights, which made a conducting filament glow in a vacuum rather than spark across a gap, were much better than arc lighting for the family home and most office settings.[27] Edison won the battle with arc lighting not so much by beating them at their own game, but by exploiting the strengths of his own bulbs as a way to replace the household gas lights.

Building an Electrical Empire

Edison built a massive monopoly on direct current power stations in the United States and Europe. He did this along two different fronts: isolated power plants in homes, offices, and steamships; and central power stations servicing city blocks, what today we call a utility.

Above: **Harold Brown demonstrating the killing power of AC by electrocuting a horse at Edison's West Orange laboratory**

Above:* S.S. *Columbia

His first isolated plant was on the S.S. *Columbia*, a steamship newly built by recurring investor and newspaperman Henry Villard.[28] Given that Edison's Electric Light Company stock had fallen from $4,000 to $500 nearly overnight because of mocking reviews of his tendency toward promising more than he could deliver,[29] Edison was happy to test his isolated plant in a private setting.[30] The ship also had the advantage of already having a steam plant onboard, so all it really needed was a system of electric lights.

In 1884 Edison installed a complete direct current system on the S.S. *Oregon*, one of the most modern ships of the time. On the *Oregon*, Edison would first put new employee Nikola Tesla to the test.[31] Both of the twin dynamos had failed, so the ship was sitting in port with no way to run. Edison had sent several men to try to fix it, but with no luck. He was desperate, so when Tesla walked into his office he sent him straight down to the docks. Tesla was eager to please Edison, so he packed up the necessary tools and arrived on board that evening. "The dynamos were in bad condition," Tesla later wrote, "with several short circuits and breaks." Seizing the initiative, Tesla put the ship's crew to work helping him, and by daybreak he had "succeeded in putting them in good shape."[32]

***Above:* Edison's employee and eventual rival Nikola Tesla**

Above: **William Henry Vanderbilt's drawing room**

Edison was impressed, and hired Tesla to repair his direct current systems in the United States, much as Tesla had done in Europe (including the famous incident in which Edison's system exploded, nearly killing Emperor Wilhelm I of Germany).[33]

Other isolated direct current systems were routinely being installed. Within a few months of going public with his new lightbulbs, the Edison companies were getting isolated plant orders faster than they could keep up.[34] Everyone wanted electrical lighting installed in their homes, offices, and factories. By early 1883, Edison had sold 330 isolated systems, lighting more than 64,000 lamps.[35] He was making money not only on manufacturing and installation, but also by providing expert technician services to keep the complicated system running. Most isolated plants went into larger installations like "commercial and industrial businesses, hotels, and theaters."[36]

A handful of incredibly wealthy industrialists also bought them. One of the first to receive a personal home power plant and electrical light installation was William Henry Vanderbilt, who had built a second fortune in the railroad industry after inheriting his first fortune from his father, Commodore Cornelius Vanderbilt.[37] Eager to have his electrical systems talked up among the wealthy elite, Edison agreed to allow a direct current system in Vanderbilt's upper Fifth Avenue mansion, which was then under construction. All went well when the system was switched on—for a few minutes—before "signs appeared of a smoldering fire with the wallpaper, which apparently had a fine metallic thread in its weave."[38] An unhappy Mrs. Vanderbilt ordered the entire power plant to be removed, and the ensuing bad press was the opposite of what Edison had hoped for.

Not one to be put off by the misfortune of others, financier and industrialist J. P. Morgan ordered an isolated power plant for his own New York City mansion. Ego did not stop him from being prudent, however, and he insisted the generators be installed in a new cellar dug at some distance from the main house. A brick-lined tunnel connected the system to the house, and Morgan hired a full-time engineer to maintain the system.[39] The more remote location of the power plant also helped keep down the noise and unpleasant odor that often accompanied the system. His neighbors, the Browns, were not so lucky. Mrs. Brown complained about sooty tarnish on her silver and stray cats settling onto the warm conduit during the winter, often "yowling" loudly all night long.[40] Morgan ignored her, and was happy with Edison. That happiness would not last forever.

Above: **J. P. Morgan**

[Entered at the Post Office of New York, N. Y., as Second Class Matter.]

A WEEKLY JOURNAL OF PRACTICAL INFORMATION, ART, SCIENCE, MECHANICS, CHEMISTRY AND MANUFACTURES.

Vol. XLVII.—No. 9.] [NEW SERIES.]

NEW YORK, AUGUST 26, 1882.

[$3.20 per Annum. [POSTAGE PREPAID.]

THE EDISON ELECTRIC LIGHTING STATION.

On Pearl street, near Fulton, under the shadow of the Third Avenue Elevated Railroad, and but a minute's walk from Fulton Ferry, is an iron front building, originally put up for commercial purposes, but which for a year or more has been in process of preparation for a central electric lighting station under the Edison system. The beginning of this great work was indicated by the laying of underground conductors around every block in that portion of the city bounded on the east by the East River, on the west by Nassau street, on the north by Spruce and Ferry streets and Peck Slip, and on the south by Wall street. This district includes 946 consumers, whose premises are already wired. The number of lamps to be used in connection with these wires is 14,311. From the basement of the building referred to radiate large semicylindrical copper conductors, insulated from each other and arranged in pairs, each pair

[*Continued on page* 130.]

THE REGULATOR.

TEST BATTERY OF 1,000 LAMPS.

THE DYNAMO ROOM.

FIRST EDISON ELECTRIC LIGHTING STATION IN NEW YORK.

While isolated systems were all the rage, Edison tried his best not to install them. He believed the best strategy was to construct central power stations that could feed direct current electricity through underground wires to entire city blocks. He leased a brownstone and moved Mary and their young children into New York City so he could embark on his next great idea.[41] While his companies were busy selling isolated plants, Edison was building the Pearl Street Central Power Station in lower Manhattan.

Pearl Street was the first of several central stations in New York. The district was "a one-mile-square area . . . bounded by the East River, Wall Street, and Spruce, Ferry, and Nassau Streets."[42] The location of this first district was no accident—it was close to New York's major newspapers and financial institutions, and thus sure to garner the right publicity and financing. While jumping through many bureaucratic hoops and dealing with uninspecting inspectors, Edison managed to lay more than fifteen miles of underground wires linking his main station with hundreds of buildings within the district.[43] Four large boilers and six huge generators produced more than 600 kilowatts of electricity, and by spring 1884 the Pearl Street station was servicing 500 buildings.[44]

While Edison was electrifying Manhattan, he also set up shop in Europe. In 1881 he had sent Charles Batchelor to Paris with the largest dynamo ever built for the first ever Electrical Exposition. "It was capable of lighting twelve hundred incandescent lamps, and weighed with its engine

Opposite: Scientific American **cover showing Edison's new Pearl Street Lighting Station**
Above: **Laying electrical cable along Pearl Street, 1882**

twenty-seven tons…it was then, and for a long time after, the eighth wonder of the scientific world."[45] The system was a great success, and Edison soon had companies in Italy, Holland, Belgium, and the Ivry-sur-Seine facility in Paris, where the young Tesla worked before crossing the Atlantic.[46] The first "jumbo" dynamo had gone to Paris, but the second and third had gone to London, where Edison's associates built a 3000-light central station in Holborn Viaduct in early 1882.[47]

By 1884 Edison had conquered both the United States and Europe with his direct current electrical power and lighting systems. He was well on his way to eliminating gas as a standard lighting source, and had successfully reduced arc lighting to limited factory and streetlight applications. With Pearl Street now providing service to the one-square-mile first district, Edison was starting to plan for his expansion into the rest of Manhattan.

Battle #3: DC vs. AC

This last battle was the one that Edison most needed to win. Arc lighting was based on alternating current (AC), as compared to Edison's direct current (DC) systems, but no sooner had Edison pushed one AC system aside than alternating current came back to haunt him in a different form—the polyphase alternating current system of Nikola Tesla.

Tesla was a Serbian engineer who had bounced around Austria, the current Czech and Slovak Republics, and Hungary before taking a job working for Continental Edison in Paris.[48] While in Budapest he had envisioned a way to solve one of the biggest problems with direct current, the sparking commutator. Like Edison, Tesla also labored eighteen to twenty hours a day, a habit that occasionally sent him into a serious bout of exhaustion. After one such incident he was walking through a downtown park reciting the epic poem *Faust* by Johann Goethe when suddenly he stopped: "The idea came to me like a flash of lightning and in an instant the truth was revealed. I drew with a stick on the sand the diagrams…The images I saw were wonderfully sharp and clear."[49]

Tesla envisioned the rotating magnetic field that would become his alternating current motor, which solves the problem that had

Above: **The Tesla AC motor**

kept alternating current from replacing direct current as a power source. It would be many more years before Tesla would have a chance to build his motor. (He created his prototype while fixing Edison's direct current dynamos in Strasbourg—the ones that nearly killed Emperor Wilhelm.[50])

By the time the unknown Tesla arrived in New York in 1884, Edison was already famous and well on his way to establishing a monopoly on providing electricity to New York and other cities. During the year that Tesla worked for Edison, in which he revamped and improved direct current dynamos, he tried repeatedly and unsuccessfully to convince Edison that it would be better to use alternating current using his unproven rotating magnetic field induction motor. But Edison had already ruled out alternating current as viable power source, and he was permanently invested in the massive infrastructure he had already created for direct current. Tesla grew fed up, and eventually quit.

Meanwhile, Edison's direct current empire continued to expand to other cities and states, although not without competition. In 1882,

George Westinghouse—famous for his invention of the air brake for railroad cars—bought out Philip Diehl's competing induction lamp patent rights, which forced Edison to lower the licensing rate for using his patents, thus reducing the price of electric lamps (and Edison's profit). Other direct current companies, like Thomson-Houston, also pressured Edison to keep his rates reasonable. The ubiquitous patent lawsuits kept everyone busy trying to protect their own businesses.

Edison was clearly the leader in this field, but that was about to change. Westinghouse formed his own electric company in 1886, and by 1888 Tesla finally had developed his complete alternating current induction motor and all the associated transformers. This revolutionized the industry. Westinghouse purchased the rights to Tesla's patents and hired him to incorporate them into his own systems. The war of the currents was officially on.[51]

War of the Currents

Edison did not give in easily. He began a public relations campaign to discredit alternating current as being too dangerous for public use. He had a point. Alternating current could be raised to incredibly high voltages, whereas direct current was held at relatively low voltages.[52] Edison published pamphlets ominously titled *A Warning from the Edison Electric Light Company* suggesting alternating current was not safe.[53] He also (falsely) suggested to suppliers and utilities that Westinghouse was in violation of Edison's patents, and thus it would be unwise to rely on the soon-to-be-departed technology. Engineering societies debated the merits, although sometimes the charges and countercharges seemed more personal than professional, with combatants "fighting tooth and nail" for the future.[54]

The battle between AC and DC also got bloody. While relatively rare, accidents sometimes occurred on the network of naked electrical wires strung on poles set alongside city streets.[55] One particularly gruesome scene occurred when John Feeks, an electrical repairman sent up to remove dead wires, accidentally found a live one and fell into a nest of wires, where he "dangled for more than forty-five minutes."[56]

Opposite: **A gruesome representation of repairman John Feeks' death by electrocution**

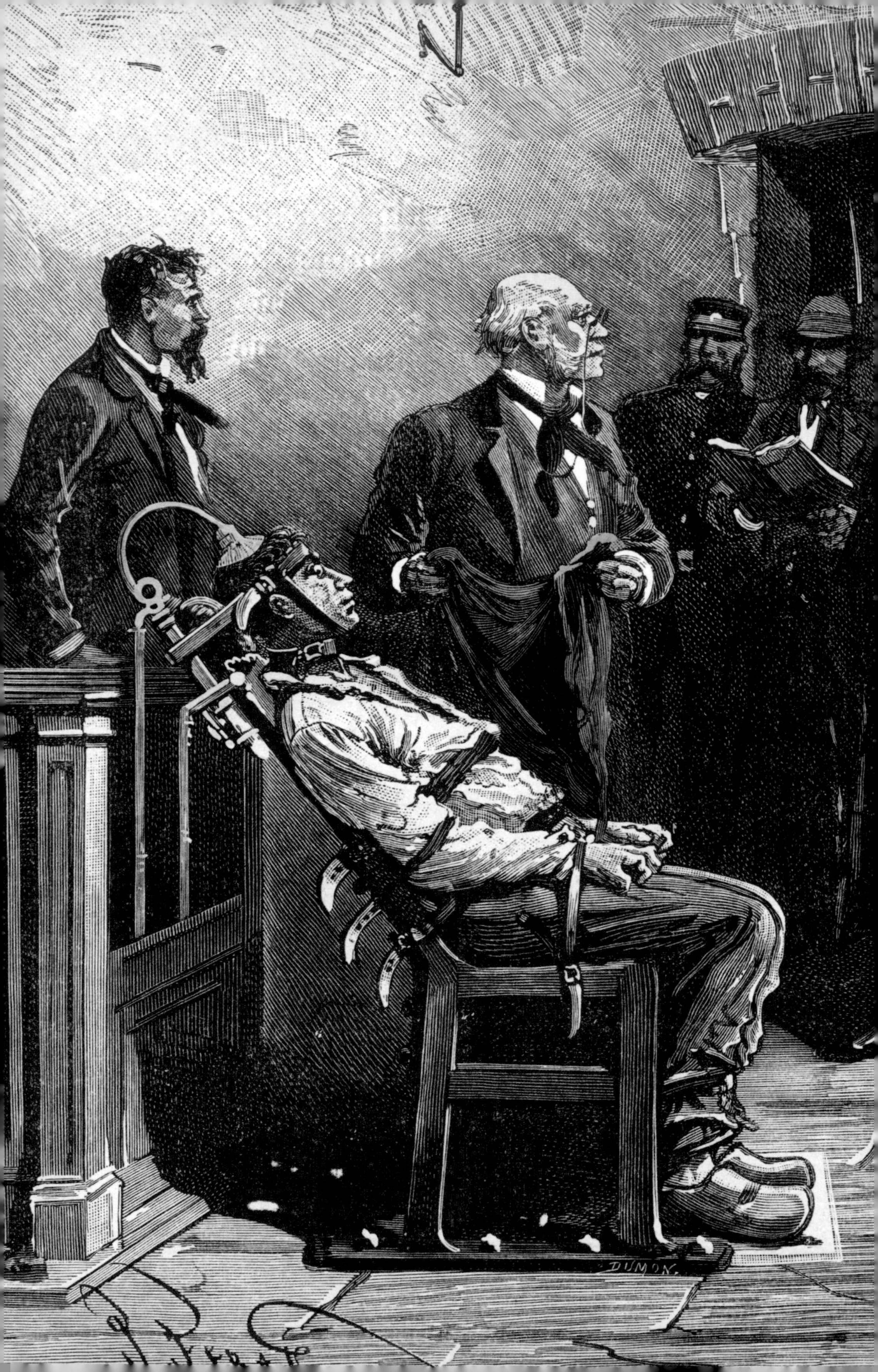
DUMON

Streaks of light flashed from his body as spectators gasped in horror below. Reporters raced from the scene to get quotes from Edison on the dangers of alternating current, which he duly provided without knowing whether the wires were AC or his own DC.

Edison also actively lobbied for use of the electric chair to replace the usual means of execution, an overdose of morphine or hanging.[57] He felt the chair would be more humane because it would provide a quicker, cleaner kill. More important, it would use alternating current, further bolstering Edison's claim that alternating current was too dangerous for humanity. Some members of the committee set up to evaluate the methods were skeptical until Edison sent a letter of support. "I certainly had no doubt after hearing his statement," one committee member said, and the recommendation was implemented.[58] Unfortunately for Edison, and for the axe murderer William Kemmler on which it was first used, the execution did not go smoothly. After supposedly being electrocuted to death, Kemmler suddenly let out a loud cry of pain, to which the attendants responded by turning the power up to full for two minutes, long enough for "the stench of burning flesh" to fill the room.[59]

Edison also allowed electrical engineer Harold Pitney Brown to use his laboratory for a series of experiments.[60] Brown paid neighborhood boys to collect stray dogs, which he then electrocuted in Edison's lab using Westinghouse's alternating current. He then wrote letters to the press exclaiming the dangers of that "damnable" alternating current.[61] To denigrate his main competitor completely, Edison called the electrocutions "getting Westinghoused."

The Battle is Lost

Two events were major factors in deciding the war of the currents. In 1893 there was a competition to determine who would get the contract to light up the World's Columbian Exposition. Also known as the Chicago World's Fair, the six-month-long exposition was to showcase new technology from all over the world. Both the General Electric Company and the Westinghouse Electric Company (powered

Opposite: **Tbe 1890 execution of William Kemmler, the first ever by electric chair**
Following: **Tbe World's Columbian Exposition, 1893**

Cable Address "Edison, New York"

From the Laboratory of Thomas A. Edison,

Orange, N.J.

(No Model.) 2 Sheets—Sheet 1.

T. A. EDISON.

Regulating the Generation of Electric Currents.

No. 239,374. **Patented March 29, 1881.**

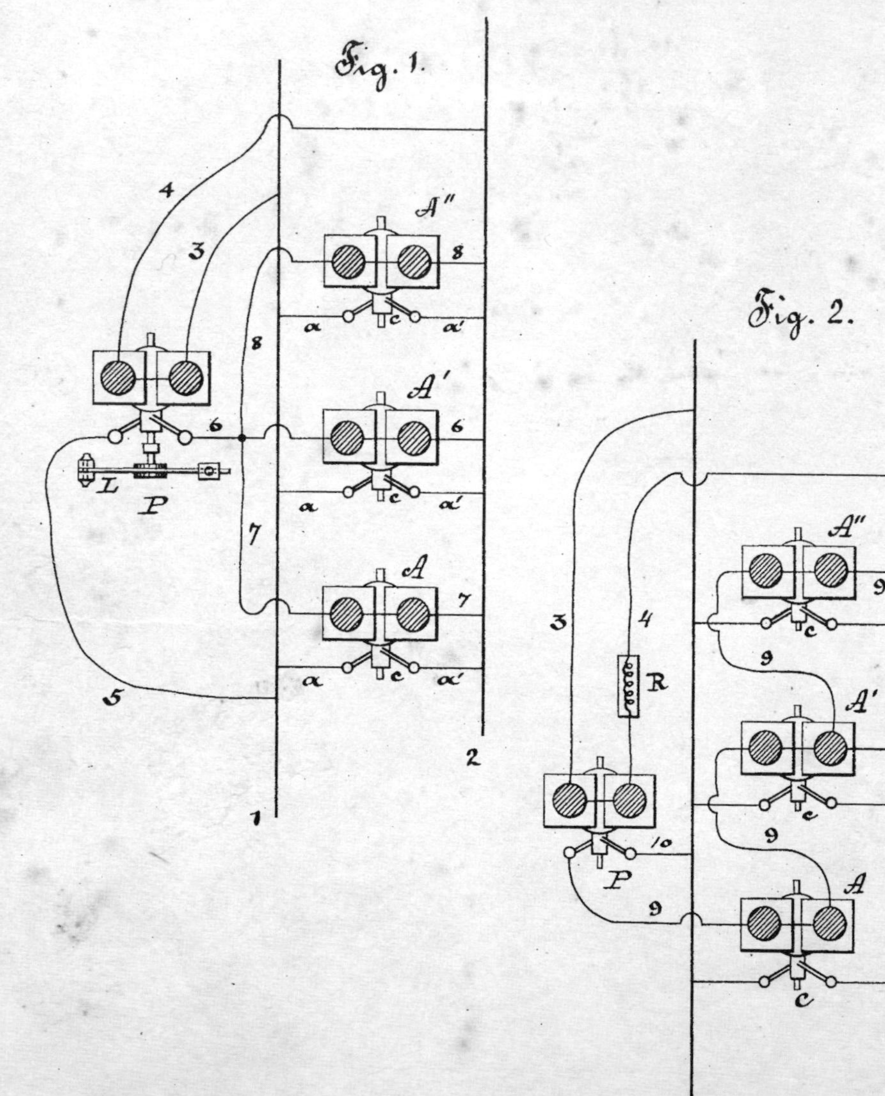

Attest:

S. D. Mott

M. J. Hagelt

Inventor:

Thos. A. Edison

by Tesla's alternating current technology) were among the competitors. Edison's direct current was pitted against Westinghouse's alternating current. Bidding was brutal as Edison and Westinghouse viciously undercut each other in an attempt to land the plum contract. Other competitors were quickly eliminated, and Westinghouse ultimately won. Tesla's polyphase alternating current system lit up the fair.[62]

The result was spectacular. Nicknamed the "White City" because of the white stucco buildings surrounding the central pool, the name also could have referred to the brilliant aura created by 92,000 outdoor incandescent lamps that lit the grounds for six months.[63] Including all the interior lamps, the fair required 250,000 modified Sawyer-Mann "stopper lamps," a competing bulb Westinghouse raced to produce because Edison refused to allow use of his patented long-life bulbs. Edison was not shut out completely, however, as he was able to display several of his own inventions in the showcase electrical building, including the dominating "Edison Tower of Light."[64]

Because of the success of alternating current at the Chicago World's Fair, the team of Westinghouse and Tesla also beat out Edison for the next major contract at Niagara Falls. The Niagara River flows north from Lake Erie to Lake Ontario, dropping up to 188 feet over some of the most spectacular falls in North America.[65] Engineers had made only limited use of the power of the falling water until the newly formed Cataract Construction Company (led by former Edison Electric Board member Edward Dean Adams) chose to base its new electrical power plant on a dozen Tesla patents. Tesla's polyphase generator system beat out Edison's direct current, but Edison won the contract to string electrical wires from Niagara to Buffalo, nearly twenty miles away.

These setbacks effectively removed Edison from the electric power generation business, a process that had already begun back in 1892, when competition and J. P. Morgan's maneuverings forced Edison to merge his Edison General Electric Company with the Thomson-Houston Company to form the new General Electric.[66] While somewhat bitter at how he had been treated, Edison turned to other pursuits, including iron ore milling and the development of motion picture projectors. Edison was about to become a movie mogul, albeit a reluctant one.

THOMAS A. EDISON
Copyright 1905 By IRVING UNDERH
New York.

CHAPTER 8

EDISON THE MOVIE MOGUL

By 1911, motion pictures had become one of Edison's most profitable businesses, at least temporarily.[1] The idea of motion pictures evolved out of the phonograph.[2] Writing in the first person in his patent caveat filed on October 8, 1888, Edison stated, "I am experimenting upon an instrument which does for the Eye what the phonograph does for the Ear Which is the recording and reproduction of things in motion."[3]

Edison's first problem with the development of motion pictures was his lack of interest. He and his colleagues were occupied with his "perfected" phonograph, in stiff competition with Bell's graphophone, and battling it out against Victor and Columbia for the home phonograph market. At the same time, he was fighting the war of the currents and electrifying Manhattan and places abroad. And then there was the budding iron ore milling business. Edison just did not have the time to work on motion pictures. He also doubted there would be much of a market for movies.

As he had done so many times before, Edison assigned someone to spearhead the development: William K. L. Dickson, one of his assistants on the mining project and an experienced photographer.[4]

Opposite: **Edison operating the invention he hoped to keep to himself: the movie camera**
Right: **William K.L. Dickson, Edison's chief collaborator on the Kinetoscope**

A natural showman, the French-born (but of Scottish and American parentage) Dickson was perfect for the job. Better yet, he had already established himself as a reliable worker in the West Orange laboratory, where he tested dynamos, supervised the metallurgical laboratory, and served as the lab's official photographer.[5]

Pictures in Motion

As with most inventions, others had already started the process that Edison's team would move forward. In June 1889, William Friese-Greene had patented a motion picture camera in England.[6] Two months later, Englishman Wordsworth Donisthorpe patented his own version of a motion picture camera. Louis Aimé Augustin Le Prince, a Frenchman working in England, developed a multiple-lens camera in 1888.[7] Le Prince also filmed two motion picture sequences using a single-lens camera and paper film; the twelve-frame-per-second

Roundhay Garden Scene runs for a grand total of 2.11 seconds.[8] In a bizarre twist reminiscent of future action movies, Le Prince and his luggage mysteriously vanished from a moving train just prior to making a trip to the United States to present his invention.[9]

These early inventors did not have the finances to continue development, but Edison did. The first version out of the Edison laboratory was "rather too ambitious,"[10] as it attempted to synchronize the sound of the phonograph with the movement of images. "Thousands of tiny images" were taken with a conventional camera, and one by one they were mounted on a modified phonograph cylinder. A second cylinder played back the sound, ideally in sync with the images.[11] But the machine did not work. The curvature of the cylinder distorted the small images, so it was nearly impossible to view them with any resolution. Increasing the size of the images to ¼ inch and applying a photographic emulsion to the cylinder failed to resolve the problem, although Edison did produce a series of short films (of a few seconds each) collectively called *Monkeyshines*.[12] Overall, however, the idea of using cylinders was abandoned.

Another Englishman, Eadweard Muybridge, came to the rescue.[13] Muybridge was a photographer who as far back as the 1870s was producing images in series, which he used mainly to study the motion of animals.[14] In one sequence, Muybridge had taken twelve rapid photos of a horse in full gallop in order to determine if all four legs were off the ground at the same time (they were). He accomplished this by using multiple cameras to record images in rapid succession.[15]

Muybridge had also invented a zoopraxiscope, a rotating glass wheel and a slotted disk that projected a series of pictures in sequence,

each slightly ahead of the other.[16] Turning the wheel made the pictures appear to be in motion. With these devices in hand, the now-famous Muybridge paid a visit to Edison during a tour of the United States in February 1888.[17] As with his earlier visit with Wallace, Edison gained considerable insights into his next steps after this meeting. Edison barely acknowledged the visit for months, but in October suddenly submitted his caveat to the patent office for "a system of motion pictures: a device to record the images, a device for viewing them, and an instrument that merged viewing pictures and listening to sound in the same experience."[18]

Above: **Galloping-horse sequence from Eadweard Muybridge's *Animals in Motion***

Above: **Étienne-Jules Marey with his chronophotographic gun**

Étienne-Jules Marey was another influence on Edison's thinking about motion pictures. After growing up in the Côte-d'Or region of France, Marey studied medicine and became interested in the science of laboratory photography; he is widely credited with being the Father of Chronophotography, or photographing motion.[19] In 1882 he invented the chronophotographic gun, a menacing-looking instrument capable of capturing images at a rate of twelve frames per second.[20] All twelve sequential still images were recorded on the same strip of film, a disk that rotated as the rapid-fire photos were taken.[21] Marey also designed a camera that captured "sixty images a second on a long continuous strip of film, which was pulled by a cam in a deliberately jerky fashion to stop the film momentarily so that the light could saturate the film and capture motion."[22] Edison sought out Marey when he attended the 1889 World's Fair in Paris.

The World's Fair's biggest attraction was the huge iron-latticed tower named after its designer, Alexandre Gustave Eiffel,[23] on whose edifice Edison wined and dined with the rich and famous during the exposition. But what really caught Edison's interest was Marey's photographic gun. Marey was more focused on the technical developments of his invention and less about the market value, and he gladly showed Edison the mechanics and examples of his work.[24] He also gave Edison a copy of his book providing all the technical details.[25] Armed with new ideas, but still lacking in substantive time to develop them, Edison passed the information to Dickson and left him to make something of it.[26]

The Kinetoscope Emerges

Edison's patent caveat was filed, with Dickson working anonymously in the background. The device they had in mind would not only show pictures in motion, but also "in such a form as to be both Cheap[,] practical and convenient. This apparatus I call a Kinetoscope 'Moving View.'"[27] (The name was derived from the Greek *kinesis*, meaning motion.) They described it as a silver emulsion-coated phonograph cylinder with 42,000 "pin-point" photographic images each 1⁄32 inch wide mounted spirally upon it, to be viewed through a binocular eyepiece salvaged from a microscope; the visual cylinder spun to the simultaneous accompaniment of a contiguous phonograph sharing the same shaft and playing the "sound track."[28] The idea of synchronized cylinders was completely unworkable, but it epitomizes how Edison worked—he built on something he already did, and he hesitated to move away from it.

But move away he did. Dickson searched for a way to take and display the thousands of pictures that would need to be strung together for any length of viewing time. The usual way of making photographs was to produce them on glass negatives, which clearly was not an option for moving pictures.[29] One option that seemed viable was celluloid, a plastic material made out of cellulose nitrate that English photographer John Carbutt successfully used.[30] Another promising option was rolls of paper that George Eastman had managed to coat with photographic film and fused into a cheap Kodak camera.[31]

Dickson experimented with celluloid and paper, and after Edison's visit with Marey filed a new patent caveat, this one describing a "sensitive film" that would "pass from one reel to another." Then, like the phonograph before it, the kinetoscope project was dropped—this

time for only a year—while Edison kept Dickson busy with his ore milling business. When Dickson was finally allowed to return to the kinetoscope, Edison assigned William Heise to give him a hand.[32]

Heise had expertise stemming from his prior work with printing telegraphs, which he now used to design the mechanical movement of film through the camera. Dickson focused on the optical components of the camera itself, along with the chemical and physical characteristics of the film.[33] Together they developed the two parts that would make it possible to film, and then display, motion pictures.

By the spring of 1891, the two men had designed a camera, which they called a kinetograph, to film moving pictures.[34] The kinetograph's horizontal-feed exposed images on strips of perforated film ¾ inch wide. A "shutter and escapement mechanism" allowed the camera to stop the film "for a fraction of a second," just long enough to expose the film before advancing to the next exposure.[35] Dickson and Heise advanced the technology with amazing rapidity: "forty-six impressions are taken each second, which is 2,760 a minute and 165,600 an hour."[36] Several short experimental films were produced, "including a lab worker smoking a pipe and another swinging a set of Indian clubs."[37]

After developing a suitable camera to create motion pictures, they needed to develop a way to watch them. The answer was a wooden box, much like those housing phonographs, which they called a kinetoscope.[38] The box stood about four feet high and was twenty inches square.[39] Inside the box was "an electric lamp, a battery-powered motor, and a fifty-foot ribbon of positive celluloid film arranged on a series of rollers and pulleys."[40] The film viewer would bend over the box, stare through an eyepiece, and watch as the film whizzed through view at forty-six frames per second.

And whiz it did. The first films were over in twenty seconds or less; basic scenes such as Dickson tipping his hat or a blacksmith banging his hammer.[41] Still, it was a start, and Dickson continued to work on perfecting both the kinetograph camera and the kinetoscope player. Edison, on the other hand, was not sure there was much of a market: "This invention will not have any particular commercial value. It will

Opposite: **The five-seconds-long *Fred Ott's Sneeze*, filmed in Edison's Black Maria in 1894, is the first copyrighted motion picture.**

be rather of a sentimental worth,"[42] something of a novelty.[43] At the same time he seemed to recognize the future attraction to the new medium, which could reproduce on the walls of their homes actors and scenes they currently had to go out to the theater to experience.[44] Despite his hesitations, Edison arranged for a kinetoscope exhibit at the Chicago World's Fair. It was a couple of years in the future, so he had plenty of time to perfect the device. Or so he thought. He assigned James Egan, one of his machinists, to build twenty-five kinetoscopes.[45]

Inventing the First Movie Studio

The first experimental films were shot in the West Orange laboratory, but as motion pictures gradually became more professional, Edison needed a professional studio in which to film. In December 1892, construction began behind Building 4 on a studio that Edison later remembered as "a ghastly proposition for a stranger daring enough to brave its mysteries."[46] Covered in black tar paper inside and out, it was dubbed the Black Maria after the slang term for the police paddy wagons of the day it resembled.[47] Not coincidentally, it looked like Marey's "barnlike studio" Edison had seen during his 1889 visit:[48]

> "It obeys no architectural rules, embraces no conventional materials, and follows no accepted schemes of color," boasted the sometimes flamboyant Dickson of the Black Maria. He did admit it had "a weird and semi-nautical appearance."[49]

The Black Maria was a "fifty-by-eighteen-foot wood building with a twenty-one-foot-high pitched roof."[50] It also had two rather unique features. The first was the roof: "Half of the roof could be raised or lowered like a drawbridge by means of ropes, pulleys and weights, so that the sunlight could strike squarely on the space before the machine [i.e., the motion picture camera]."[51] The studio had to allow in sunlight, even though it was outfitted with electricity; Edison's incandescent bulbs were not bright enough for filmmaking, and arc lighting was too harsh. This need for light led to the second odd feature: The whole building was mounted "on a graphite pivot that allowed the staff to turn the studio on a wood track." As the sun arced across the sky during the day, they simply turned the building to keep pace.[52] Edison wistfully noted in later years how the building could "turn like a ship in a gale."[53]

Because Edison pulled Dickson away from the movie business to work on other projects, progress on the kinetoscope moved ahead in fits and starts. Without Dickson around, James Egan was unable to get quick responses on technical issues and would not complete manufacturing the two dozen kinetoscopes contracted until the year after the World's Fair at which Edison hoped to showcase them.[54] This was yet another missed opportunity for Edison, who had already lost the contract to light the fair to George Westinghouse and Nikola Tesla.[55]

Eventually back on the job, Dickson managed to complete the work developing the camera and turned from technical developer to moviemaker. As with the phonograph, Edison wanted films that focused on high art, like performances of the Metropolitan Opera House.[56] Instead, Dickson's first film was *Sandow, the Strongman*, who struck various poses and flexed his muscles in front of the camera before unexpectedly picking up one of the assistants and chucking him out the door. Unfortunately for posterity, however, this last feat happened too fast for the camera to capture, and the unappreciative assistant refused to do a retake.[57]

Above: **A scene from Edison's 1894 short film, *Boxing Cats***
Following: **The Black Maria film studio**

Other early films produced in the Black Maria included a five-second, forty-five-frame film created in January 1894, officially called *Edison's Kinetoscopic Record of a Sneeze* but remembered more by its unofficial name—*Fred Ott's Sneeze*. Other equally unexciting early films were the aptly named *Blacksmith Scene* and *Horse Shoeing*, which brought the feature length up to a stunning thirty seconds.[58] Trying to liven up the medium a little more, they also filmed *Carmencita*, the eponymously named twenty-one-second film showing the flashing footwork and twirls of a Spanish vaudeville dancer.[59] For the more violent set there was the very PETA-unfriendly *Cockfight* pitting two roosters in combat while avid bettors spur them on.[60]

Still more films were made; some silly, like boxing cats and wrestling dogs,[61] others more seductive, like Annabelle Whitford's *Butterfly Dance*.[62] Most of these were short, but they also started filming boxing matches and other more entertaining fare. Because of high demand for longer features, Dickson filmed "a six-round boxing match between former world champion James J. Corbett and Peter Courtney, a heavyweight from Trenton, New Jersey." Corbett was guaranteed $4,750 of the $5,000 purse, but payable only if he would knock out Courtney in the sixth round (not in earlier or later rounds, in order to maximize profit margins). Once the sixth round started, Corbett dutifully knocked Courtney to the mat for the win—and the big payday.[63]

The new medium grabbed the public's attention. It helped that big names such as Buffalo Bill brought the popular stars of his Wild West show, including Native American dancers and rifle-shooting ace Annie Oakley, into the studio to create lively entertainment.[64] In 1894, the first year of moviemaking, Dickson and his crew produced seventy-five films in the Black Maria.[65]

Inventing Movie Theaters

Filmmaking took off so quickly because of the foresight of individuals other than Edison, who as usual was often distracted by other activities. Unlike the modern multiplex theaters of today, the first efforts at

Right: **Early Edison star Eugene Sandow, ready to throw someone out the door**

Above: **Watching movies on a Kinetoscope wasn't always a comfortable experience.**

showing films to the public were much more personal and intimate.[66] Largely driven by a narrow view of the technology and experience with phonograph cabinetry, the kinetoscope required the viewer to lean over a cabinet and peer through a peephole as the film moved within the box. The first movie emporium was started in April 1894 with this technology.

Edison did not establish this premier theater. Alfred Tate, an Edison colleague and one of his greatest salesmen, contracted with two brothers to set up ten newly built kinetoscopes in a former shoe shop on Broadway near Herald Square in Manhattan.[67] The machines were outfitted with coin slots, and they charged customers twenty-five cents to see up to five short films.[68] The response was more than they bargained for. Before they were even ready to open to the public, they saw curious customers outside on the street, "faces pressed against the glass for a better glimpse."

> Tate had a thought as he looked out onto the eager gawkers: "Why shouldn't we make that crowd pay for our dinner tonight?," as he thought about the juicy steaks at Delmonico's just a block away from the shop.
>
> "Bert," said Tate, "you take charge of the machines. I'll sell the tickets, and Lombard, you stand near the door and act as reception committee. We can run till six o'clock and by that time we ought to have dinner money."
>
> We "all thought it would be a good joke all right but the joke was on us," Tate remembered years later. Rather than finish up by six p.m. in time for dinner, it was past one o'clock

> in the morning before they could shut down the shop with their unexpected bounty of $120 in cash. Starved from their opening night exertions, Tate and his colleagues set off "to an all-night restaurant to regale on broiled lobsters."[69]

More kinetoscope parlors popped up in San Francisco, Atlantic City, Boston, Washington, D.C., and even London. The kinetoscope business was incredibly profitable for Edison, at least during its first year, in which $177,847 ($4.91 million today) worth of kinetoscopes and films were produced.[70] This initial fascination rapidly faded, however, and the following year saw only $49,896 in sales.[71] Edison tried to recapture the novelty by connecting a kinetoscope to a phonograph—he called it a kinetophone—so viewers could hear a soundtrack through earphones as they bent over the cabinet to watch the film. It was not popular.[72] Something else had to be done.

Above: **A Kinetoscepe parlor in San Francisco, ca. 1894**

EDISON'S
THE VITASC

GREATEST
MARVEL

PE

"Wonderful is The Vitascope. Pictures life size and full of color. Makes a thrilling show."
NEWYORK HERALD, April 24, '96.

From Personal Viewing to Projection to the Masses

One of the issues hindering sales—in addition to the distinct lack of interesting films being produced—was that each film had to be viewed individually. This worked for the short films initially produced, but was not particularly viable as advancements in film technology allowed production of the longer films customers craved. Motion picture viewing has a social element—people wanted to watch films together. In order to accomplish this, the film had to be projected across the room to a screen on the wall.

Edison was slow to adapt. As with his hesitancy to switch from phonograph cylinders to disks, and from direct to alternating current, Edison initially did not want to develop projection machines that would instantly make obsolete his fine cabinet–encased kinetoscopes. But as the kinetoscope business faded away, he finally acknowledged the need to move forward. In 1895 William Dickson decided to leave Edison's employment and set up his own competing operation, and Edison had difficulty finding someone who could take his place. Initial attempts within the lab were not successful, so when he had the opportunity to gain control of the independently produced phantascope, Edison took it. The Phantoscope was a projector invented in late 1895 by C. Francis Jenkins and Thomas Armat.[73] They were unable to get

Above: **The Phantoscope, considered by some to be the first true movie projector**

financing to manufacture it, and allowed it to be marketed under Edison's now-famous name.[74] It was renamed the Vitascope and made its debut in the spring of 1896,[75] but even Edison's great influence was not enough to make it successful. After dismal sales, Edison finally introduced his own projector the following year.[76]

Edison also developed a portable motion picture camera that could be carried outside to film scenes around New York City and elsewhere (previous cameras were huge and studio-bound).[77] He filmed a fountain in Central Park; parades in Scranton, Pennsylvania; amusements at Coney Island; and President William McKinley's inauguration in Washington, D.C.[78] He also shot the majestic waters of Niagara Falls, where Tesla and Westinghouse had beat him in gaining electrical power from the Falls (and where McKinley would be assassinated a few years later).[79]

Further advancements came quickly, and Edison's company moved moviemaking operations out of the Black Maria and into a new studio on the penthouse level of a building on East Twenty-First Street in Manhattan.[80] An even larger studio was built in the Bronx

Above: **Scene from *The Life of Abraham Lincoln* (1915) showing the Lincoln–Douglas Debates**
***Following*:** **Joseph Keppler lampoons Edison in *Puck* for his ties to Wall Street.**

"Now, gentlemen, I will show you the Great Inve
Money, and here's your Share; now you see them, a

ick. Here's your

seven years later. The public was clamoring for films that were longer and told interesting stories. The advent of Edison's home-projecting kinetoscope only accentuated this desire for good movies.[81] In order to meet the demand, Edison and his staff became movie moguls.

Edison still wanted to focus on educational and culturally lofty films, but the masses wanted action films like *Kansas Saloon Smashers* and *Terrible Teddy, the Grizzly King* (a parody of Vice President Theodore Roosevelt's "hunting exploits").[82] One action film showed firefighters rescuing a mother and child from a burning building, with additional scenes showing "firefighters responding to the alarm, sliding down poles, hitching their horses to a fire engine, and dashing to the fire."[83]

Perhaps the two most famous Edison company films were *The Great Train Robbery* (1903) and *The Life of Abraham Lincoln* (1915). *The Great Train Robbery* was a ten-minute Western filmed in the studio and on location. It showcased the innovative nature of early filmmaking, including multiple camera angles, composite editing, and even hand-coloring of the prints for some scenes.[84] It was considered "absolutely the superior of any moving picture ever made."[85]

The Life of Abraham Lincoln was another silent film (with musical soundtrack) presenting highlights from Lincoln's life.[86] Motion pictures were getting longer, and some of Edison's films now took up two reels.

Above: **Final scene from Edison's *The Great Train Robbery*, in which the outlaw appears to fire his gun directly at the camera**

Above: **A 1903 newspaper ad featuring the ill-fated Topsy**
Following**: Edison's Bronx movie studio**

The Life . . . was a "two-part drama" that ran "from the scene in front of the log cabin to the assassination at Ford's Theater in Washington." The sales catalog claimed, "Nothing has been left undone to make this a consummate review of Lincoln's life."[87] For the 100th anniversary of Lincoln's birth in 1909, Wanamaker's huge department store in lower Manhattan hosted a screening of Edison's ten-minute film *The Blue and the Grey, or the Boys of '61*, accompanied by "favorite war songs" of the era.[88]

Edison was also involved in the making of a more infamous film. In 1903, an Asian elephant named Topsy held at a Coney Island amusement park had become unmanageable, in large part because of abusive treatment by her handlers. The park's owners decided to have her euthanized by electrocution. Electricians associated with New York Edison handled the electrocution and employees from Edison's filmmaking company filmed the event.[89] The short but gruesome film can still be viewed on YouTube today.[90]

By 1911 the movie business was one of Edison's most profitable, but while he continued to make movies through 1915, profits dropped off, and by 1914 his market share was down to only 8 percent.

26

Cable Address "Edison, New York"

From the Laboratory of Thomas A. Edison,

Orange, N.J.

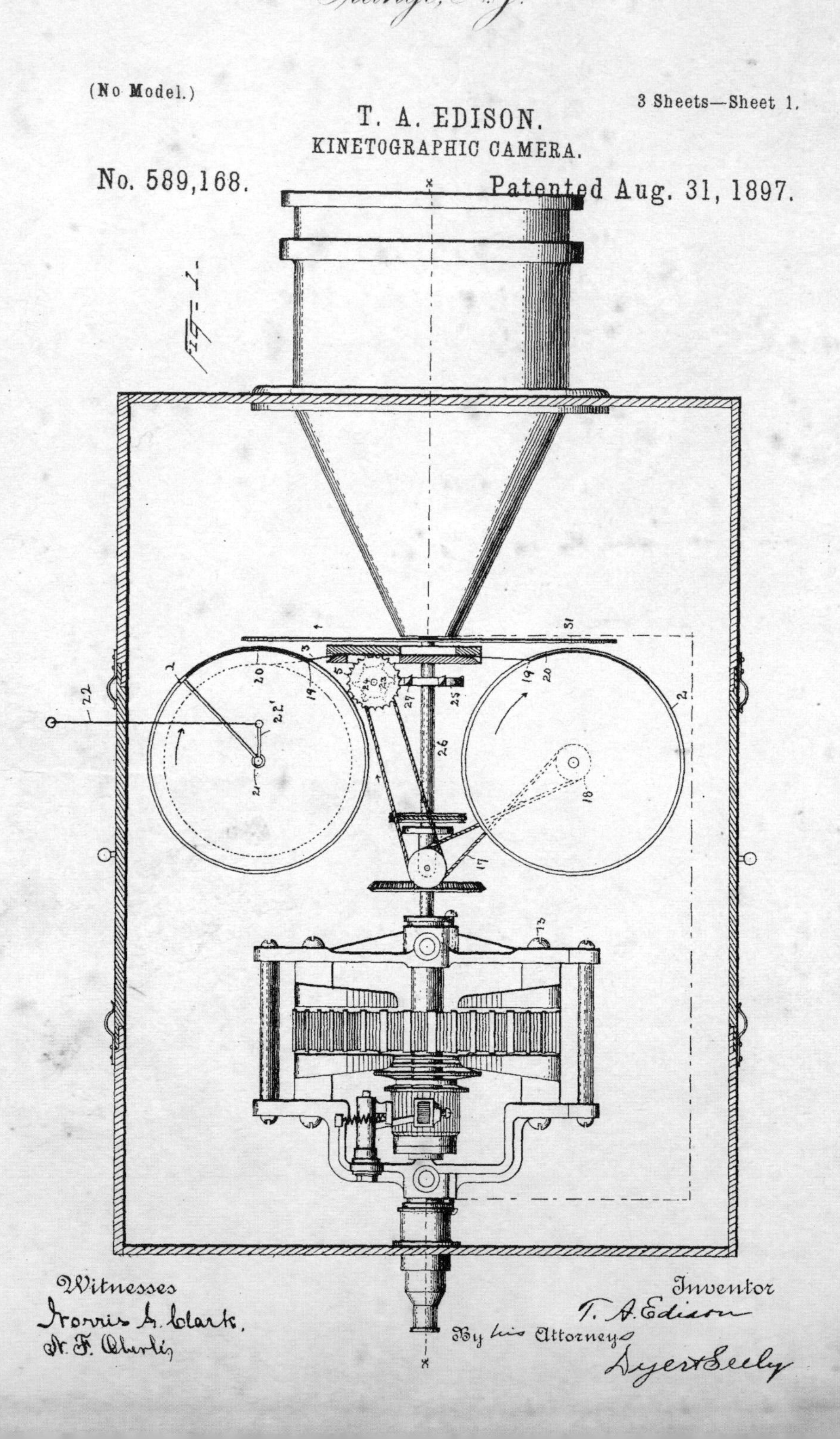

Above: **Topsy the elephant being electrocuted on film**

It declined from there. Frustrated with low profits and never quite enthusiastic on the business, Edison sold his equipment and film rights in 1918. His departure was not because of lack of demand—plenty of people were willing to pay for longer features and better-produced films—but it would be left to others to build the empire that created the golden age of movies.[91]

Edison did not miss a beat; he was already working on his next venture.

CHAPTER 9

A MAN OF MANY TALENTS

Thomas Edison is responsible for far more inventions and industries than those for which he is generally credited. Did you know he pioneered the milling of low-grade iron ore? Or that he built houses out of cement? Or created storage batteries for electric cars and houses? Did you know that he was a prolific writer, and even started a science fiction novel? This chapter looks at some of his less famous endeavors.

Iron Ore Milling

If you asked most people to list the inventions and industries of Thomas Edison, hardly anyone would answer, "iron ore milling." But Edison spent nearly a decade of his life obsessed with the practice. Samuel Insull once said Edison was "practically intoxicated by the business."[1] Iron ore had been mined and milled for many years, but there was always the problem of how to extract iron from low-grade ore, which consisted of a lot of rock and very little iron. Low-grade ore also has higher phosphorus levels, which tends to make the extracted iron more brittle. Most companies just left the ore in the ground and moved on to more lucrative sites in the Midwest. But Edison, ever excited by a challenge, decided to find a way to extract the iron profitably.[2]

He used his electrical and telegraphy expertise to come up with a method of extraction based on the use of electromagnets.[3] Early attempts on Long Island and Rhode Island did not work out as

Opposite: **Edison's iron ore system at Ogdensburg, New Jersey**

planned, but by late 1888 he had organized a new company in New Jersey and, with a few false starts elsewhere, built an ore milling plant in Ogden.[4] He was ready to mill some ore.

It was not easy. Edison had difficulty overcoming the problems that had turned others away. Phosphorus levels were too high for many customers, the crushing rolls and separators left too much valuable residue behind, and management problems resulted in severe inefficiencies and failures to meet orders.[5] By the summer of 1891, Edison moved to Ogden to "fix all the problems." Eventually he decided the plant design was unworkable, so he tore it down and built a new plant—the most massive and complicated milling operation in existence.[6] New crushing rolls were brought in to replace the jaw-type crushers, steam shovels did the work of twenty men, and giant new overhead cranes moved ore and iron from one place to another. All of this improved the output, but constant engineering challenges required Edison to use all the money he was making in his other businesses. In 1900, he closed the mine.[7]

Above: **Edison's cement houses**

On to Portland—Cement

The expertise Edison gained from developing new engineering systems for low-grade iron ore gave him an idea for his next great adventure: cement. Portland cement (named after a British Island that inspired its developer) is "a mixture of limestone and specific proportions of silica, alumina, and iron oxide that is burned in a kiln at a high temperature."[8] Portland cement was more consistent in composition than natural cement, which also made it more economical.

Edison had Francis Upton research the necessary physical and chemical properties, and in 1899, a year before closing Ogden, he started a new company to manufacture cement. Buying up land in New Jersey with the appropriate limestone deposits, Edison set himself the task of expanding capacity of the standard kiln from 250 to 1,000 barrels of cement every twenty-four hours.[9] Crushing rolls handled up to 300 tons per hour.[10] Conveyor belts moved the cement around the plant. Engineering difficulties and marketing problems were constant challenges, and a fatal plant explosion shut down the facility temporarily, but Edison was able to start turning out products made from cement and selling the traditional bags of cement to contractors. The "long kiln" he invented turned out to be one of his most profitable; long after he left the business—well into the 1920s—he received a royalty of "one cent on every barrel of cement produced by other companies."[11]

Above: **Edison's cement phonographs**

Among the products produced were street curbs, septic tanks, flowerpots, and other traditional items. But Edison had bigger ideas. He built phonograph cabinets out of cement, along with floors, fence posts, and decorative items.[12] His most ambitious project, however, was to have contractors build entire houses out of poured concrete. With the proper molds installed onsite, these homes could be erected in only twelve hours.[13]

Naval Consulting Board

Edison's friends in government and the military turned to him regularly for technical advice on a variety of topics. While not particularly war-mongering, Edison did recognize how warfare was bound to change with the advancement of technology. Echoing rival Nikola Tesla, whose

Above: **Secretary of the Navy Josephus Daniels breaking ground for the Naval Research Laboratory on December 6, 1920**

own "death ray" talk would later tickle the ears of pre–Second World War military generals, Edison thought peace could be attained through technological power. With the First World War on the horizon, Edison noted, "Science is going to make war a terrible thing—too terrible to contemplate. Pretty soon we can be mowing men down by the thousands or even millions almost by pressing a button."[14]

As early as 1915, after the Secretary of the Navy named him head of a new Naval Consulting Board, Edison suggested to military and civilian leaders that they stockpile weapons and ships in preparedness for possible war.[15] He also recommended the military set up a network of research laboratories. These would be patterned after Edison's own West Orange lab, of course, and would allow rapid development of whatever technical needs warranted as they arose.[16]

It took years for the Naval Research Laboratory to be built. It finally opened in Washington, D.C., in 1923, five years after World War I had ended. Funding had been cut to a fraction of the amount Edison felt was needed, and the military ignored his preference for siting the lab in Sandy Hook, New Jersey.[17] Edison and colleagues did most of the work at a makeshift lab on Eagle Rock Mountain near West Orange.[18] Edison was frustrated that the Navy gave little priority to the Board's recommendations (Nikola Tesla felt similarly; his proposals were submitted to the Board but never acted upon one way or the other).[19] Edison disagreed with the Navy's focus and methods—and young college-educated scientists—and very few of the recommended programs were ever put into battle.[20] Still, the creation of the Naval Research Laboratory did put the federal government on a path toward better research and preparedness, all because of the Navy's confidence in Edison.[21]

Science and Science Fiction

Surprisingly, in addition to all of his other activities and interests, Thomas Edison also wrote a science fiction novel, or at least part of one.[22] His first foray into writing, not counting the notes he took while doing chemistry experiments in his parent's Port Huron basement, was during his days as a news butch on the Grand Trunk Railroad. In between stations, and during layovers before the return train, Edison

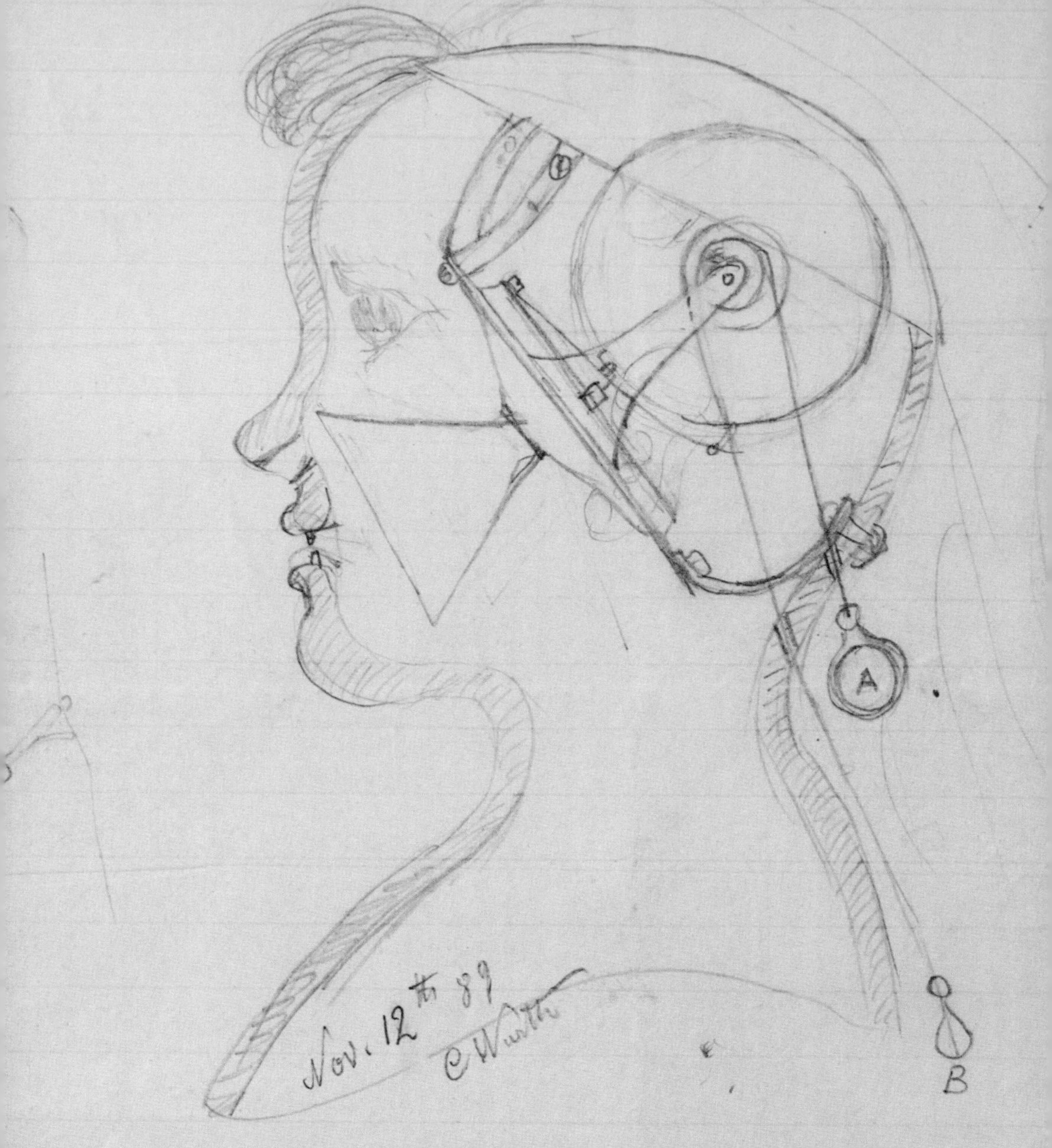

A

Nov. 12th 89
C Wurth

B

Cheap Toy Phonogr.

To be mounted in the head

The head only to be sold. Talk only short

such as: I love you mamma. For talking, pull

For rewinding pull string B

T. A. EDISON.

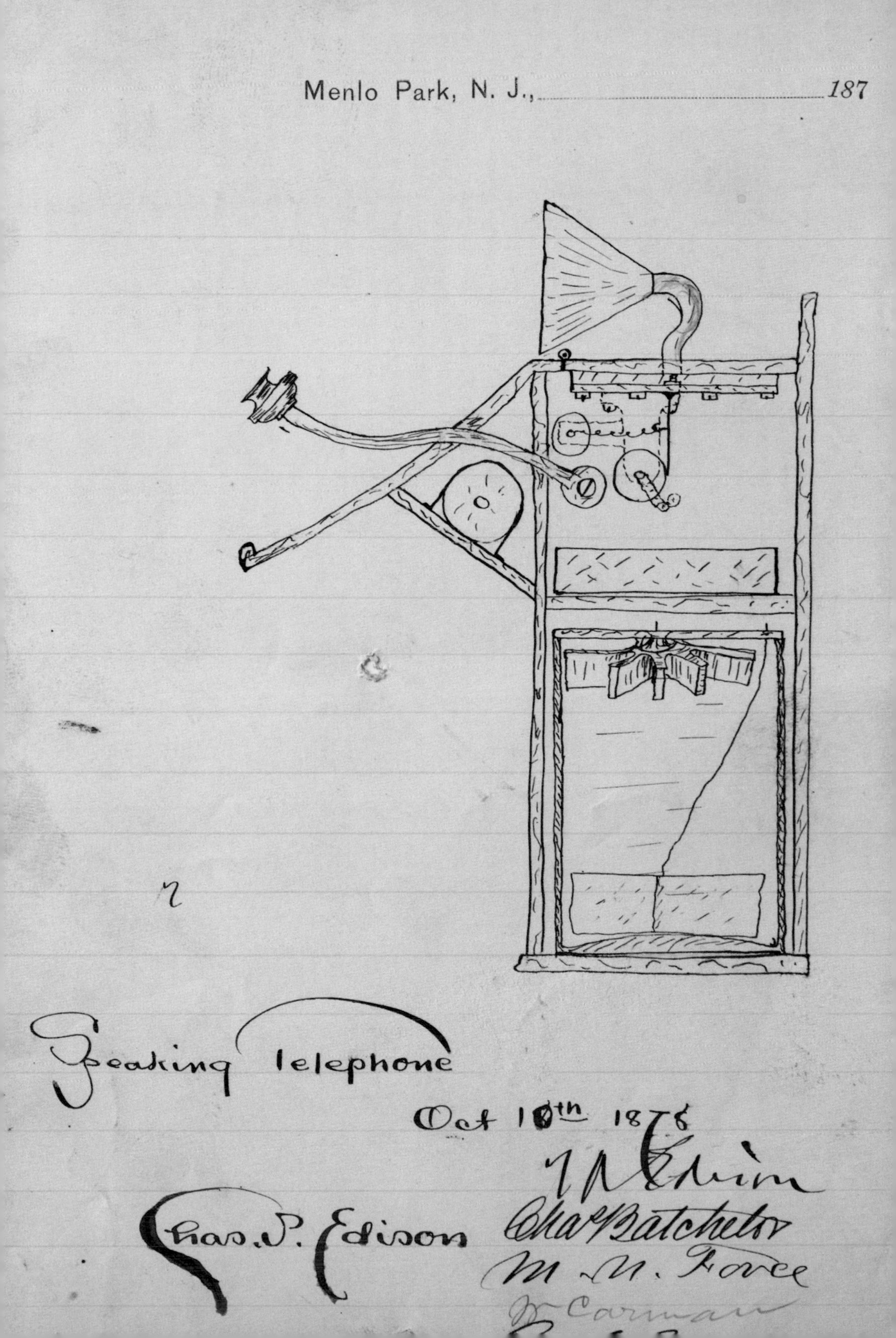
35
Menlo Park, N. J., 187
Speaking telephone
Oct 10th 1878
T A Edison
Chas. P. Edison
Chas Batchelor
M. N. Force

wrote and printed his own newspaper, the *Weekly Herald*.[23] From there he graduated to writing for *The Telegrapher*.[24]

The Telegrapher was a journal created by the National Telegraphic Union, founded in 1863 during the Civil War. Edison and his fellow itinerant telegraphers had formed the Union "as an attempt to consolidate this rather makeshift, exponentially growing, unruly profession of drifting young men, and give them a united arbitration voice."[25] Thomas Edison, still a teenager, became its most prolific editorial

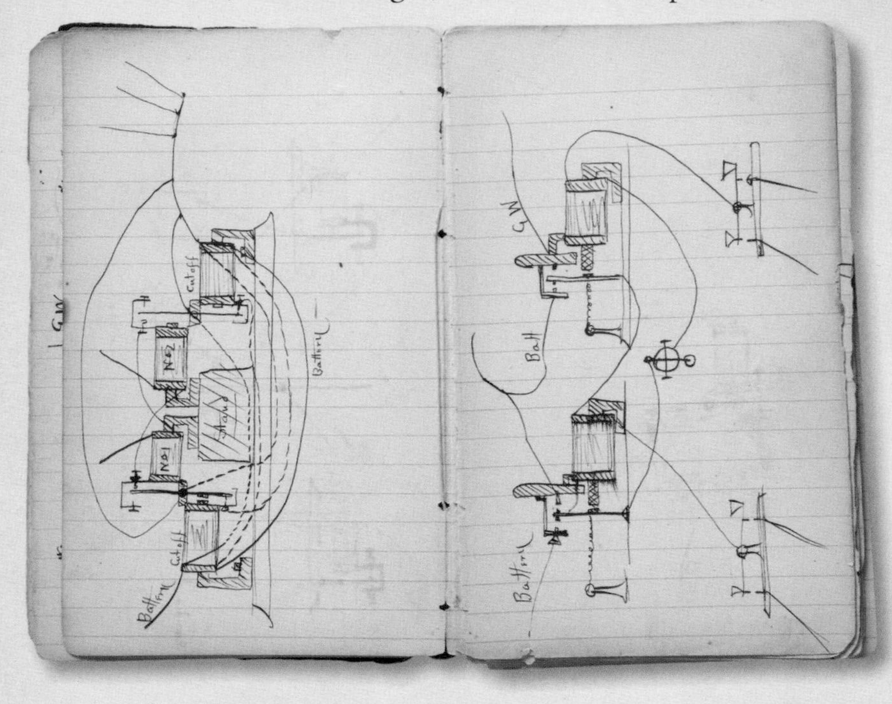

writer.[26] Always researching and recording technological advances, Edison wrote at least seven articles in one year alone documenting his earliest discoveries. When he went to work for Western Union in Boston, he also wrote for their corporate newsletter, the *Journal of the Telegraph*.[27]

To be sure, these were highly technical pieces and not the most exciting reading to outsiders. Perhaps more interesting was his writing during the one time in his life he kept a personal diary. The diary was required of all participants in a summer social gathering at the Gilliland estate in New England during the time shortly after the death

***Previous, above, and following*: Edison's laboratory notes and letters**

of Edison's first wife, Mary. Among his references to Mina, the much junior young woman whom he would marry a year later, Edison waxed poetic on a variety of subjects in language that comes unexpected from the pen of a man always jiggering with technical details.

> This is by far the finest day of the season, neither too hot nor too cold. It blooms on the apex of perfection–an Edensday. Good day for an angels' picnic. They could lunch on the smell of flowers and new mown hay, drink the moisture of the air, and dance to the hum of bees. Fancy the soul of Plato astride of a butterfly riding around Menlo Park with a lunch basket.[28]

Or this one:

> Arose early, went out to flirt with the flowers. Then my dream changed. Thought I was looking out upon the sea. Suddenly the air was filled with millions of little cherubs as one sees in Raphael's pictures. Each, I thought, was about the size of a fly. They were perfectly formed and seemed semitransparent. Each swept down to the surface of the sea, reached out both their tiny hands, and grabbed a very small drop of water, and flew upward, where they assembled and appeared to form a cloud.[29]

While he continued to scribble and draw and notate in his 3,500 laboratory journals throughout his career, Edison's most interesting writing may be his attempt at science fiction. At one point he started a book on telegraphy, but put it aside because of lack of time.[30] He also dabbled in poetry,[31] and during the Civil War briefly considered becoming a Shakespearian actor. All that got pushed into the background as he built his inventing career. Sometime in 1890 he was approached by author George Lathrop, who was interested in facilitating the writing of a science fiction novel, something that he and Edison had discussed in the past.[32] Keeping with Edison's visions of continuing technological improvements in the future, the novel was to be called *Progress*, and a commitment to publish was obtained from *McClure's Magazine*.[33]

With Lathrop's prodding, Edison produced notes for the book, thirty-three pages of which now exist in the Thomas Edison Papers

LETTERS
THE
IDEAL
LETTERS
FROM
TO

FROM
TO
Central Stationery Co.
New York
THE IDEAL FILE
LETTERS
GENERAL
BOX No. 96
MARCH 1923
THE COMMERCIAL FILE
LETTERS.
GENERAL
Box 139
August 1925

Project.[34] The notes reveal a somewhat disjointed concept, with one page talking about "the experimental station of the international Darwinian Society at Para on the Amazons," the next finding a literate civilization in the unexplored parts of Antarctica, and the next jumping to the "Saharan Sea" near the Mediterranean.[35] As might be expected, Edison filled his notes with obscure technology, including "etheric forces are used instead of electricity" and "force is generated by the action of the vibrations of light beyond . . . the ultraviolet of the spectrum."

Lathrop continued to urge Edison to produce further pages and even wrote five chapters on his own, which he sent to Edison for approval. Edison promptly lost them. Frustrated and in debt to *McClure's* for the advance payment, Lathrop desperately begged Edison to supply more material—or, at the very least, approve what Lathrop had written. But Edison, who by this time had moved to Ogden to salvage his ore-milling operations, was too busy to comply. Ultimately nothing ever came of the science fiction novel.[36] Edison continued with his frantic schedule, and Lathrop—who was married to Nathaniel Hawthorne's daughter, Rose—died in 1898 at only forty-seven years old.[37]

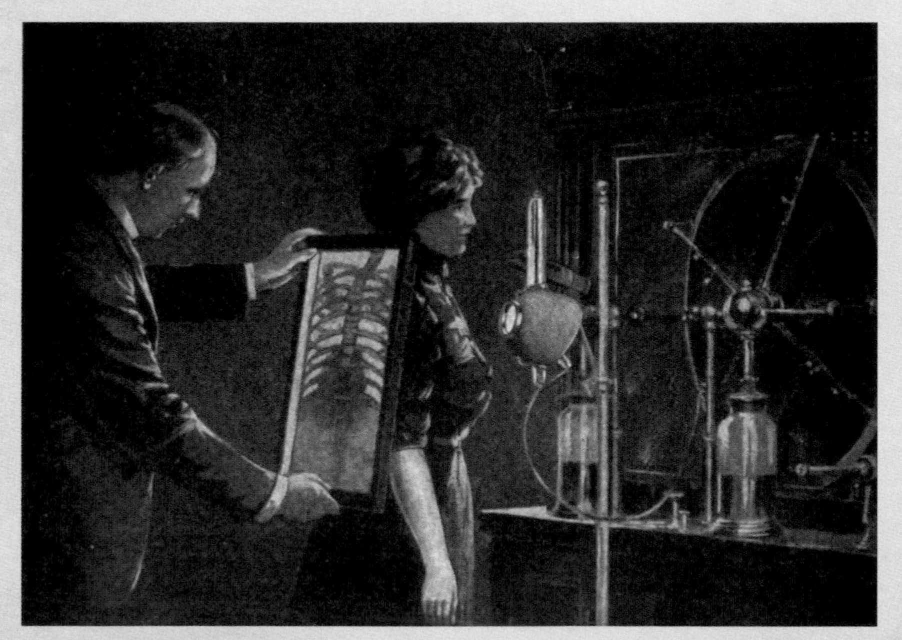

Above: **A fluoroscopic image**

Edison had one more writing-related accomplishment of note: He helped start the iconic and prestigious scientific journal *Science*.[38] Edison was a friend of the publisher of *Nature*, the already preeminent British journal, and was interested in starting up an American version. Edison hired a young freelance writer named John Michel, provided an assistant and writing space, and agreed to finance the operation as long as the journal would reach at least marginal profitability in a short time frame. It was called *Science: A Weekly Journal of Scientific Progress*. Edison kept his participation anonymous, although he controlled the content.[39] This led to some self-serving articles in early editions, but despite grumbling from some competitors and would-be authors, the journal caught on and slowly evolved into the journal *Science* as we know it today.[40] After Edison withdrew support a few years later, Alexander Graham Bell published it for the next decade.

A Little Bit of Everything

Edison spent decades inventing. Some of his ideas became huge and others drifted away, but no one else's contributions to society are likely to exceed his. In addition to the major industries already described, Edison experimented with many other technologies.

After Wilhelm Röntgen invented what we know today as X-rays, Edison did considerable experimentation to improve on the concept and develop a practical device for using it. Focusing first on improving the vacuum tubes, Edison eventually developed a way to view the fluorescence produced by X-rays, and such was born the fluoroscope.[41] Sadly, Edison's fluoroscope, already on display at the 1901 Pan-American Exposition in Buffalo, could have been used to save the life of President William McKinley after he was shot, but presidential aides refused to use it for fear of radiation poisoning. McKinley died several days later from the lead bullet still lodged in his body.[42]

Edison also built home appliances like toasters under the name Edicraft,[43] talking dolls,[44] electric trains,[45] and, despite his reluctance, radio (his sons Charles and Theodore pushed him into it). He even got into solar eclipses, developing a tasimeter to measure infrared radiation, which he used to measure the heat from the sun. This was one of many offshoots from Edison's research on telephones.[46]

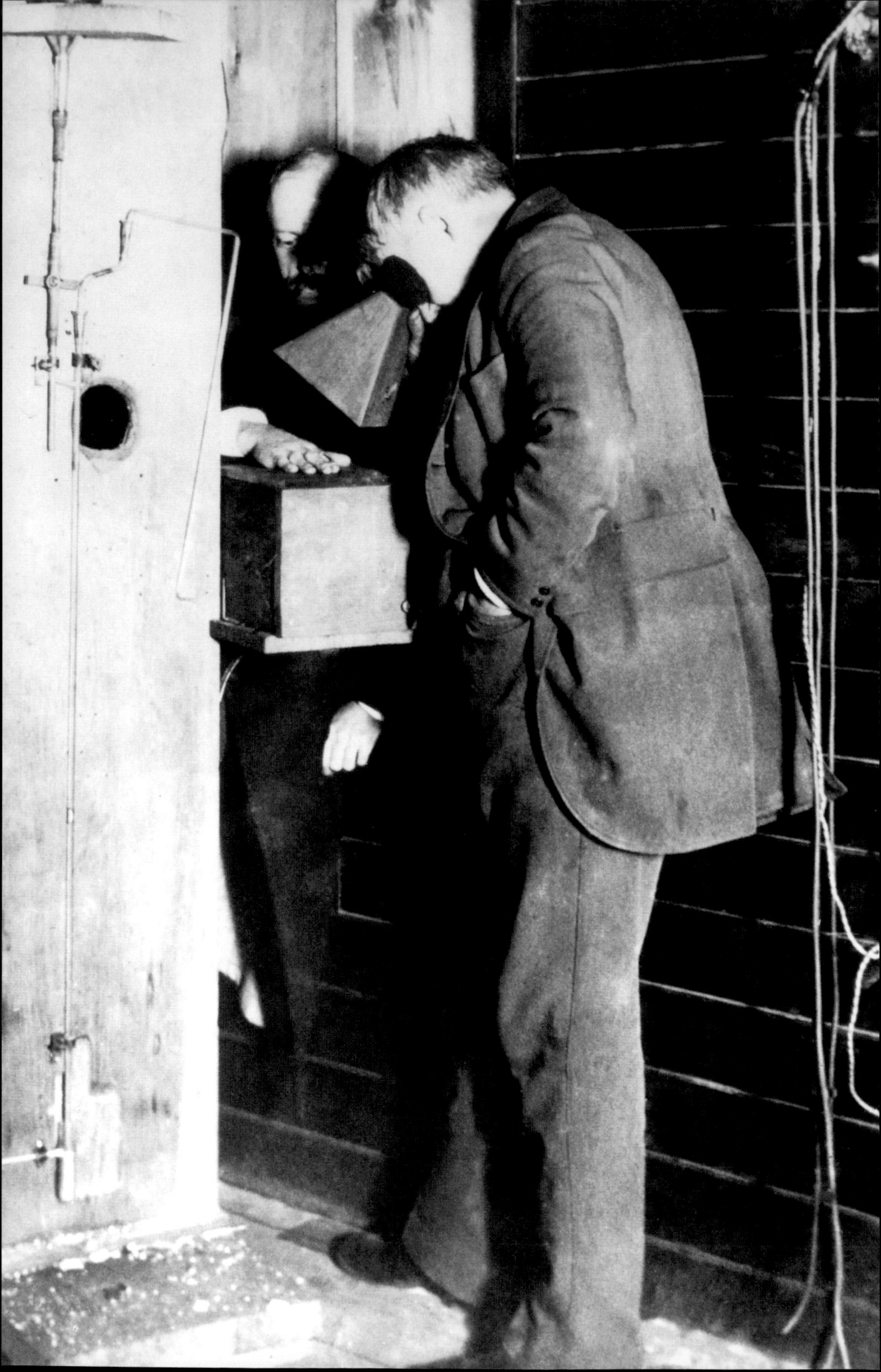

Rubber

By 1927 Edison had largely turned the management of Thomas A. Edison Inc. over to his son Charles, who would run it until it merged with McGraw Electric Company in 1957.[47] More content than usual to relax with Mina in their Fort Myers estate, Edison was not entirely retired. Good friends Henry Ford and Harvey Firestone were looking for someone to find a domestic source of rubber to offset the increasing costs of natural rubber from South America, Malaysia, and other distant parts of the world.[48] Eager to remain active, Edison converted his laboratory in Fort Myers to the study of new plant sources. In 1927 he set up the Edison Botanic Research Corporation[49] and told people who met him at the Fort Myers train station, "I'm here to work on my rubber experiments, and nothing else!"[50]

Edison started by identifying the characteristics of plants that would provide the most likely sources. He noted, "we are looking

***Opposite*: Edison looking into a fluoroscope**
***Above*: Edison and Harvey Firestone watch rubber expert and Firestone employee M. A. Cheek tap a rubber tree at Fort Myers, March 1925**

Cable Address "Edison, New York"

From the Laboratory of Thomas A. Edison,

Orange, N.J.

(No Model.)

T. A. EDISON.

Magnetic Ore-Separator.

No. 228,329. Patented June 1, 1880.

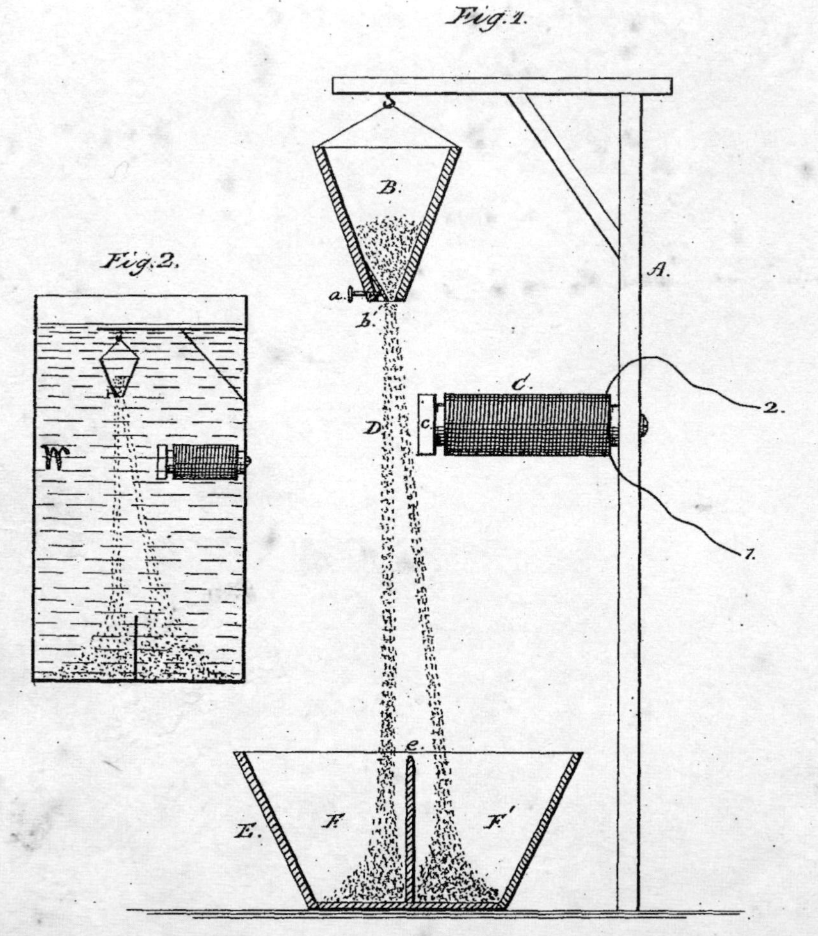

Attest:

F. W. Howard

H. C. Hall

Inventor:

Thomas A. Edison

by Dyer & Wilber

Attys

for an annual crop…which will come to maturity in eight or nine months, which can then be harvested by machinery…It must be something that will stand light frosts, for there is no part of the United States where there are not occasional frosts."[51] As with his quest for incandescent lightbulb filaments decades earlier, Edison sent people all over the world collecting samples of as many plants as they could find. Cuttings were sent back to the lab, where they were tested for rubber content using a new process Edison had developed.[52] While his staff of more than a dozen was traveling the world, Edison himself was collecting plants in Florida. At least 17,000 different species were tested.[53]

As always, Edison surrounded himself with a team consisting of chemists, machinists, and other experts. The lab was renovated to include a nursery, extra storage, drying ovens, and whatever else was needed for botanical experimentation.[54] They diligently tested everything, narrowing the best options to promising plants like "oleander, flame vine, and black mangrove."[55] Eventually Edison settled on goldenrod, which was a ubiquitous wildflower (some would say weed). It grew quickly, and its rubber was easily extracted. Goldenrod was not as easy to harvest mechanically as Edison wanted, but overall it was the best option for a domestic source of natural rubber.[56]

And then the Great Depression hit, and with it came less demand for rubber, as no one could afford cars, and a surplus of natural rubber on the market. Synthetic rubber would make the use of natural rubber obsolete and not cost-effective. Edison was getting old, and his last inventive spurt would go to its grave shortly after he did.

CHAPTER 10

A LEGACY LIKE NO OTHER

In the early morning hours of October 18, 1931, Thomas Alva Edison passed away peacefully in his Glenmont mansion in West Orange, New Jersey, not far from the laboratory where he had toiled many long days for many long years.[1] He was eighty-four years old and had been inventing for seven decades. His health had been failing for months, and he had struggled with the cumulative effects of diabetes, Bright's disease (kidney disease), stomach ulcers, and uremic poisoning, the final stages of kidney failure. His family was by his side, although he seemed to recognize only Mina, his wife of the past forty-two years.[2]

His legacy was immediately obvious. Sculptor James Earle Fraser, as was the fashion for famous people of the day, prepared a death mask and cast of Edison's hands. Edison's body lay in state in the library of the laboratory, and more than 50,000 mourners passed by to pay their respects.[3] After two days the casket was moved back to Glenmont for a private funeral. Besides Mina and the family, nearly 400 friends attended the service, including camping buddies Henry Ford and Harvey Firestone, First Lady Lou Henry Hoover (representing the U.S. President), and many other friends. Sympathy letters were received from world dignitaries such as Pope Pius XI and German President Paul von Hindenburg, as well as from more notorious personages as fascist dictator Benito Mussolini and Gus Winkler, a hit man for Al Capone.[4] *Science* magazine published a glowing obituary of the famed inventor, declaring him a "benefactor of humanity."[5]

Opposite: **Edison in the West Orange lab with his Edison Effect lightbulb, 1919**

EDISON

Edison is buried behind the family home at Glenmont, a half mile from his West Orange laboratory. His inventive legacy lives on to this day.

Legacy of Invention

Edison is credited with 1,093 patents in the United States alone, with many more in the United Kingdom, France, and Germany. Most of the earliest patents were related to improvements made to the telegraph, from duplex and biplex to quadruplex and printing telegraphs. Many others revolved around the phonograph, from the earliest tinfoil device to the cylinders and up to the flat disk phonographs that became the mainstay of recording and listening devices until the advent of cassettes, compact discs, and the MP3. Each phonograph type required many individual patents to cover the carbon transmitters (also used in telephones), styluses, cranks and motors, recording materials, and horn-like amplifiers.

The incandescent lightbulb and first systems of electric light and power also resulted in a large number of associated patents, as did motion picture and sound recording technology. Edison's patents include systems of ore-milling and concrete production (including concrete housing), fluoroscopes (X-rays), storage batteries, fuel cells, and dozens of other smaller inventions.[6]

Edison's legacy includes not only individual inventions, but also entire new industries like electric power generation, phonographs, and motion pictures. He began thinking about renewable resources long before it was fashionable. While he did not pursue it as much as his rival Nikola Tesla,[7] Edison recognized the limitations of fossil fuel energy. Not long before his death, he noted to his friends Henry Ford and Harvey Firestone:

> We are like tenant farmers chopping down the fence around our house for fuel when we should be using Nature's inexhaustible sources of energy–sun, wind, and tide. I'd put my money on the sun and solar energy. What a source of power! I hope we don't have to wait until oil and coal run out before we tackle that.[8]

Opoosite: **Edison demonstrating the phonograph**

EDISON
LIGHT-O-MATIC
RADIO
EDISON
NEW SPEED IRON
FROM EDISON
LABORATORIES!
WINGS ON YOUR IRONING!
The first iron to bear the signature of Thomas A. Edison because it's the first iron worthy of his famous name! It's new! It's handsome! It's fast! It combines so many revolutionary features that it makes all other irons old-fashioned!
DOES AN HOUR'S IRONING IN 39 MINUTES!—Fastest of them all! Impartial tests prove that the Edison saves 21 minutes an hour compared to your old iron.
EDISON SIZE
ORDINARY SIZE
15% TO 22% BIGGER IRONING SURFACE!—The Edison irons quicker because it does 15% to 22% more ironing with every stroke. It has a bigger ironing surface without extra weight.
FREE-ACTION HANDLE GETS SLEEVE WRINKLES QUICKER!—Permits you to iron inside of sleeves and between difficult folds without wasting a second or leaving a crinkle.
STREAMLINED FOR SPEED!—Smartly designed with streamlined sides, the Edison flashes through the heaviest wash with tugless ease.
$7.95
Thomas A. Edison
PEED IRON
A6
Edicraft
REG. U.S. PAT. OFF.
AUTOMATIC
Toaster
THOMAS A. EDISON, INC.
ORANGE NEW JERSEY
THE
Edicraft
Siphonator
TRANS-ILLUMINATION
The Edison Dental and Surgical Mouth Lamp with Flexible Handle.
Price complete, with connecting cord 6 feet long. . . . $4.00
PRICE EXTRA LAMPS TO FIT HANDLE $1.50 EACH.
The Edison Lamp Outfit,
Consisting of Edison Mouth Lamp complete, 8 Edison Lalande Cells type Q, Regulating Lamp Rheostat and connecting cords.
Price complete, $27.50
This outfit will last physicians fully six months without needing any attention, after which it can be renewed at a slight cost.
ON VIEW AND FOR SALE BY
The Edison Manufacturing Co.,
110 East 23d St., N. Y. City.
Noted Psychologists
get remarkable and enjoyable sensation out of Mr. Edison's unique Realism Test
From actual photograph taken in the Edison Shop, Fifth Ave., New York, when Messrs. Bingham, Farnsworth and Follett came in and asked to hear the Realism Test.
The second stirred himself: "I felt the presence of a living singer. She was singing—free and unrestrained. The accompaniment seemed by a separate instrument."
The third spoke up: "The music filled my mind with thoughts of peace and beauty."
The Realism Test
It was Mr. Edison's unique Realism Test—given specially for three men of international renown in art and science. The first who spoke was Dr. W. V. Bingham, Director of the Department of Applied Psychology, Carnegie Institute of Technology. His two colleagues were Prof. C. H. Farnsworth, Director of the Department of Music, Teachers College, Columbia University, and Wilson Follett, Esq., distinguished author and music critic.
Perhaps no similar group of men could combine, to an equal degree, the viewpoint of scientist, musician, and music-lover.
The reactions of these highly critical minds demonstrated that Mr. Edison has succeeded in devising a new and fascinating way for you to judge the New Edison. It brings into play your whole temperament and your fullest capacity to feel the finer
The NEW EDISON
with Edison BATTERIES

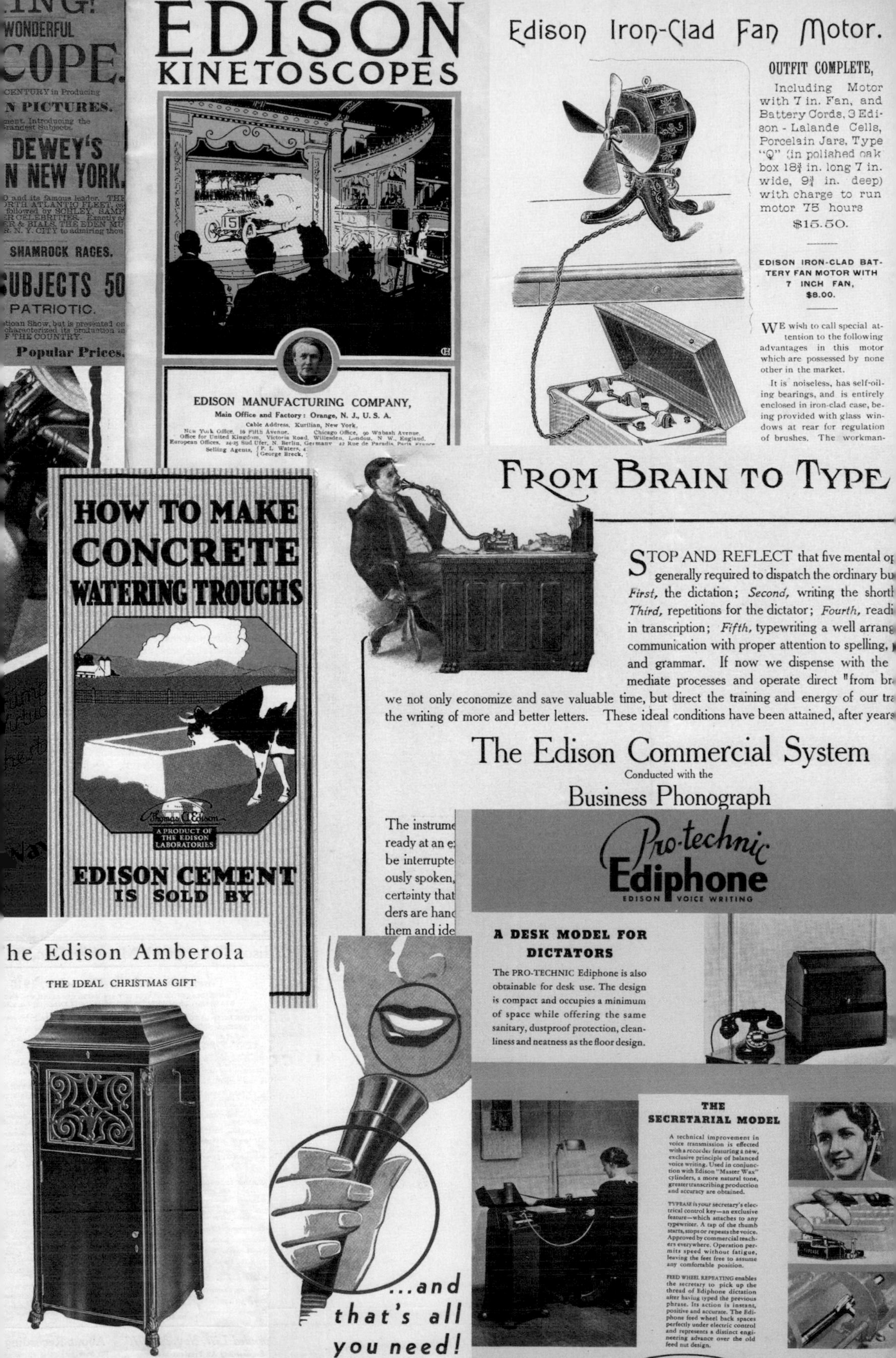

.ING!
WONDERFUL
COPE.
CENTURY in Producing
N PICTURES.
ment. Introducing the
Grandest Subjects.
DEWEY'S
N NEW YORK.
O and its famous leader. THE
ORTH ATLANTIC FLEET, es
followed by SCHLEY, SAMP
R CELEBRITIES. Exactly as
ER & BIALS, THE EDEN MU
R. N. Y. CITY to admiring thou
SHAMROCK RACES.
SUBJECTS 50
PATRIOTIC.
tican Show, but is presented on
characterized its production in
F THE COUNTRY.
Popular Prices.
EDISON
KINETOSCOPES
15
EDISON MANUFACTURING COMPANY,
Main Office and Factory: Orange, N. J., U. S. A.
Cable Address, Kurilian, New York.
New York Office, 16 Fifth Avenue. Chicago Office, 90 Wabash Avenue.
Office for United Kingdom, Victoria Road, Willesden, London, N. W., England.
European Offices, 24-25 Sud Ufer, N. Berlin, Germany. 42 Rue de Paradis, Paris, France.
Selling Agents, P. L. Waters,
George Breck,
Edison Iron-Clad Fan Motor.
OUTFIT COMPLETE,
Including Motor with 7 in. Fan, and Battery Cords, 3 Edison - Lalande Cells, Porcelain Jars, Type "Q" (in polished oak box 18¾ in. long 7 in. wide, 9¾ in. deep) with charge to run motor 75 hours
$15.50.
EDISON IRON-CLAD BATTERY FAN MOTOR WITH 7 INCH FAN,
$8.00.
WE wish to call special attention to the following advantages in this motor which are possessed by none other in the market.
It is noiseless, has self-oiling bearings, and is entirely enclosed in iron-clad case, being provided with glass windows at rear for regulation of brushes. The workman-
FROM BRAIN TO TYPE
STOP AND REFLECT that five mental op
generally required to dispatch the ordinary bu
First, the dictation; Second, writing the shorth
Third, repetitions for the dictator; Fourth, readi
in transcription; Fifth, typewriting a well arrang
communication with proper attention to spelling,
and grammar. If now we dispense with the
mediate processes and operate direct "from br
we not only economize and save valuable time, but direct the training and energy of our tr
the writing of more and better letters. These ideal conditions have been attained, after years
The Edison Commercial System
Conducted with the
Business Phonograph
The instrume
ready at an e
be interrupte
ously spoken,
certainty that
ders are hand
them and ide
HOW TO MAKE
CONCRETE
WATERING TROUGHS
Thomas A. Edison
A PRODUCT OF THE EDISON LABORATORIES
EDISON CEMENT
IS SOLD BY
Pro-technic
Ediphone
EDISON VOICE WRITING
A DESK MODEL FOR DICTATORS
The PRO-TECHNIC Ediphone is also obtainable for desk use. The design is compact and occupies a minimum of space while offering the same sanitary, dustproof protection, cleanliness and neatness as the floor design.
THE SECRETARIAL MODEL
A technical improvement in voice transmission is effected with a recorder featuring a new, exclusive principle of balanced voice writing. Used in conjunction with Edison "Master Wax" cylinders, a more natural tone, greater transcribing production and accuracy are obtained.
TYPEASE is your secretary's electrical control key—an exclusive feature—which attaches to any typewriter. A tap of the thumb starts, stops or repeats the voice. Approved by commercial teachers everywhere. Operation permits speed without fatigue, leaving the feet free to assume any comfortable position.
FEED WHEEL REPEATING enables the secretary to pick up the thread of Ediphone dictation after having typed the previous phrase. Its action is instant, positive and accurate. The Ediphone feed wheel back spaces perfectly under electric control and represents a distinct engineering advance over the old feed nut design.
Thomas A. Edison
INCORPORATED
he Edison Amberola
THE IDEAL CHRISTMAS GIFT
Price: United States, $200.00; Canada, $240.00.
...and
that's all
you need!

Edison worked on a way to generate electricity from a wind turbine, then store that energy for short-term use, suggesting as early as 1901 that rural citizens "could bottle up enough current to give . . . light at night."[9] He even made drawings of a windmill that could power four to six homes. Working with Henry Ford, Edison developed storage batteries and electric automobiles, suggesting that people could recharge at plug-in sites along trolley lines. He was not particularly successful pursuing renewable resources, but he was at least aware of the benefits of doing so.

His legacy and contributions to invention go beyond individual products. Edison invented the art of invention. Previously, companies relied on in-house expertise or itinerant workers to tweak old ideas into new. Edison changed that. At his Menlo Park and West Orange invention factories, he created what amounted to the first industrial research and development laboratories. He hired fellow invention-minded colleagues and allowed them the freedom to figure out how to achieve the set goals. He also hired skilled artisans so he could provide conceptual drawings from his notebooks and be confident the team could build what he had envisioned. This collaborative approach freed him to think up new ideas while others were doing the busy work of ongoing projects. His full-capacity laboratories—complete with metal shops, glass-blowing facilities, testing stations, and storerooms full of every supply and chemical imaginable—allowed for a system of mass production. Edison not only designed new products, but also manufactured them, and often used the "American System of Manufacture," a sort of assembly-line process where laborers could put together products using prefabricated parts. This system allowed him to increase production of phonographs from ten to fifty per day.[10]

Edison also pioneered what we now call external consulting. Big corporations like Western Union contracted large sums of money to Edison and his companies to find technical solutions and improvements to existing systems, then manufacture the new devices in quantities that meet the growing demand. This brought in a near-constant stream of funding, which, along with commercialization of other Edison inventions, provided the necessary financing to develop even newer technologies.

Finally, Edison created the concept of branding. He started dozens of companies, most of which highlighted the Edison name, and everyone knew to call him when they needed something done. To secure the branding concept even more tightly, eventually all his businesses were held under the umbrella of one corporate brand—Thomas A. Edison, Inc. Even Edison's new official signature incorporated the now-iconic umbrella motif.[11]

Pop Culture

The workaholic Edison, often in juxtaposition with archrival Nikola Tesla, was a perfect model for science fiction fantasy stories. In fact, there is an entire genre of "fantastic fiction" named after him—Edisonade. While the Edisonade name is a modern invention, the genre started back in the nineteenth century; it generally features a young inventor (including "Tom Edison Jr.") who travels to distant places and has fantastic adventures.[12]

Thomas Edison himself appears in *Edison's Conquest of Mars*, a science fiction novel published in 1898 that features a proactive attack on Mars after a failed Martian invasion of Earth. When Martians

Above and following: **Art from *Edison's Conquest of Mars*, originally serialized in the *New York Journal*, 1898**

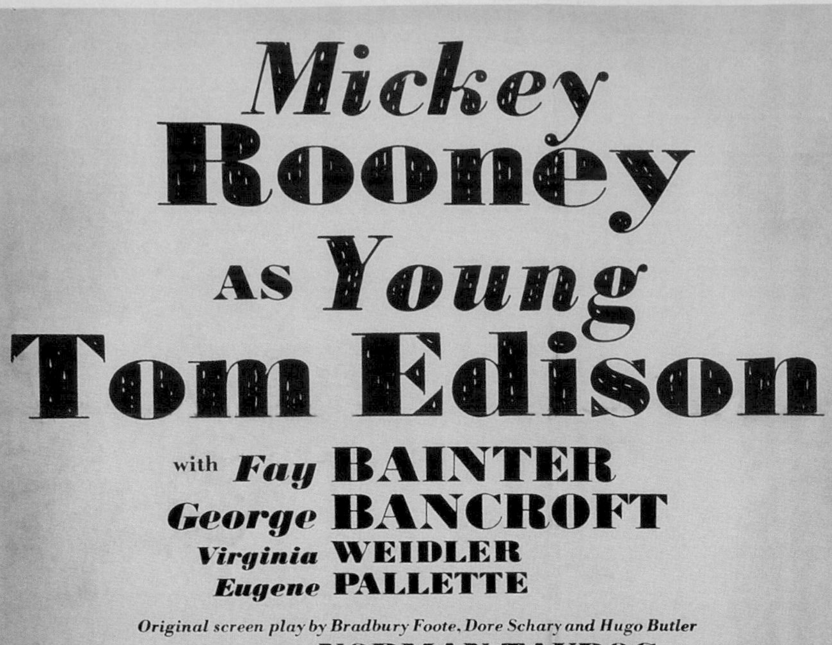
Mickey
Rooney
as Young
Tom Edison
with Fay BAINTER
George BANCROFT
Virginia WEIDLER
Eugene PALLETTE
Original screen play by Bradbury Foote, Dore Schary and Hugo Butler
Directed by NORMAN TAUROG
Produced by John W. Considine, Jr.-Associate Producer: Orville O. Dull
A Metro-Goldwyn-Mayer
PICTURE

attacked, Edison invented a "disintegrating ray" (based on his work with X-rays at the time) to save Earth and the Universe.[13] The book is a sequel to *Fighters from Mars*, an unauthorized version of H. G. Wells' *The War of the Worlds*, then in serialization in *Pearson's Magazine* in the United Kingdom.[14]

Edison and Nikola Tesla both make appearances in *The Great Abraham Lincoln Pocket Watch Conspiracy*, by Jacopo della Quercia, in which a globetrotting President Taft and companion Robert Lincoln fight unknown terrorists in an action-packed attempt to save the world.[15] In *Tesla's Signal*, by L. Woodswalker, Thomas Edison offers his inventive services to villains after falling under the spell of a mind-bender.[16] Even famed author Kurt Vonnegut, Jr., highlighted the inventive genius in the short story "Tom Edison's Shaggy Dog," about Edison's discovery that dogs have superintelligence and the ability to speak English.[17] A 1978 novel by Donald R. Bensen called *And Having Writ…* has Thomas Edison serving one term as President of the United States after three hapless aliens get stranded on Earth.[18] If video games are your thing, check out the *Assassin's Creed* series, in which Edison is once again up against his favorite rival, Tesla.[19]

If you are interested in more serious books about Thomas Edison, explore the bibliography for excellent biographies by Neil Baldwin, Leonard DeGraaf, Paul Israel, Randall Stross, and others.

Appropriately, given his pioneer work in motion pictures, several movies have been made that feature the life of Edison. In the year 1940, less than a decade after his death, two movies starring two icons of cinematography were released. Mickey Rooney played *Young Tom Edison*,[20] while Spencer Tracy portrayed a more mature *Edison, The Man*.[21] Musicians have also referred to Edison, including the song "Edison's Medicine" by the band Tesla,[22] "The Wizard of Menlo Park" by Chumbawamba,[23] and, for a more disco/pop crowd, "Edison" by the Bee Gees.[24]

***Opposite*: Movie poster from *Young Tom Edison* starring Mickey Rooney**

Edison also appears in a variety of time-travel fiction, science fiction film, and television (including, of course, *The Simpsons*). The best-known modern appearance of Edison may be in the YouTube video *Epic Rap Battles in History*, in which Edison goes up against, you guessed it, Nikola Tesla.[25]

It is safe to say that virtually everyone above the age of ten has heard of Thomas Edison.

Honors

Thomas Edison received many honors and awards over the course of his long career. Patrons did not wait until he was gone before bestowing these honors upon him. On the fiftieth anniversary of the invention of the incandescent lightbulb, Treasury Secretary Andrew Mellon created a special Congressional Gold Medal to acknowledge Edison. It reads "He illuminated the path of progress by his inventions."[26] The newly formed Academy of Motion Pictures Arts and Sciences gave him the very first honorary Academy Award (more familiarly known today as an Oscar) in 1929, the first year of its existence.[27]

The number of awards he received is substantial, including:

- **The Matteucci Medal, 1887 (an Italian award for physicists)[28]**
- **John Scott Medal, 1889 (City Council of Philadelphia)[29]**
- **Edward Longstreth Medal, 1899 (Franklin Institute in Philadelphia)[30]**
- **John Fritz Medal, 1908 (American Association of Engineering Societies)[31]**
- **Franklin Medal, 1915 (Franklin Institute of Philadelphia)[32]**
- **Navy Distinguished Service Medal, 1920 (U.S. Navy)[33]**
- **Edison Medal, 1904 (AEEE, later the IEEE)[34]**
- **Congressional Gold Medal, 1928[35]**

In addition, Edison was inducted into the Royal Swedish Academy of Sciences, the U.S. National Academy of Sciences, and the New Jersey Hall of Fame. In 2010 he even received a technical Grammy Award for his contributions to the development of sound recording.[36]

There are innumerable high schools, state and community colleges, streets, hotels, and fountains named after Edison. At least three bridges carry his name, as does Lake Thomas A. Edison in California.[37] Two U.S. Navy surface ships and an Ethan Allen-class ballistic-missile submarine are called *Edison*. There is even an asteroid named in his honor—742 Edisona.[38] If you want to honor Edison yourself, you can order from a wide selection of T-shirts featuring Edison,[39] for yourself and for your dog.[40] And you can purchase various inventor lab kits for any budding inventors-to-be.[41]

Edison started many companies bearing his name, and you can still find several today, including electric utilities such as Consolidated Edison, Commonwealth Edison (now part of Exelon), Detroit Edison (now part of DTE Energy), and Southern California Edison. Perhaps his greatest legacy is the company formerly called Edison General Electric, today known simply as General Electric, one of the most successful companies in existence and whose catchphrase "Imagination at Work" certainly evokes its founder.[42]

Awards named in his honor include the previously mentioned Edison Medal created in 1904 and given out annually by the Institute of Electrical and Electronic Engineers (IEEE);[43] the Edison Award, granted by the Netherlands each year for outstanding achievements in the music industry;[44] and the Thomas A. Edison Patent Award, given out annually by the American Society of Mechanical Engineers.[45]

Keeping the Edison Name Alive

Many organizations have worked hard to honor the man who has more than 1,000 patents spanning the fields of telegraphy, electric power, lighting, batteries, phonograph, motion pictures, cement, and mining. Many locations associated with Edison have established museums, preserved landmarks, and even erected giant lightbulbs in remembrance of his work.

The Edison Birthplace Museum stands in commemoration of his birth in Milan, Ohio. While the home was sold when the Edison family left Milan, Edison's sister Marion reacquired it forty years later. Several years after her death, Edison himself bought the property again and had a cousin live there to maintain its heritage.[46] On his last visit in 1924 he was shocked to find out that it was still being lit with oil lamps and candles. Many years after Edison's death, Mina bought the house. On the 100th anniversary of Edison's birth, February 11, 1947, it was opened as a museum.[47]

Not to be forgotten is the Thomas Edison Depot Museum in Port Huron, Michigan, where Edison plied his news butcher trade on the Grand Trunk Railroad, and the Thomas Edison House (*edisonhouse.org*) in Louisville, Kentucky, where he lived for a while during his days as an itinerant telegraph operator. There is even an Edison Museum in Beaumont, Texas, despite the fact that Edison never visited.

And then there are the laboratories that Edison made famous. The Thomas Edison Center at Menlo Park stands on the site of Edison's original "invention factory." After Edison had moved out of Menlo Park and to New York City, then to West Orange, New Jersey, the Menlo Park facility became severely dilapidated and most of its usable equipment was shuttled to the new facilities. A fire destroyed Edison's home in 1914, and five years later another fire burned down the office and library.[48] On May 16, 1925, the state of New Jersey dedicated a memorial tablet on the now-vacant site. Edison and Mina attended

Above: **Edison's Megaphone, which could reportedly amplify voices at a distance of up to two miles**

the ceremony, along with the Governor of New Jersey, the President of Princeton University, General Electric Chairman Edward W. Rice, Vice-President of New York Edison Company John Leib, and Samuel Insull, President of Commonwealth Edison Company of Chicago.[49] The tablet, embedded in a large rock monument, still stands today.[50]

The Menlo Park site contains perhaps one of the most iconic monuments to Edison's legacy. On the fiftieth birthday of the perfection of the lightbulb, Edison Pioneers—a group of current and former workers in Edison's companies—erected a steel-framed tower where the main laboratory building once stood. The tower included a steel-frame lightbulb at the top, which was lit on October 21, 1929. The structure remained in place for several years, until lightning destroyed it in 1937.[51] Interestingly, the Edison Pioneers had started working on a new permanent Art Deco tower five months earlier, and it was dedicated on Edison's birthday in 1938. Paying homage to Edison's venture into cement housing, this tower was built of much sturdier cement and stretched 135 feet skyward. On top was a 19-foot-diameter replica of an incandescent lightbulb constructed of segmented Pyrex glass and made by the Corning Glass Works from a sketch of the first commercial lightbulb.[52] That tower remains standing today.

Alongside the tower is a small but information-packed museum highlighting the history of the Menlo Park laboratory. Volunteer tour guides regale visitors not just with facts about the many inventions, but also personal stories that bring Thomas Edison to life.[53] Exhibits showcase his early telegraph and electricity inventions, and guides play a 115-year-old wax cylinder on a phonograph that sounds like it was built yesterday.

The original Menlo Park laboratory is in Dearborn, Michigan. Henry Ford opened the Henry Ford Museum, sometimes referred to as the Edison Institute, to showcase American heritage. Part of the museum complex includes a 240-acre tract of land called Greenfield Village that includes nearly 100 historical buildings along with pasture, forest, and river habitats.[54] Among the many historic structures is a replica of Edison's Menlo Park lab. Because Ford was a good friend, Edison

Opposite: **Edison in his workshop**

permitted him to move the only two surviving buildings—the Glass House and Sarah Jordan's Boarding House—to Deerfield Village.[55] Any other material left from the original Menlo Park laboratory buildings was also shipped to Dearborn, including dirt from the site.

The Wizard of Menlo Park spent much of his inventing life up the road from Menlo Park in West Orange, New Jersey. Today the West Orange laboratory and Glenmont, where Edison and Mina raised their own plus Edison's older children, makes up the Thomas Edison National Historical Park and is run by the National Park Service. The complex includes all the original laboratory buildings and equipment, so visiting it is like going back in time. Onsite is also a replica of the Black Maria movie studio, where the earliest films were produced and filmed. One of the highlights is the library where beautiful bookcases are filled with books that Edison and his colleagues used to research new solutions to old problems. A cot tucked in one corner is a reminder of the long hours Edison worked, although he was just as likely to cozy up on the nearest laboratory bench.[56]

Even before Edison's death there was a recognition that something needed to be done to preserve his papers and facilities. By 1938 a company executive was lamenting to the Edison family the deteriorating state of organization, which to him resembled "a jackdaw's nest."[57] Just prior to Mina's death in 1947, she sold the property to the Thomas A. Edison Company, and by the middle of the 1950s it was transferred to the National Park Service to preserve. On September 5, 1962, Congress officially designated the West Orange laboratory and nearby Glenmont the Edison National Historical Site.[58] It would take many more years before it would be adequately maintained and opened as a valuable public trust that gives all of us supreme insight into the working life of Thomas A. Edison.

Yet another organization has preserved Edison's life for the public. Donated by Mina Edison to Fort Myers six months before her death, and in recognition of the importance of friend and neighbor Henry Ford, the Edison and Ford Winter Estates are open for public tours.[59] The twenty acres include both Edison's and Ford's homes, guest houses, and gardens, as well as Edison's Botanic Research Lab. The Edison Ford Museum showcases hundreds of inventions, exhibits, and artifacts.

Opposite: **Edison in his true home, the workshop**

The Research Continues

While Thomas Edison has been gone for many decades, the work of compiling his important papers continues. The Thomas Edison Papers is a project started in 1978 and run by Rutgers University to organize, and now digitize, all of Thomas Edison's papers, notebooks, and other resources, which total more than five million pages.[60] A major goal of the project is:

> . . . to produce a selective fifteen-volume book edition of transcribed and annotated documents. The book volumes provide not only an overview of Edison's life and career but also significant resources for understanding the development and other technology, as well as the emergence of new technology industries.[61]

Work on the project is expected to continue for many more years, but already there are editions in digital, microfilm, and book formats. Online resources include links to chronologies, Edison's inventions and patents, his companies, and a bibliography of works.[62]

Above and opposite: **Menlo Park as it looks today**

Cable Address "Edison, New York"

From the Laboratory of Thomas A. Edison,

Orange, N.J.

T. A. EDISON.

STARTING AND CURRENT SUPPLYING SYSTEM FOR AUTOMOBILES.

APPLICATION FILED JULY 31, 1912.

1,255,517. Patented Feb. 5, 1918.

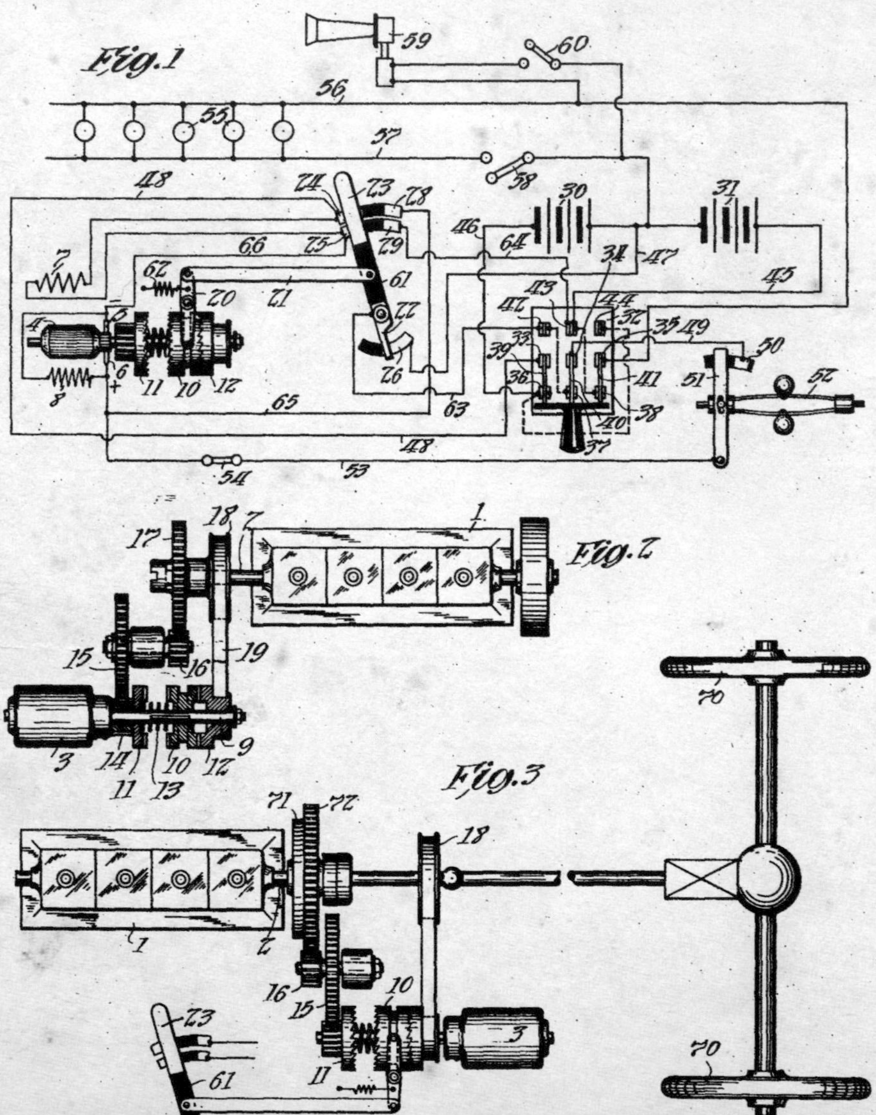

Fig. 1

Fig. 2

Fig. 3

Witnesses:

C.E. Brown

Henry Lanahan

Inventor

Thomas A. Edison

by Frank L. Dyer

his Atty.

The full expanse of Edison's contributions to society is still being debated. He played a large role in the improvement of telegraphy, the telephone, the development of a reliable electric lighting system and lightbulb, the phonograph, and motion pictures. His less well-known achievements in iron ore milling, concrete building materials, storage batteries for electric cars, and the search for a domestic source of rubber for automobile and bicycle tires contributed greatly to the future endeavors of others who expanded the commercial breadth of Edison's inventions and discoveries.

Edison's name has become synonymous with innovation. His "invention factories" integrated the product design, manufacturing, and marketing functions of the business, and his team-based approach became the inspiration for later research laboratories by the most innovative companies.[63] His 1913 prediction that "books will soon be obsolete," as scholars would learn through motion pictures, anticipated today's reliance on visual learning via tablets and smartphones.[64]

Edison has also inspired such visionaries as Larry Page, cofounder and CEO of Google. Page had read a biography of Nikola Tesla when he was only twelve, but as he grew up Page realized that "you also need leadership skills":[65]

> You'd want to be more like Edison. If you invent something, that doesn't necessarily help anybody. You've got to actually get it into the world; you've got to produce, make money doing it so you can fund it.[66]

Perhaps Edison's most important contribution is, as Alfred North Whitehead put it, "the invention of the *method* of invention."[67]

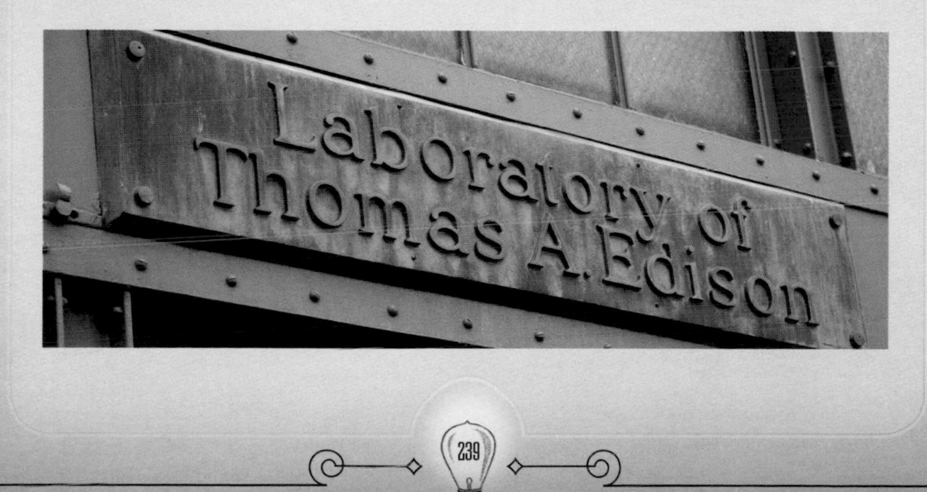

ACKNOWLEDGMENTS

FOR REGINALD AND FLORENCE AND BRYAN

As with all books of this type, there are many who came before to pave the path forward. I want to acknowledge all the previous biographers who have spent many hours researching the life of Thomas Edison. Their tireless efforts have brought to light millions of pages of letters, laboratory notebooks, and published documents that allow the rest of us to have it easy in comparison. Special thanks go out to Paul Israel (Thomas Edison Papers), Leonard DeGraaf (Thomas Edison National Historical Park), and Chuck Perillo, whose engaging tour of the Edison Museum at Menlo Park brought Thomas Edison to life.

I also want to thank my agent, Marilyn Allen of Allen O'Shea Literary Agency, and my editor, Chris Barsanti at Sterling Publishing, for allowing me this opportunity to bring to life the amazing accomplishments of Thomas Edison. Special thanks to Scott Russo, the designer at Sterling who pulled together all the graphics and photographs for this book and my previous book on Nikola Tesla.

Thank you to the people who made *Tesla: The Wizard of Electricity* such a success. The response to *Tesla* laid the groundwork for this book on Edison.

Finally, thank you to all my friends, family, and fellow scientists and writers who have inspired and encouraged my scientific and writing careers. Extra special thanks go to Ru Sun for her constant encouragement, constructive criticism, and amazing attention to detail. This book and I are much better because of her efforts.

SELECTED BIBLIOGRAPHY

Baldwin, Neil. 1995. *Edison: Inventing the Century*. Hyperion, New York.

Carr, Nicholas. 2009. *The Big Switch: Rewiring the World, From Edison to Google*. W.W. Norton & Company, New York.

Conot, Robert. 1979. *Thomas A. Edison: A Streak of Luck*. Da Capo Press, New York.

DeGraaf, Leonard. 2013. *Edison and the Rise of Innovation*. Sterling Publishing, New York.

Dyer, Frank Lewis and Martin, Thomas Commerford. 1910. *Edison: His Life and Inventions*. Harper & Brothers Publishers, New York.

Essig, Mark. 2003. *Edison & The Electric Chair: A Story of Light and Death*. Walker & Company, New York.

Freeberg, Ernest. 2013. *The Age of Edison: Electric Light and the Invention of Modern America*. Penguin Press, New York.

Israel, Paul. 1998. *Edison: A Life of Invention*. John Wiley & Sons, New York.

Jonnes, Jill. 2003. *Empires of Light: Edison, Tesla, Westinghouse, and the Race to Electrify the World*. Random House, New York.

Josephson, Matthew. 2003. *Edison: A Biography*. History Book Club edition.

Kent, David J. 2013. *Tesla: The Wizard of Electricity*. Fall River Press, New York.

Kent, David J. 2014. *Nikola Tesla: Renewable Energy Ahead of Its Time*. E-book available from Amazon Digital Services.

Kent, David J. 2015. *Abraham Lincoln and Nikola Tesla: Connected by Fate*. E-book available from Amazon Digital Services.

Stross, Randall. 2007. *The Wizard of Menlo Park: How Thomas Alva Edison Invented the Modern World*. Crown Publishers, New York.

Additional sources:

http://www.pbs.org/wgbh/amex/edison/timeline/index.html

http://www.absoluteastronomy.com/timeline/Thomas_Edison

http://www.thomasedison.com/Inventions.htm

http://edison.rutgers.edu/

http://www.davidjkent-writer.com/

Opposite: **Arthur Williams, Thomas Edison, John Lieb, Nicholas Brady, and Thomas Murray**

TIMELINE

1847—Born February 11, Milan, OH; seventh and last child of Samuel Ogden Edison, Jr.
1854—The Edison family moves to Port Huron, Michigan
1859—Gets a job as a news butch on the Grand Trunk Railroad, selling newspapers and candy; sets up a chemistry lab and a printing press on the train
1863–1867—Works as a telegraph operator in various cities of the Midwest
1867—First sketches of ideas for improving telegraph equipment
1868—Becomes a telegraph operator in the main Western Union office in Boston
1869—On January 30 announces his resignation from Western Union and intention to devote himself full time to invention
1869—Receives his first patent for the electric voting machine
1869—Sells rights for first successful printing telegraph; receives first telegraph patent; moves to New York City
1869—Opens a short-lived stock quotation business
1870—Moves to Newark, New Jersey, and with money from a contract with the Gold and Stock Telegraph Company opens a telegraph manufacturing shop where he also conducts his inventive work
1871—Devises several important improvements in printing telegraph (stock ticker) technology
1871—Marries 16-year-old Mary Stilwell on Christmas Day
1872—Forms partnership with Joseph Murray
1873—Daughter born, Marion Estelle Edison (1873–1965), nicknamed "Dot"
1874—Invents the quadruplex telegraph for Western Union, which transmits four messages simultaneously (two in each direction)
1875—Ends partnership with Murray and separates his laboratory from the manufacturing shop
1875—Invents the electric pen, an early copying device, and works on various telegraph inventions
1876—Son born, Thomas Alva Edison, Jr. (1876–1935), nicknamed "Dash"
1876—Alexander Graham Bell invents telephone
1876—Opens first industrial research lab in Menlo Park (now called Edison), New Jersey
1876—Receives patent for mimeograph machine
1877—Invents the carbon transmitter, a crucial improvement in telephone technology
1877—July 17, first envisions recording diaphragms; November 29, envisions the tinfoil phonograph, which he demonstrates at the offices of *Scientific American* on December 7
1878—Son born, William Leslie Edison (1878–1937)
1878—Demonstrates phonograph to National Academy of Sciences in Washington, D.C., then drops work on phonograph until 1886
1878—Goes to Wyoming to see total eclipse of the sun and test "tasimeter"
1878—Shifts attention to electric lighting; forms Edison Electric Light Company in New York City "to own, manufacture, operate and license the use of various apparatus used in producing light, heat, or power by electricity"

1879—Invents carbon filament lamp and a direct-current generator for incandescent electric lighting; makes first public demonstration of incandescent lightbulb on December 31 by lighting up Menlo Park

1880—Hires a larger staff to help him develop the components of his electric lighting system for commercial use and sets up a factory for the manufacture of electric lamps at Menlo Park

1880—In May, installs first isolated electrical plant in the steamship S.S. *Columbia*

1880—Performs first test of his electric railway on the grounds of Menlo Park

1881—Leaves Menlo Park and opens new offices in New York City; establishes factories to make various parts of the electric light and power system and begins construction of the first permanent central power station, on Pearl Street, which opens in September 1882

1881—In February, first land-based isolated electric plant

1881—Edison and Alexander Graham Bell form the Oriental Telephone Company

1882—George Westinghouse's company buys Philip Diehl's competing induction lamp patent rights for $25,000

1882—Nikola Tesla moves to Paris to work for Continental Edison Company; advances induction motor and rotating magnetic fields ideas

1883–1884—Edison spends a year promoting the installation of central stations for small manufacturing cities and towns

1883—The first electric lighting system employing overhead wires, built by Thomas Edison, begins service at Roselle, New Jersey

1884—Wife Mary Edison dies at age 29 on August 9 of unknown causes

1884—Tesla arrives in U.S. with a letter of introduction from Charles Batchelor to Thomas Edison; meets Edison and fixes lighting plant in S.S. *Oregon*; quits in 1885

1886—George Westinghouse forms Westinghouse Electric Company

1886—On February 24 at age 39, Edison marries 20-year-old Mina Miller; moves to West Orange, New Jersey, with a winter retreat in Fort Myers, Florida

1886—Charles Tainter, working in Alexander Graham Bell's Volta Laboratory, develops an improved wax-recording phonograph called the graphophone

1887—Edison moves into new laboratory in West Orange, New Jersey

1888—Daughter born, Madeleine Edison (1888–1979)

1888—Expands search for bamboo, grass, and other fibers to be used in the incandescent lamp filament

1888—Tesla invents the first practical alternating current motor and polyphase power transmission system, which revolutionizes industry and commerce

1888—On February 27, Muybridge visits Edison to discuss combining his zoopraxiscope with Edison's phonograph; in October, Edison files patent caveat on a motion picture system

1888—Spurred by the graphophone, Edison develops his "perfected" phonograph; "war of the currents" begins

1889—Organizes iron ore milling companies and begins processing at Ogden mine in New Jersey

1889—Files a lawsuit against former associates Tomlinson and Gilliland for alleged fraud in negotiations with Jesse Lippincott and the North American Phonograph Company

1890—Son born, Charles Edison (1890–1969); takes over his father's company and experimental laboratories upon his father's death; also becomes Governor of New Jersey

1890—William Kemmler becomes the first man executed with an electric chair
1891—First public display of Edison's prototype kinetoscope; Edison builds "Black Maria" motion picture studio at West Orange
1891—Moves to Ogden mine to "fix all the problems"
1892—The Thomson-Houston Company and Edison General Electric merge to form General Electric
1893—Columbian Exposition in Chicago is powered by alternating current and the Niagara Falls Commission approves AC as the system for the first large-scale electrical generator in the world
1893—Demonstrates his system for making and showing motion pictures
1896—Introduces the Home Phonograph, an inexpensive, spring-motor phonograph
1897—Patents the Home Projecting Kinetoscope, the first home movie projector
1898—Son born, Theodore Edison (1898–1992)
1899—Closes Ogden mine and shifts efforts to building Portland cement business
1900—General Electric organizes the first modern research-and-development laboratory; Edison begins work on a storage battery for use in electric cars
1901–1903 Mining prospector in Sudbury, Ontario; credited with the original discovery of the Falconbridge ore body
1902—Begins commercial production of cement; introduces "moulded" records commercially
1903—Topsy, an elephant, is electrocuted and filmed by Thomas Edison's company
1903—Releases *The Great Train Robbery* film, which sets new standards for live-action filming
1904—Marconi gets patent for the invention of radio
1904—Kaiser Wilhelm II of Germany becomes the first person to make a sound recording of a political document, using Edison's phonograph cylinder
1909—Markets his alkaline storage battery, which is used extensively in a host of commercial applications after the market for electric automobiles declines
1912—Introduces the Diamond Disc phonograph
1915—Secretary of the Navy Josephus Daniels convinces Edison to head a Naval Consulting Board to investigate new military technology
1916—With Henry Ford and Harvey Firestone, begins a tradition of vacationing together and the three are followed by the press
1927—Begins an effort to find a natural substitute for rubber that can be grown and processed in case of shortages caused by war, eventually settling on goldenrod as the best material
1928—Joins Fort Myers Civitan Club (volunteer community service club); receives special Congressional Medal to honor his life's work
1929—Re-enacts the invention of the incandescent light at the Golden Jubilee celebration in Dearborn, Michigan, where Henry Ford has reconstructed the Menlo Park laboratory
1931—Submits his last patent application
1931—Dies at age 84 on October 18 from complications of diabetes; the nation dims its lightbulbs for one minute on the day of his funeral

1947—Mina dies at age 82 on August 24

INVENTIONS AND PATENTS

Thomas A. Edison was perhaps the most prolific and diversified inventor in history. He received 1093 patents in the United States alone, with an even greater number in foreign markets. These numbers do not include the more than 500 estimated patent applications that failed or were abandoned. Dyer and Martin provided a list of all the patents Edison had received as of 1910, but he continued to patent inventions for many years to come. A full compilation of all of his patents (including those after 1910) can be found on the website of the Thomas Edison Papers project (http://edison.rutgers.edu/).

Edison's United States patents can be grouped into several main categories, with the number of patents for each category in parentheses.

Electric Lighting and Power (424)

By far the greatest number of individual patents was related to the development of electric lighting, power generation, and electricity distribution. These patents included many specific kinds of electric lights, methods for making carbon and other incandescent filaments, and the manufacturing process for all. Edison's patents also cover the design and manufacture of various dynamos and their improvements, electric meters, primary and secondary batteries, and thermal regulators. Edison even had patents for electric chandeliers and locomotives for his electric railway systems.

Phonographs and Sound Recording (199)

The second-largest number of patents came from Edison's work with phonographs and other means of recording sound. Each type of phonograph had many intricate parts that carried their own designs. Patents covered everything from reproducers to feed and return mechanisms to on/off switches to automatic determining devices. Other patents were for office dictating machines, home phonographs, and even specialty miniature phonographs for talking dolls. Coating methods, the process for making recording cylinders and discs, and design of the cabinets got their own patents.

Telegraphy and Telephony (186)

As might be expected, given how he started in the invention business, Edison has many patents related to improvements made to telegraphs and its inevitable expansion into telephones. These include patents for duplex, diplex, quadruplex, and sextuplex telegraphs, as well as printing, acoustic, automatic, chemical, and speaking telegraphs. Other patents cover various electrical switches, recording instruments, and relays. Telephone-related patents include those for Edison's version of the telephone, his carbon transmitter, and telephone repeater devices.

Batteries (147)

Edison had 147 patents for different types of batteries, including galvanic, reversible galvanic, voltaic, thermoelectric, and storage. He also patented processes for charging batteries, electroplating apparatuses, and electrodes.

Mining and Ore Milling (53)

Edison spent more than a decade attempting to extract iron from low-grade ore. He invented many new ways to get at valuable materials others had left behind. To support this endeavor he patented multiple magnetic ore separation devices, as well as associated dryers, mixers, screeners, grinders, and concentrators. Edison also patented methods for bricking fine ores, dust-proof swivel shaft bearings that worked under the most extreme conditions, and conveyor systems to move the ore and product around the plant.

Cement (49)

Many of the same processes used for ore milling came into play for Edison's development of a cement industry. In addition, he had separate patents for cement-specific uses, including various screening, mixing, averaging, and sampling apparatuses. He also patented several types of rotary kilns, crushing rolls, apparatuses for production of concrete structures (e.g., houses), and even methods for using waste heat from the kilns (possibly the first form of energy recycling).

Miscellaneous (50+)

Many of Edison's inventions cannot be categorized. These include his vote recording device, his electric pens, and his processes for extracting rubber from plants. The group also includes more obscure and unexpected patents like those for the "art of malleableizing iron," a process for preserving fruit, and "a method and means for improving the rendition of musical compositions."

Foreign Patents (1249)

Dyer reports that by 1910 Edison had more than 1200 foreign patents in 34 countries, with most of them mirroring his patents in the United States. The greatest numbers were in the United Kingdom, Germany, France, Canada, and Austria, with more than 100 patents in each. A full breakdown of the patents per country is available at http://edison.rutgers.edu/dmforpat.htm.

Above: **Rock crusher. "The giant rolls are what might be called the spectacular feature of the whole plant . . . to see them seize a 5-ton rock and crunch it with less show of effort than a dog in crunching a bone gives one a vivid sense of the meaning of momentum."**
—*Scientific American*, January 22, 1898

ENDNOTES

Prologue

1...... Baldwin, *Edison: Inventing the Century*, 35–36; Dyer, *Edison: His Life and Inventions*, 49–50
2...... Dyer, 49–50; Israel, *Edison: A Life of Invention*, 18; Personal communication between the author and Chuck Perillo at the Menlo Park Museum on 7/2/15
3...... Dyer, viii

Chapter 1: Birth of an Inventor

1...... Baldwin, 17
2...... Conot, *Thomas A. Edison: A Streak of Luck*, 3
3...... Ibid.; Baldwin, 19
4...... Dyer, 16
5...... Baldwin, 17
6...... Conot, 4
7...... Dyer, 15
8...... Conot, 3
9...... Edison, as quoted in Israel, 3
10.... Baldwin, 15
11.... Ibid., 9; Israel, 4
12.... Israel, 4
13.... Baldwin, 9–15
14.... Ibid., 15
15.....DeGraaf, *Edison and the Rise of Innovation*, xx
16.... Baldwin, 20
17.... DeGraaf, xxi
18.... Baldwin, 23
19.... Rote learning refers to the process of strict memorization and practice in order to remember specific facts
20.... Baldwin, 24–25; Dyer, 16
21.... Israel, 8
22.... Ibid., 7; http://www.menloparkmuseum.org/history/thomas-edison-and-menlo-park/, 1853; DeGraaf, xxii, reports a slightly different title: *First Lessons in Natural Philosophy* 1859
23.... Israel, 11
24.... Dyer, 26
25.... Ibid., 16
26.... Baldwin, 19; citing W. E. Wise, *Young Edison: The True Story of Edison's Boyhood*, Chicago, 1933
27.... Dyer, 17
28.... Ibid.
29.... Ibid., 18
30.... Ibid., 28
31.... Ibid., 29
32.... www.Phonojack.com/Edison.htm
33.... Dyer, 30
34.... DeGraaf, xxii
35.... Dyer, 30
36.... DeGraaf, xxiii; Israel, 16
37.... Israel, 16
38.... DeGraaf, xxiii
39.... Dyer, 33
40.... DeGraaf, xxxiii; Israel, 17
41.... Israel, 16
42.... Dyer, 35
43.... Ibid., 34
44.... Ibid., 36
45.... Ibid., 32
46.... Ibid., 37
47.... Ibid.
48.... Israel, 18
49.... Baldwin, 37
50.... Ibid., 426, citing Gabler, Edwin, *The American Telegrapher: A Social History, 1860–1900*, Class and Culture Series, Rutgers University Press, New Brunswick, 1988
51.... Baldwin, 33
52.... Israel, 18
53.... Baldwin, 33–34
54.... Dyer, 50
55.... Israel, 19
56.... Dyer, 51
57.... Ibid., 52
58.... Ibid., 53
59.... Ibid., 53–54
60.... Ibid., 55
61.... Ibid., 56
62.... Israel, 25
63.... Ibid.
64.... Baldwin, 38; Dyer, 74
65.... Israel, 21
66.... DeGraaf, xxv
67.... Ibid., xxvi
68.... Baldwin, 44
69.... Ibid., 46

Chapter 2: A Better Telegraph: The Beginnings of Invention

1...... Israel, 40
2...... Wheeler, Tom. 2006. *Mr. Lincoln's T-Mails: The Untold Story of How Abraham Lincoln Used the Telegraph to Win the Civil War*, HarperBusiness, New York
3...... Dyer, 99

4...... Ibid., 99–100
5...... Baldwin, 43
6...... Dyer, 101
7...... Ibid., 100
8...... TAE Papers, PA051; TAEM 0:0, *Telegrapher*, 30 Jan. 1869
9...... Dyer, 102; Patent was filed October 11, 1868, received June 1, 1869; Patent No. 90,646
10.... Ibid., 103
11.... Ibid., 102–103
12.... Stross, *The Wizard of Menlo Park: How Thomas Alva Edison Invented the Modern World*, 8
13.... DeGraaf, 3
14.... Dyer, 103
15.... Ibid.
16.... DeGraaf, 3
17.... Israel, 40–47
18.... DeGraaf, 3–4
19.... Dyer, 115; DeGraaf, 4
20.... Dyer, 110; DeGraaf, 4 notes that this number could have been as few as 25
21.... Dyer, 115
22.... Ibid., 124; the company was eventually taken over by Gold & Stock Telegraph Company
23.... Conot, 33
24.... Dyer, 122
25.... Ibid., 123; Edison is recounting this experience years later
26.... Ibid.; Conot, 33
27.... Dyer, 123
28.... DeGraaf, 5
29.... Dyer, 124–127
30.... Ibid., 129; DeGraaf, 5
31.... DeGraaf, 5
32.... Dyer, 128; DeGraaf, 5
33.... Dyer, 129
34.... Israel, 54
35.... Dyer, 131
36.... Israel, 66
37.... Ibid., 54
38.... DeGraaf, 6
39.... Conot, 40
40.... Dyer, 132
41.... Ibid., 133
42.... See Chapter 3 for more on Edison's invention factory
43.... Israel, 6
44.... Dyer, 134
45.... Ibid.
46.... Israel, 105
47.... Conot, 37; Israel, 56
48.... Dyer, 141; DeGraaf, 7
49.... Conot, 37; DeGraaf, 7
50.... DeGraaf, 7; Conot, 37
51.... DeGraaf, 8
52.... Conot, 39–40
53.... Dyer, 144
54.... Ibid.
55.... Ibid., 145
56.... Ibid.
57.... Stross, 19, citing PTAED, 18 Jan. 1878, D7110B
58.... DeGraaf, 14; Israel, 99
59.... DeGraaf, 12
60.... Israel, 97
61.... DeGraaf, 13
62.... Dyer, 158; DeGraaf, 13
63.... Israel, 101–102; Dyer, 157
64.... Israel, 102; Dyer, 159
65.... Dyer, 159
66.... DeGraaf, 14
67.... Dyer, 159; Israel, 102
68.... DeGraaf, 15; Israel, 104
69.... Dyer, 160
70.... Israel, 109–110
71.... DeGraaf, 15
72.... Israel, 110
73.... DeGraaf, 15
74.... Dyer, 168
75.... Israel, 100
76.... Stross, 18
77.... Ibid.
78.... Israel, 106
79.... Dyer, 168–169
80.... Ibid., 169

Chapter 3: Inventing the Art of Invention

1...... See, e.g., Stross's book by that title
2...... Israel, 167–170
3...... Baldwin, 27
4...... DeGraaf, xxii
5...... Israel, 15
6...... Ibid., 41
7...... DeGraaf, 3
8...... Israel, 42
9...... DeGraaf, 3
10.... Israel, 42
11.... Dyer, 132; Israel, 54; Baldwin, 72
12.... Dyer, 129; DeGraaf, 5
13.... Israel, 100
14.... Ibid., 54
15.... Israel, 191; DeGraaf, 19
16.... DeGraaf, 20; Note that Menlo Park was a section of Raritan Township, which has now been renamed Edison
17.... Dyer, 269
18.... DeGraaf, 21
19.... Baldwin, 68; Dyer, 271
20.... Dyer, 269
21.... Ibid.
22.... Baldwin, 68; Stross, 47

23.... Stross, 47, citing newspaper reporter Amos Cummings
24.... Dyer, 271
25.... Israel, 121, citing G. M. Shaw's article "Sketch of Thomas Alva Edison" in *Popular Science Monthly*, 13 (Aug. 1878), 489–90
26.... Dyer, 270
27.... Ibid.
28.... Ibid.
29.... Baldwin, 69
30.... Dyer, 270
31.... Ibid., 271
32.... Ibid., 272
33.... DeGraaf, 20
34.... Ibid., 23
35.... Israel, 353; Edison starting calling his researchers "Muckers." It was taken as a positive nickname since Edison was often in the lab "mucking" alongside his workers. Later his workers would form a sort of fraternal organization known as the Muckers of the Edison Laboratory (see Endnote No. 45 of Chapter 18 in Israel)
36.... DeGraaf, 24
37.... Ibid., 24
38.... Ibid., 23
39.... Dyer, 276
40.... Israel, 86
41.... Baldwin, 111
42.... Dyer, 274
43.... Baldwin, 55
44.... Ibid., 74
45.... Dyer, 276
46.... Baldwin, 74
47.... Dyer, 276, quoting Upton
48.... Ibid., 276–277
49.... See longer discussions in Baldwin, Conot, Israel
50.... Stross, 60
51.... Ibid.
52.... Conot, 86
53.... Dyer, 268
54.... Ibid., 278
55.....See HMLR. 1932, September, *Harper's Magazine*, Volume 165, "Edison in His Laboratory by M. A. Rosanoff"; Also see http://quoteinvestigator.com/2012/04/19/edison-no-rules/
56.... Dyer, 278
57.... Ibid., 280, quoting Francis Jehl
58.... DeGraaf, 24
59.... Dyer, 281
60.... Ibid., 279, quoting Francis Jehl
61.... DeGraaf, 24, quoting Charles Clarke
62.... Dyer, 280
63.... Ibid., 297
64.... DeGraaf, 73
65.... Ibid., 28
66.... Israel, 260
67.... DeGraaf, 20
68.... Ibid., 77
69.... Ibid., 78
70.... Ibid., 79
71.... Israel, 261
72.... Ibid., 265
73.... DeGraaf, 86–87; Israel, 261–263
74.... DeGraaf, 129
75.... ENHS, personal visit, 7/2/15
76.... Ibid.; DeGraaf, xi
77.... Baldwin, 152
78.... Ibid., 56
79.... DeGraaf, xxvi
80.... Ibid., 6
81.... Ibid., 26
82.... Baldwin, 56
83.... Ibid.
84.... Stross, 260–262

Chapter 4: Of Phonographs and Celebrity

1...... Stross, 23
2...... Ibid.
3...... Baldwin, 61
4...... DeGraaf, 30–31
5...... A caveat is the initial application for a patent describing the basic principles of a new technology in order to establish precedence; generally this is followed up with a full patent application
6...... Dyer, 174
7...... Conot, 168
8...... Dyer, 176
9...... Conot, 94
10.... DeGraaf, 31
11.... Ibid.
12.... Conot, 94
13.... Israel, 132–134
14.... DeGraaf, 31
15.... Dyer, 180; Israel, 141
16.... DeGraaf, 31
17.... Dyer, 189–198; Edison still had telephone patents in the UK (e.g., see Israel p185) and there were other companies using his technology; as with any new technology, the reality is much more complicated than attributing "discovery" to any one person
18.... Baldwin, 77; a motograph was a music-transmitting apparatus
19.... Israel, 157–161
20.....Stross, 29; Baldwin, 79; TAED Document ID:TI2196; [TI2196;TAEM 11:366]; Israel, 143 notes a July 17 first conception

as "a way to record telephone messages so they could be played back and transcribed at a slower speed in a manner similar to his Morse recorder practice instrument"
21.... Stross, 29 (see the footnote on Stross, 300 for more details)
22.... Dyer, 205
23.... Stross, 29
24.... Dyer, 206
25.... Stross, 29
26.... DeGraaf, 35
27.... Stross, 30
28.... Ibid.
29.... Ibid.; additional [*sic*] notations removed for clarity
30.... Baldwin, 79
31.... Ibid., 79–80
32.... Israel, 147
33.... Baldwin, 80
34.... DeGraaf, 36
35.... Baldwin, 82
36.... DeGraaf, 36
37.... Israel, 145, see figure
38.... Baldwin, 81, see figure
39.... Ibid., 82
40.... DeGraaf, 36
41.... Baldwin, 82
42.... Ibid.
43.... Ibid.
44.... Israel, 147
45.... Ibid., 17
46.... Stross, 31; Conot, 106
47.... Stross, 31; DeGraaf, 36
48.... Baldwin, 84
49.... DeGraaf, 36
50.... Israel, 147
51.... Baldwin, 84
52.... Stross, 55
53.... Dyer, 210
54..... Batchelor and others usually gave the commentary at demonstrations as Edison's hearing loss and hesitancy to speak generally relegated him to sitting and watching
55.... DeGraaf, 38
56.... Ibid., 40
57.... For a history of the National Academy of Sciences, see http://www.nasonline.org/about-nas/ history/; See also Kent 2015 *Abraham Lincoln and Nikola Tesla: Connected by Fate*
58.... Baldwin, 96
59.... Israel, 147
60.... Baldwin, 96
61.... Dyer, 108–109
62.... Israel, 153; Baldwin, 109
63.... Dyer, 210
64.... Israel, 154
65.... Dyer, 211
66.... Ibid., 214
67.... DeGraaf, 41
68.... Dyer, 216–217
69.... DeGraaf, 45
70.... Dyer, 217
71.... Israel, 280
72.... Dyer, 218
73.... DeGraaf, 99
74.... Israel, 282–283
75.... DeGraaf, 99
76.... Ibid., 100
77.... Dyer, 221
78.... DeGraaf, 101
79.... Ibid., 102
80.... Israel, 293; DeGraaf, 104
81.... DeGraaf, 104
82.... Ibid.
83.... Ibid., 102, quoting Batchelor
84.... Those wanting to hear creepy examples can now do so at http://www.npr.org/2015/08/01/428311627/edisons-little-monsters-restored-to-their-original-freakishness
85.... DeGraaf, 105
86.... Israel, 288
87.... DeGraaf, 106
88.... Israel, 425; DeGraaf, 108; the Columbia company was another competitor
89.... DeGraaf, 108
90.... Israel, 424–425
91.... DeGraaf, 108
92.... Chuck Perillo, a guide at the Menlo Park museum, tells the story of how the "Gold Moulded" cylinders—copies of original music cylinders—led to the first "gold records" given out by the music industry (Personal communication, 7/2/15)
93.... Israel, 425; Baldwin, 318
94.... DeGraaf, 110, citing Nov 1911 letter
95.... Stross, 260 notes that Edison once received a glowing letter from a Mrs. W. C. Lathrop praising him lavishly for…the Victrola!

Chapter 5: Edison's Family and Friends

1...... DeGraaf, 10
2...... Paraphrasing, with apologies, the first line of Jane Austen's *Pride and Prejudice*
3...... DeGraaf, 10
4...... Stross, 15
5...... DeGraaf, 11; Stross, 15
6...... After working for Edison his whole life, Ottwould die within hours of Edison, thus losing out on the $10,000 bequeathed

him in Edison's will; see Baldwin, 412
7...... Conot, 46
8...... Mary had many brothers, sisters, stepsisters, and a stepbrother; her father was a sawyer (i.e., worked in a saw mill) and they struggled financially (See Conot, 47)
9...... Israel, 73; Baldwin, 53
10.... Stross, 295. Stross also relates a "more sinister version" of this story on 15
11.... DeGraaf, 11
12.... Ibid.; Conot, 47
13.... Stross, 16
14.... Ibid.
15.... DeGraaf, 11; Conot, 48
16.... DeGraaf, 11; Conot, 47
17.... Conot, 47
18.... Israel, 123; Baldwin, 61
19.... Stross, 16
20.... Israel, 122; there is no evidence Edison ever called William "Stop"
21.... Conot, 48
22.... Ibid., 53, 55
23.... Israel, 122–123
24.... Ibid., 390
25.... For more details, see http://www.thomasedison.org/index.php/education/the-edison-family/
26.... Stross, 212, 248–249; Baldwin, 294
27.... Israel, 259
28.... Ibid., 387
29.... Baldwin, 295
30.... Ibid.
31.... Ibid.
32.... DeGraaf, 70
33.... Ibid., 234, Note 1, Chapter 5
34.... Conot, 219
35.... For example, see http://news.rutgers.edu/research-news/thomas-edison%E2%80%9s-first-wife-may-have-died-morphine-overdose/20111115#.VvFPixhEpTG
36.... Conot, 219
37.... DeGraaf, 70
38.... Remorse for his inattentiveness did not seem to extend to Edison's sons, who remained relegated to boarding schools
39.... Stross, 143
40.... Baldwin, 147; DeGraaf, 70
41.... Baldwin, 147, 149
42.... Ibid., 147
43.... DeGraaf, 71
44.... Ibid.
45.... Baldwin, 147
46.... Ibid., 148; The term "Chautauquas" became widely used for rambling introspection, most notably in Robert M. Pirsig's *Zen and the Art of Motorcycle Maintenance*
47.... Baldwin, 153
48.... Ibid. (see footnote)
49.... Thomas Edison's Diary, July 12, 1885 [MA001; TAEM 0:0]
50.... Ibid.
51.... DeGraaf, 72
52.... A version of this story was told to the author by Chuck Perillo at Menlo Park Museum on 7/3/15
53.... Israel, 247
54.... DeGraaf, 72; Israel, 247
55.... Baldwin, 153
56.... Israel, 249
57.... Baldwin, 224–226
58.... Israel, 255
59.... See http://www.edisonmuckers.org/mina-miller-edison/
60.... Israel, 437–438
61.... DeGraaf, 70–71; Israel, 237
62.... Conot, 265
63.... Stross, 159
64.... Israel, 289–290
65.... Baldwin, 303
66.... Stross, 233–4; Baldwin, 303
67.... Stross, 236
68.... Israel, 423
69.... Stross, 254
70.... Ibid., 253–4
71.... See more at http://www.dnr.state.md.us/feature_stories/FamousTravelersPart1.asp.
72.... Baldwin, 328–331
73.... Stross, 254
74.... Ibid.
75.... Ibid.
76.... Ibid., 255
77.... Baldwin, 330
78.... Stross, 255
79.... Ibid., 257
80.... Dyer, 368

Chapter 6: Building a Better Lightbulb

1...... DeGraaf, 48
2...... Dyer, 239
3...... DeGraaf, 48
4...... Dyer, 236
5...... Ibid., 238
6...... Ibid.; Israel, 165; Stross, 81
7...... Dyer, 238
8...... Israel, 168
9...... Dyer, 240
10.... Ibid.
11.... Ibid.
12.... Ibid., 241
13.... Israel, 171
14.... Dyer, 242

15.... Ibid., 244
16.... Israel, 165
17.... Dyer, 245
18.... Ibid.
19.... Israel, 165
20.... Dyer, 245
21.... Ibid.
22.... Ibid., 245–246
23.... Dyer, 302; See also http://quoteinvestigator.com/2012/07/31/edison-lot-results/
24.... Israel, 164
25.... Dyer, 248
26.... Ibid.
27.... Ibid.
28.... Israel, 36
29.... Baldwin, 111–113
30.... Dyer, 249
31.... Ibid., 250
32.... Israel, 199
33.... Dyer, 252
34.... Ibid.
35.... Ibid., 258
36.... DeGraaf, 52
37.... Dyer, 258; DeGraaf, 52
38.... DeGraaf, 53
39.... Dyer, 261
40.... Stross, 86
41.... Dyer, 276; quoting Upton
42.... Ibid., 320
43.... Ibid., 262
44.... Ibid.
45.... Ibid., 263
46.... Israel, 196
47.... Dyer, 300
48.... Baldwin, 122
49.... Dyer, 300
50.... Ibid., 301
51.... Conot, 174
52.... Dyer, 302
53.... Ibid., 303
54.... Ibid., 304
55.... Ibid.
56.... Ibid., 305; citing article in the *Evening Sun*
57.... Ibid., 306
58.... Ibid.
59.... Ibid., 308
60.... Ibid., 310
61.... Ibid.
62.... Ibid., 313
63.... Ibid., 314

Chapter 7: War of the Currents

1...... DeGraaf, 48; Israel, 208
2...... Dyer, 319, quoting Rathenau
3...... Ibid., 321
4...... For example, Israel, 204–205
5...... Joseph Henry had been an early electrical experimenter prior to becoming the first Secretary of the Smithsonian Institution. He made groundbreaking discoveries related to telegraphy and induction. For more information see Jahns, Patricia, 1970, *Joseph Henry: Father of American Electronics*
6...... For more, see Jonnes, *Empires of Light*; Kent *Wizard*; Israel; Baldwin
7...... Dyer, 290–295
8...... Ibid., 296
9...... Ibid.
10.... Ibid., 325
11.... Israel, 168–169
12.... For a history of gas production, see http://www.cganet.com/docs/100th.pdf
13.... http://www.encyclopedia.chicagohistory.org/pages/504.html
14.... Baldwin, 104
15.... Ibid., 105
16.... Ibid.
17.... Stross, 124
18.... Ibid.
19.... Ibid., 128
20.... Ibid.
21.... Ibid., 122
22.... Ibid. (see footnote for details)
23.... Essig, 135
24.... Stross, 123
25.... Ibid., 125; Arc lighting works by generating a large spark passing over a gap between two carbon electrodes in air
26.... Israel, 328. Incandescent eventually took over those uses as well
27.... DeGraaf, 48
28.... Villard had been a journalist during the Civil War and did not particularly like Abraham Lincoln; he later became an influential corporate executive
29.... Stross, 105
30.... Ibid., 106
31.... For a more in-depth discussion, see Kent, *The Wizard of Electricity,* 80
32.... Kent, *Wizard,* 80
33.... Ibid., 47
34.... Stross, 126
35.... DeGraaf, 57
36.... Ibid.
37.... For example, see http://www.biography.com/people/william-henry-vanderbilt-21010571#professional-success
38.... Stross, 130
39.... Ibid.
40.... Ibid., 131

41.... Baldwin, 129
42.... DeGraaf, 57
43.... Ibid., 60
44.... Ibid., 61
45.... Dyer, 326
46.... Ibid., 335; Kent, *Wizard,* 46
47.... Dyer, 336
48.... Kent, *Wizard,* 4
49.... Ibid., 43
50.... Ibid., 47
51.... Ibid., 110
52.... Ibid., 113
53.... Essig, 135
54.... Ibid.
55.... Kent, *Wizard,* 113
56.... Ibid., citing *New York Times*, Oct 12, 1889
57.... Essig, 92
58.... Ibid.
59.... Essig, 252–253
60.... Jonnes, 197, citing "For Shame Brown!" *New York Sun*, August 25, 1889
61.... Carr, 39
62.... See Kent, *Wizard* for a full discussion of the Chicago World's Fair competition
63.... Ibid., 96
64.... Baldwin, 234
65.... For an interesting look at Niagara Falls, see http://www.niagaraparks.com/about-niagara-falls/geology-facts-figures.html.
66.... Baldwin, 227–228

Chapter 8: Edison the Movie Mogul

1...... DeGraaf, 144
2...... Stross, 195; Baldwin, 211
3...... Thomas Edison Papers, 8 Oct 1888, PT031AAA1;TAEM 113:238
4...... Stross, 196; DeGraaf, 125
5...... DeGraaf, 125; Baldwin, 211
6...... DeGraaf, 122
7...... Ibid.
8...... See https://archive.org/details/Roundhay_Garden_Scene and https://www.youtube.com/watch?v=nR2r__ZgO5g and for more on Le Prince see http://www.nationalmediamuseum.org.uk/~/media/Files/NMeM/PDF/Collections/Cinematography/PioneersOfEarlyCinemaLouisLePrince.ashx
9...... Le Prince gained the honorarium "Father of Cinematography," although his estate and Edison engaged in many lawsuits over who invented motion pictures
10.... Stross, 195
11.... Ibid.
12.... DeGraaf, 125–126
13.... Muybridge's birth name was Edward Muggeridge. For a recent biographical treatment, see Hendricks, Gordon (2001). *Eadweard Muybridge: The Father of the Motion Picture.* Mineola, New York: Dover. ISBN 978-0-48641-535-2
14.... DeGraaf, 123
15.... Ibid., 124
16.... Ibid.
17.... Israel, 292
18.... DeGraaf, 124
19.... See http://americanhistory.si.edu/muybridge/htm/htm_sec1/sec1p3.htm.
20.... For a recent biography of Marey, see Braun 1992 Picturing Time, http://americanhistory.si.edu/muybridge/htm/htm_sec1/sec1p3.htm]
21.... Baldwin, 209
22.... Stross, 196
23.... See http://www.toureiffel.paris/en/everything-about-the-tower/the-eiffel-tower-at-a-glance.html.
24.... Baldwin, 209
25.... Stross, 196
26.... Baldwin, 211
27.... Ibid., 212
28.... Ibid.
29.... DeGraaf, 126
30.... Ibid.
31.... Israel, 442
32.... Baldwin, 219
33.... DeGraaf, 127
34.... Israel, 296
35.... DeGraaf, 127
36.... Ibid., citing *Literary Digest* 1894
37.... Ibid.
38.... Israel, 296
39.... Stross, 197
40.... DeGraaf, 127–8
41.... Ibid., 128; Stross, 197
42.... DeGraaf, 128, as quoted in the *Chicago Evening Press*
43.... Stross, 199
44.... DeGraaf, 128
45.... Ibid., 129; Baldwin, 220
46.... DeGraaf, 129
47.... Ibid., 130; Stross, 199
48.... Baldwin, 232
49.... Ibid., 232–233
50.... DeGraaf, 129
51.... Ibid., 129–130
52.... DeGraaf, 129
53.... Ibid.
54.... DeGraaf, 130
55.... Kent, *Wizard,* 95

56.... Stross, 199
57.... Ibid., 200
58.... DeGraaf, 130
59.... Video at https://www.youtube.com/watch?v=-15jwb1ZTMA; Stross, 200
60 See https://www.youtube.com watch?v=U5OtuzEGi6M
61.... DeGraaf, 133
62.... Ibid.
63.... Stross, 203
64.... DeGraaf, 133
65.... Ibid.
66.... Baldwin, 221
67.... Ibid., 241; DeGraaf, 132; Five others were sent to Atlantic city and ten to Chicago, making up the 25 Egan was contracted to build
68.... Cabinets were set up in two rows of five, so people could watch the five in one row for their 25 cents, another 25 cents for the other five; each showed one short film; DeGraaf, 132
69.... Story is adapted from Baldwin, 242
70.... DeGraaf, 133
71.... Ibid.
72.... DeGraaf, 133–134
73.... Ibid., 134
74.... Ibid.
75.... Ibid.
76.... Ibid.
77.... Ibid., 135
78.... Ibid.
79..... Ibid.; Kent, *Lincoln and Tesla: Connected by Fate*
80.... DeGraaf, 136
81.... Ibid., 140
82.... Ibid., 136
83.... Ibid., 137
84.... Video at https://www.youtube.com/watch?v=jxqg21tfqCg; Also see Baldwin, 297
85.... For example, see Smith, Michael Glover; Selzer, Adam (2015). *Flickering Empire: How Chicago Invented the U.S. Film Industry*. Columbia University Press. p. 71; This assessment came from Edison's own agents so is likely biased
86.... See at https://www.youtube.com/watch?v=h6CgmQsQQxA.
87.... DeGraaf, 142–144
88.... Fox, Richard Wightman. 2015. *Lincoln's Body: A Cultural History*, 192 citing Wanamaker ad in New York Times
89.... Edison Papers project, http://edison.rutgers.edu/topsy.htm
90.... https://www.youtube.com/watch?v=NoKi4coyFw0
91.... DeGraaf, 145

Chapter 9: A Man of Many Talents

1...... Israel, 347
2...... DeGraaf, 149
3...... Ibid., 148
4...... Israel, 346; DeGraaf, 151
5...... DeGraaf, 152
6...... Ibid., 153, 148
7...... Baldwin, 279; DeGraaf, 161
8...... DeGraaf, 164
9...... Ibid., 166
10.... Ibid., 167
11.... Baldwin, 279
12.... DeGraaf, 171
13.... Ibid., 172
14.... Ibid., 193
15.... Israel, 446; The U.S. did not enter the war until 1917.
16.... DeGraaf, 193
17.... The author worked for several years at the National Marine Fisheries Service laboratory on Sandy Hook. The location is also the site of a Coast Guard base and was a Nike missile base during the cold war; see http://weirdnj.com/stories/abandoned/bizarre-art-inside-abandoned-sandy-hook-bunker/
18.... DeGraaf, 198
19.... Israel, 449; Kent, *Wizard*
20.... DeGraaf, 202
21.... Ibid., 203
22.... Conot, 341
23.... DeGraaf, xxxiii
24.... Baldwin, 39
25.... Ibid.
26.... Ibid.
27.... Ibid., 46
28.... Thomas Edison's Diary, July 12, 1885 [MA001; TAEM 0:0]
29.... Thomas Edison's Diary, July 21, 1885 [MA039; TAEM 0:0]
30.... Israel, 94–95
31.... Baldwin, 58
32.... Conot, 341
33.... Ibid.
34.... http://edison.rutgers.edu/
35.... Papers of Thomas Edison Papers, D9004AFW; TAEM 128:747
36.... Conot, 341–342
37.... For more on Lathrop, see John Howard Brown, Rossiter Johnson, John Howard Brown, eds. (1904). *The twentieth century biographical dictionary of notable Americans* 6. The Biographical Society. 360
38.... Baldwin, 120
39.... Ibid., 121

40.... *Science* magazine, 7 Feb 1947, "Thomas A Edison and the Founding of Science: 1880," Vol 05, 2719, 142–148; See also, Baldwin, 122
41.... DeGraaf, 158
42.... This incident is discussed in greater depth in Kent, *Lincoln and Tesla: Connected by Fate*
43.... DeGraaf, 210
44.... Stross, 195
45.... DeGraaf, 58
46.... Baldwin, 99–100
47.... For a biography of the equally well-accomplished Charles Edison, see Venable, John. 1978. *Out of the Shadow: The Story of Charles Edison*
48.... Baldwin, 380–385
49.... DeGraaf, 206
50.... Baldwin, 385
51.... DeGraaf, 208, citing *Science Monthly*
52.... Ibid., 209
53.... Ibid., 213
54.... Ibid., 212
55.... Ibid., 213
56.... Ibid., 214

Chapter 10: A Legacy Like No Other

1...... Israel, 462; DeGraaf, 219
2...... DeGraaf, 218–219
3...... Ibid., 219
4...... Ibid., 222
5...... *Science*, 23 Oct 1931, 74 (1921): 404–405
6...... For more information on his inventions, see the Edison papers project at http://edison.rutgers.edu/inventions.htm
7...... For a complete discussion of Tesla's efforts with renewable energy, see Kent, *Nikola Tesla: Renewable Energy Ahead of Its Time*
8...... See http://ecogeek.org/2007/06/thomas-edison-1931-id-put-my-money-on-solar/; In conversation with Henry Ford and Harvey Firestone (1931); as quoted in *Uncommon Friends: Life with Thomas Edison, Henry Ford, Harvey Firestone, Alexis Carrel & Charles Lindbergh* (1987) by James Newton, 31
9...... http://www.nytimes.com/2007/06/03/magazine/03wwln-essay-t.html?ref=magazine
10.... DeGraaf, 100
11.... Ibid., 29
12.... For more on Edisonade, see http://www.sf-encyclopedia.com/entry/edisonade and https://cogpunksteamscribe.wordpress.com/tag/edisonade/
13.... Conot, 342
14.... See John L. Flynn (2005). "War of the Worlds: From Wells to Spielberg." p.5v
15.... https://www.goodreads.com/book/show/13564114-the-great-abraham-lincoln-pocket-watch-conspiracy
16.... https://www.goodreads.com/book/show/25425896-tesla-s-signal
17.... The story appears in Vonnegut's short story collection *Welcome to the Monkey House* and was first published in *Collier's Magazine*, March 14, 1953; http://www.amazon.com/Welcome-Monkey-House-Kurt-Vonnegut/dp/0385333501
18.... http://www.uchronia.net/bib.cgi/label.html?id=bensandhav; also, http://www.amazon.com/Having-Writ/dp/044102274X/ref=sr_1_1?s=books&ie=UTF8&qid=1438476726&sr=1-1&keywords=and+having+writ
19.... http://assassinscreed.ubi.com/en-us/home/
20.... http://www.imdb.com/title/tt0033289/
21.... http://www.imdb.com/title/tt0032432/
22.... http://teslatheband.com/tesla2015/
23.... http://www.chumba.com/index.php
24.... http://www.metrolyrics.com/edison-lyrics-bee-gees.html
25.... https://www.youtube.com/watch?v=gJ1Mz7kGVf0
26.... DeGraaf, 222
27.... Ibid.
28.... http://www.accademiaxl.it/en/awards/120-medaglia-matteucci.html
29.... http://www.garfield.library.upenn.edu/johnscottaward.html
30.... https://www.fi.edu/franklin-institute-awards
31.... http://www.aaes.org/john-fritz-medal-past-recipients
32.... https://www.fi.edu/franklin-institute-awards
33.... http://www.homeofheroes.com/valor/02_awards/index_dsm/01_navyDSM.html
34.... http://www.ieee.org/about/awards/medals/edison.html
35.... http://history.house.gov/Institution/Gold-Medal/Gold-Medal-Recipients/
36.... https://www.grammy.org/recording-academy/producers-and-engineers/awards
37.... http://codes.ohio.gov/orc/5533.18
38.... http://ssd.jpl.nasa.gov/sbdb.cgi?sstr=742
39.... http://www.amazon.com/s/ref=nb_sb_noss?url=search-alias%3Daps&field-keywords=Thomas+Edison+t-shirt&rh=i%3Aaps%2Ck%3AThomas+Edison+t-shirt

40.... http://www.amazon.com/CafePress-Inventor-Thomas-Edison-T-Shirt/dp/B00YH50VX0/ref=sr_1_48?ie=UTF8&qid=1438476838&sr=8-48&keywords=Thomas+Edison

41.... http://www.amazon.com/Pearson-Software-0743503805-InventorLabs-Technology/dp/B00004UB6L/ref=sr_1_64?ie=UTF8&qid=1438477112&sr=8-64&keywords=Thomas+Edison

42.... http://www.ge.com/

43.... http://www.ieee.org/about/awards/medals/edison.html

44.... http://www.edisons.nl/edisons

45.... https://www.asme.org/about-asme/participate/honors-awards/achievement-awards/thomas-a-edison-patent-award

46.... DeGraaf, 228

47.... Ibid., 229

48.... http://www.menloparkmuseum.org/history/thomas-edison-and-menlo-park/

49.... DeGraaf, 226; http://www.menloparkmuseum.org/history/commemorative-history/

50.... Personal observation, 7/2/15

51.... http://www.menloparkmuseum.org/history/thomas-edison-and-menlo-park/

52.... DeGraaf, 228; http://www.menloparkmuseum.org/history/thomas-edison-and-menlo-park/; Personal tour to author by Chuck Perillo, 7/2/15

53.... Chuck Perillo, a tour guide at the current Menlo Park Museum, tells a story about how he had long ago received a tour at Glenmont, Edison's home in West Orange, by none other than Madeleine Edison, Edison's daughter

54.... See, e.g., Bryan, Ford R. (1996). *Henry's Attic: Some Fascinating Gifts to Henry Ford and His Museum.* Wayne State University Press. ISBN 978-0814326428

55.... http://www.menloparkmuseum.org/history/thomas-edison-and-menlo-park/#menlo-park

56.... DeGraaf, 225; Also, personal visit by the author on 7/2/15

57.... Ibid., 226

58.... Ibid.

59.... Ford Estate was obtained by Fort Myers in 1991 and the properties combined; see also DeGraaf, 230

60.... The project is a collaboration between Rutgers University, the National Park Service, the New Jersey Historical Commission, and the Smithsonian Institution; see http://edison.rutgers.edu/mission.htm

61.... http://edison.rutgers.edu/mission.htm

62.... http://edison.rutgers.edu/index.htm

63.... DeGraaf, 231-233

64.... Smith, Frederick James. *The New York Dramatic Mirror,* "The Evolution of the Motion Picture: VI – Looking into the Future with Thomas A. Edison,' July 9, 1913.

65.... https://www.youtube.com/watch?v=YNGZu3WGstw

66.... Ibid.

67.... As quoted in Baldwin, 48

IMAGE CREDITS

Christopher Bain: front & back endpapers (cylinders courtesy Michael Cumella), 5, 29, 40–41, 47, 57, 58–59, 77, 86, 95, 210–211, 236, 237, 239

© Corbis: 66

Courtesy The Bostonian Society: 26

Courtesy Dover Publications: 27

Edison Birthplace Museum: 2

Getty © Science & Society Picture Library: 157

© The Granger Collection/Granger: NYC 8–9

Hake's Americana Auctions/www.hakes.com: 192–193

Courtesy Heritage Galleries: ii–iii, 4 bottom, 226

Courtesy Internet Archive: 34–35

Library of Congress: 1, 19, 30–31, 33, 36 (frame), 44, 60 (frame), 64 (frames), 81, 146, 178, 188–189

Metropolitan Museum of Art: 142–143

National Archives: 123

National Park Service, Thomas Edison National Historic Park: front & back cover, i, vi, vii, 1 bottom, 3, 4 top, 28, 43, 45, 46, 49, 53, 54–55, 61, 68, 69, 70–71, 72, 74–75, 78, 82–83, 91, 93, 96, 100–101, 102, 103, 107, 110–111, 113, 114, 116, 117, 119, 120, 121, 154, 172, 173, 176, 182–183, 186, 187, 196–197, 200, 202, 206, 207, 208, 214, 215, 218, 222–223, 235, 246, 258

Private Collection: front & back endpapers (Detroit & New York City), iv–v, viii, xiv, 1 top, 6, 7, 10, 11, 12, 13, 15, 16, 17, 18, 20–21, 22, 24, 37, 39, 42, 48, 50, 62–63, 67, 73, 76, 80, 84, 88, 89, 90, 97, 104, 106, 108, 126, 128, 130–131, 132, 135, 140, 148, 150, 152–153, 159 bottom, 162, 163, 165, 170, 181, 191, 194, 195, 198, 199, 216

Courtesy Robin & Joan Rolfs: 98, 99

Scott Russo Archive: 23

Science Source: © Sheila Terry: 167, 168

Smithsonian Institution: 240

Toronto Public Library: 14

U.S. Naval Research Laboratory: 204

Courtesy Wikimedia Foundation: ix, x–xi, 36 (portrait), 60 (portrait), 64 top & bottom (portraits), 79, 94, 105, 124–125, 136, 158, 159 top, 160, 161, 184, 190, 212

Yale University Library/Beinecke Rare Book and Manuscript Library: 138–139

ABANDONED.

DIV. 23 **1912** (EX'R'S BOOK) 17/8

NUMBER (Series of 1900),

169868 **PATENT No.** 53-A-16

Name Thomas A. Edison,

Do not destroy
JAB

of West Orange,

County of

State of New Jersey.

Invention Method of Recording Sounds.

ORIGINAL		RENEWED
Petition	Jany 6, 1912	, 191
Affidavit	" ", 1912	
Specification	" ", 1912	
Drawing	, 191	
Model or Specimen	, 191	
First Fee Cash	$15. Jany 6, 1912	
" " *Cert*	, 191	, 191
Appl. filed complete	Jan 6, 1912	, 191

This application referred to in Patent No. Order
Do not destroy. (See order No. 3166, 400 O.G. 1)
JaBrosky

DO NOT DETACH

Examined		
Allowed		
	For Commissioner.	*For Commissioner.*
Notice of Allowance	, 191	, 191
Final Fee Cash	, 191	, 191
" " *Cert*	, 191	, 191
Patented		, 191

Attorney Frank L. Dyer, Orange, N.J.

Associate Attorney

Brush St
1440.
EDISON

EDISON
FOUR MINUTE
BY NATIONAL PHONOGRAPH COMPANY.
EDISON
AMBER